Food Labelling Data for Manufacturers

based on

McCance and Widdowson's

The Composition of Foods

Fifth revised and extended edition

The Royal Society of Chemistry
and
Ministry of Agriculture, Fisheries and Food

The Royal Society of Chemistry
Thomas Graham House
Science Park
Milton Road
Cambridge CB4 4WF
UK

Tel.: (0) 223 420066 Telex: 818293
Fax: (0) 223 423429

ISBN 0-85186-993-9

Orders should be addressed to:
The Royal Society of Chemistry
Turpin Distribution Services Ltd
Letchworth
Herts. SG6 1HN
UK

Tel.: (0) 462 672555 Telex: 825372
Fax: (0) 462 480947

Xerox Ventura Publisher™ output photocomposed by
Goodfellow & Egan Phototypesetting Ltd, Cambridge

Printed in the United Kingdom by
The Bath Press, Lower Bristol Road, Bath

Food Labelling Data for Manufacturers

based on

McCance and Widdowson's

The Composition of Foods

COMPILERS Ailsa Welch, *The Royal Society of Chemistry*
Bridie Holland, *The Royal Society of Chemistry*
Ian Unwin, *Food Information Consultant*
David Buss, *Ministry of Agriculture, Fisheries and Food*

CONTENTS

	Page
Introduction	1
Tables	
Symbols and abbreviations used in the Tables	9
Cereals and cereal products	10
Milk and milk products	34
Eggs	50
Fats and oils	52
Meat and meat products	56
Fish and fish products	88
Vegetables	104
Herbs and spices	128
Fruit	130
Nuts and seeds	146
Sugars, preserves and snacks	150
Beverages	156
Alcoholic beverages	164
Soups, sauces and miscellaneous foods	168
Appendices	
Alternative and taxonomic names	181
References to tables	191
Food index	193

INTRODUCTION

Nutrition information is increasingly being demanded and given on food labels. The values in this book may be used for this purpose.

The label should show the typical nutritional value of the product as sold, and this could require chemical analysis of representative samples. For many fresh and processed foods, however, the products will be sufficiently similar to those described in this book that the values shown here may be used. The values in this book are also useful for manufacturers and retailers whose foods differ from those shown but are prepared from known amounts of basic ingredients. In such cases, the nutritional value of the final product can be calculated from the nutritional values of the ingredients in the recipe, after allowance for any losses of water and other components during preparation.

All the values in this book have been derived from those given in the 5th edition of *McCance and Widdowson's The Composition of Foods* (***1***), to which the reader is referred for further details of the samples and how the values were derived. The numbering of the foods in this book has been retained from that in the 5th edition for ease of cross-reference, except that the letter *L* has been added to numbers in the present book. There are, however, two important differences from the values shown in the 5th edition, which make the present work more useful for nutrition labelling purposes.

The first difference from the 5th edition is that the values have been recalculated where necessary so that they are now exactly as required by the EC Directive on Nutrition Labelling for Foodstuffs (***2***). All the values for energy (both in kilojoules and kilocalories), protein, total carbohydrate and sugars have been recalculated as described below, and the sodium has been expressed in grams as well as milligrams per 100 grams because expression in grams is required by the EC Directive. Furthermore, the alcohol content of alcoholic drinks has been given as a percentage by volume rather than as grams per 100 ml, as required by separate Community Directives Nos. 86/197/EEC and 87/250/EEC. The second difference is that although the coverage of foods is exactly the same in each book, the number of nutrients has been restricted here to those of most relevance to food labelling.

The EC Directive sets out two groupings of nutrients that may be given on food labels as described overleaf, and under certain circumstances allows information on other nutrients to be given in addition to these. These extra nutrients include monounsaturated and polyunsaturated fatty acids, cholesterol, and vitamins and minerals present in significant amounts in the food. Those who wish to give information on these nutrients will find representative values in the 5th edition of The Composition of Foods, and they require no recalculation. Values for starch may also be shown but do require recalculation, so the values from the 5th edition have been recalculated for the present book.

The format of nutrition labelling

The European Directive on Nutrition Labelling of Foodstuffs sets out rules on the amount of information and the way in which it is presented on food labels. These rules supersede the UK Food Labelling Regulations 1984 (***3***). The Directive sets out the following conditions:

When nutrition information is provided on a food label, the information shall be given per 100 grams or 100 millilitres of the food as sold, and shall consist of:

either

- the energy value of the food in kilojoules (kJ) and kilocalories (kcal)
- the amounts in grams of protein, total carbohydrate and fat (in that order), **and**
- the amount of any other nutrient for which a claim is made

or *(optionally until October 1995)*

- the energy value of the food in kJ and kcal
- the amounts in grams of protein, total carbohydrate, total sugars, fat, saturated fatty acids (saturates), fibre and sodium (in that order), **and**
- the amount of any other nutrient for which a claim is made.

In addition, the nutritional value may be shown per serving as quantified on the label or per portion provided that the number of portions in the package is stated.

The way in which many of these nutrients are calculated and expressed differs from that previously required in UK food legislation and from the scientifically more accurate values used in the 5th edition of *The Composition of Foods*. The values in this book have therefore been recalculated where necessary and shown as required by the new EC Directive. The differences are as follows:

	As required by the EC Directive	*Traditional method*
Protein	N x 6.25 for all foods	N x 6.38 for dairy products N x 5.7 for most cereals Specific factors for certain foods N x 6.25 for all other foods
Total carbohydrate Sugars Starch	As the actual weight of the carbohydrate	After conversion to mono-saccharides

Energy yield per gram (with previous values in brackets)

	kJ	*kcal*
Protein	17 (17)	4 (4)
Carbohydrate	17 (16)	4 (3.75)
Fat	37 (37)	9 (9)
Alcohol	29 (29)	7 (7)
All organic acids	13 (0)	3 (0)
Sorbitol and other polyols	10 (16)	2.4 (3.75)

Special points

Branded products:– Many foods in this book are manufactured products whose composition may change if the product has been reformulated. Manufacturers should ensure that, if this has happened, the information given on the label accurately reflects the nutritional value of the product as sold rather than that given here.

Fatty acids:– There are marked differences in the proportion of saturated fatty acids (saturates) and of other fatty acids in different types of fat. The fat used in recipes in this book is usually a typical margarine, so manufacturers quoting the amount of saturates in their products should check the source and composition of the fat used with their supplier to ensure that the values quoted are truly representative.

Sugars and sodium:– The amounts of sugars and sodium added to products can vary widely. Manufacturers should make adjustments to the values shown in this book if they add amounts which differ from those in the products described here.

Organic acids and polyols: Few foods in this book contain organic acids or polyols so, apart from allowance for the acetic acid in vinegar, their contributions to energy have been ignored. Those who wish to allow for the citric and malic acids in fruit will find information on the amounts present in the supplement to the 5th edition on *Fruit and Nuts* (***4***).

Nutrients in meat:– The amount of fat on retail cuts of meats is particularly variable, and the amount of fat has also decreased since the values in this book were obtained. This can affect the amounts of other nutrients too, so those labelling meat with its nutritional value should take particular care to ensure that the values reflect their own product.

Missing values:– The letter N has been used in the tables where a nutrient is present in a food, but the exact amount is unknown. In these cases, the exact amount present must be determined by the manufacturer to ensure that the information given on the label is complete.

The layout of this book

The foods in this book have been listed alphabetically within groups, exactly as in the 5th edition. The main groups are: cereals and cereal products; milk and milk products; eggs; fats and oils; meat and meat products; fish and fish products; vegetables; herbs and spices; fruit; nuts; sugars, preserves and snacks; beverages; alcoholic beverages; soups, sauces and miscellaneous foods. There are also some sub-groups of food within these. A number of foods are known by more than one name, and the most common one has in general been used for the main table. For ease of location and identification, this book includes an appendix of alternative and taxonomic names, and there is also a detailed index of all the names used at the end of the book.

The nutrient values for each food are given on two facing pages, and are expressed per 100 grams (or, for alcoholic beverages, per 100 ml). If values for other foods are to be given per 100ml, then the amounts of Group 1 and Group 2 nutrients will first have to be multiplied by the specific gravity of the food. Some typical specific gravities are shown overleaf. The first page of values for each food group covers the Directive's Group 1 nutrients (energy, protein, carbohydrate and fat) and the second shows the extra nutrients required in Group 2 (sugars,

Table:– Specific Gravities

Milk products and eggs

Skimmed milk	1.036	Whipping cream	0.99
Semi-skimmed milk	1.034	Double cream	0.99
Whole milk	1.031	Yogurts	1.08
Condensed milk (sweetened)	1.160		(range 1.03 - 1.2)
Evaporated milk (unsweetened)	1.066	Ice cream	variable, 0.5 - 0.6 approx
Single cream	1.00	Eggs	1.02

Fats and oils

Palm oil	0.89	Other vegetable oils	0.91 - 0.925

Selected beverages

Coca-cola	1.039	Lucozade	1.074
Lemonade, bottled	1.015	Orange drink, undiluted	1.116
Lime juice cordial, undiluted	1.102	Ribena, undiluted	1.283

Alcoholic beverages

Beers	
Beer, bitter, *canned*	1.008
draught	1.004
keg	1.001
mild, *draught*	1.009
Brown ale, *bottled*	1.008
Lager, *bottled*	1.005
Pale ale, *bottled*	1.003
Stout, *bottled*	1.014
extra	1.002
Strong ale	1.018
Ciders	
Cider, dry	1.007
sweet	1.012
vintage	1.017
Wines	
Red wine	0.998
Rosé wine, medium	1.003
White wine, dry	0.995
medium	1.005
sparkling	0.995
sweet	1.016
Fortified wines	
Port	1.026
Sherry, dry	0.988
medium	0.998
sweet	1.009
Vermouths	
Vermouth, dry	1.005
sweet	1.046
Liqueurs	
Advocaat	1.093
Cherry brandy	1.093
Curacao	1.052
Spirits	
40% volume	0.950

saturates, fibre as non-starch polysaccharides, and sodium), together with some additional useful values for recipe calculations.

Further details of the foods, the derivation of the values, and the factors to be taken into account in using them, may be found in the introduction to the 5th edition, to which the reader is referred. The nutritional value of many more foods is included in the more detailed supplements to the 4th and 5th editions of *McCance and Widdowson's The Composition of Foods* (***5***,***6***,***7***,***4***). Although the information is not specifically in the form required for nutrition labelling, it can nevertheless provide a useful resource for food manufacturers and retailers.

References

(*1*) Holland, B., Welch, A.A., Unwin, I.D., Buss, D.H., Paul, A.A. and Southgate, D.A.T (1991) *McCance and Widdowson's The Composition of Foods 5th edition*, Royal Society of Chemistry, Cambridge

(*2*) EC Council Directive on Nutrition Labelling for Foodstuffs (90/496/EEC), Official Journal of the European Communities, L276/40 (1990)

(*3*) The Food Labelling Regulations 1984. Statutory instrument No. 1305. HMSO, London

(*4*) Holland, B., Unwin, I.D. and Buss, D.H. (1992) *First supplement to McCance and Widdowson's The Composition of Foods, 5th edition: Fruit and Nuts*, Royal Society of Chemistry, Cambridge

(*5*) Holland, B., Unwin, I.D. and Buss, D.H. (1988) *Third supplement to McCance and Widdowson's The Composition of Foods, 4th edition: Cereals and Cereal Products*, Royal Society of Chemistry, Cambridge

(*6*) Holland, B., Unwin, I.D. and Buss, D.H. (1989) *Fourth supplement to McCance and Widdowson's The Composition of Foods, 4th edition: Milk Products and Eggs*, Royal Society of Chemistry, Cambridge

(*7*) Holland, B., Unwin, I.D. and Buss, D.H. (1991) *Fifth supplement to McCance and Widdowson's The Composition of Foods, 4th edition: Vegetables, Herbs and Spices*, Royal Society of Chemistry, Cambridge

The

Tables

Symbols and abbreviations used in the Tables

Symbols

0	None of the nutrient is present
Tr	Trace
N	The nutrient is present in significant quantities but there is no reliable information on the amount. The amount must not be given as 'N' on a label; the exact amount must be determined
(N × 6.25)	Total nitrogen multiplied by the factor 6.25

Abbreviations

IFR	Institute of Food Research, Norwich
LGC	Laboratory of The Government Chemist, Teddington
calcd.	calculated

Notes

Recipe	Where the term 'Recipe' appears in the 'Description and main data sources' column, the values are the result of calculations based on the recipe given in the 5th edition of *The Composition of Foods*

Labelling information for Group 1 nutrients per 100g food

No.	Food	Description and main data sources	Edible proportion	Energy kJ	Energy kcal	Protein (N × 6.25) g	Carbohydrate (actual wt.) g	Fat g
	Flours, grains and starches							
1L	**Bran**, wheat	Analytical and literature sources	1.00	860	204	14.0	24.6	5.5
2L	**Chapati flour**, brown	1 sample, single supplier	1.00	1399	330	12.6	67.1	1.2
3L	white	2 samples, different suppliers, same weights	1.00	1402	330	10.8	70.6	0.5
4L	**Cornflour**	3 samples from different shops	1.00	1457	343	0.6	83.6	0.7
5L	**Custard powder**	Taken as cornflour except Na, Cl and Cu	1.00	1457	343	0.6	83.6	0.7
6L	**Oatmeal**, quick cook, *raw*	10 samples, 8 brands	1.00	1564	371	12.0	60.0	9.2
7L	**Rye flour**, *whole*	Analytical and literature sources	1.00	1397	329	8.8	69.0	2.0
8L	**Sago**, *raw*	2 samples from different shops	1.00	1466	345	0.3	85.5	0.2
9L	**Soya flour**, *full fat*	Analytical and literature sources	1.00	1927	460	40.3	21.9	23.5
10L	*low fat*	Analytical and literature sources	1.00	1557	368	49.6	26.3	7.2
11L	**Tapioca**, *raw*	4 varieties, medium pearl, seed pearl, coarse and flake	1.00	1479	348	0.4	86.4	0.1
12L	**Wheat flour**, brown	VFSS, 1977-81, and literature sources	1.00	1362	321	13.8	62.4	1.8
13L	white, *breadmaking*	Data from Voluntary Flour Sampling Scheme (VFSS), 1977-81 plus literature sources. Biscuit and cake flours are similar in composition to plain flour	1.00	1432	337	12.6	68.6	1.4
14L	white, *plain*		1.00	1427	336	10.3	70.8	1.3
15L	white, *self-raising*		1.00	1381	325	9.8	68.8	1.2
16L	wholemeal		1.00	1304	307	13.6	58.3	2.2
17L	**Wheatgerm**	Literature sources	1.00	1527	362	28.4	41.4	9.2

No.	Food	Labelling information for Group 2 nutrients per 100g food				Additional nutrients and information per 100g food		
		Sugars (actual weight) g	Saturates g	Fibre (Englyst) g	Sodium g	Sodium mg	Starch (actual weight) g	Water g
	Flours, grains and starches							
1L	**Bran**, wheat	3.7	0.9	36.4	Tr	28	20.9	8.3
2L	**Chapati flour**, brown	3.0	0.2	N	Tr	39	64.1	12.2
3L	white	2.0	0.1	N	Tr	15	68.6	12.0
4L	**Cornflour**	Tr	0.1	0.1	0.1	52	83.6	12.5
5L	**Custard powder**	Tr	0.1	0.1	0.3	320	83.6	12.5
6L	**Oatmeal**, quick cook, *raw*	1.0	1.6	7.1	Tr	9	59.0	8.2
7L	**Rye flour**, *whole*	Tr	0.3	11.7	Tr	1	69.0	15.0
8L	**Sago**, *raw*	Tr	0.1	0.5	Tr	3	85.5	12.6
9L	**Soya flour**, *full fat*	10.7	2.9	11.2	Tr	9	11.2	7.0
10L	*low fat*	12.8	0.9	13.5	Tr	14	13.5	7.0
11L	**Tapioca**, *raw*	Tr	Tr	0.4	Tr	4	86.4	12.2
12L	**Wheat flour**, brown	1.7[a]	0.2	6.4	Tr	4	60.7	14.0
13L	white, *breadmaking*	1.4[a]	0.2	3.1	Tr	3	67.2	14.0
14L	white, *plain*	1.5[a]	0.2	3.1	Tr	3	69.3	14.0
15L	white, *self-raising*	1.3[a]	0.2	3.1	0.4	360[b]	67.5	14.0
16L	wholemeal	2.1[a]	0.3	9.0	Tr	3	56.2	14.0
17L	**Wheatgerm**	15.3	1.3	15.6	Tr	5	26.1	11.7

[a] Includes the glucofructan levosin

[b] The amount present will depend on the nature and level of the raising agent used

Labelling information for Group 1 nutrients per 100g food

No.	Food	Description and main data sources	Edible proportion	Energy kJ	Energy kcal	Protein (N × 6.25) g	Carbohydrate (actual wt.) g	Fat g
Rice								
18L	**Brown rice**, *raw*	5 assorted samples	1.00	1479	349	6.9	74.0	2.8
19L	*boiled*	Water content weighed, other nutrients calculated from raw	1.00	583	138	2.7	29.2	1.1
20L	**Savoury rice**, *raw*	10 samples, 5 varieties, meat and vegetable	1.00	1729	410	8.8	70.5	10.3
21L	*cooked*	Calculation from raw, boiled in water	1.00	590	140	3.0	24.1	3.5[a]
22L	**White rice**, easy cook, *raw*	10 samples, 9 different brands, parboiled	1.00	1590	375	7.7	78.0	3.6
23L	easy cook, *boiled*	Calculation from raw	1.00	573	135	2.8	28.1	1.3
24L	fried in lard/dripping	Recipe	1.00	545	129	2.3	22.8	3.2
Pasta								
25L	**Macaroni**, *raw*	10 samples, 7 brands; literature sources	1.00	1462	345	13.2	68.9	1.8
26L	*boiled*	10 samples, 7 brands boiled in water	1.00	360	85	3.3	16.8	0.5
27L	**Noodles**, egg, *raw*	10 samples, 8 brands	1.00	1638	388	13.3	65.2	8.2
28L	egg, *boiled*	10 samples, 8 brands boiled in water	1.00	262	62	2.5	11.8	0.5
29L	**Spaghetti**, white, *raw*	10 samples, 7 brands	1.00	1435	338	13.2	67.3	1.8
30L	white, *boiled*	10 samples, 7 brands boiled in water	1.00	434	102	3.9	20.1	0.7
31L	wholemeal, *raw*	10 samples, 5 brands	1.00	1361	321	14.4	60.2	2.5
32L	wholemeal, *boiled*	Water content weighed, other nutrients calculated from raw	1.00	479	113	5.1	21.1	0.9

[a] Calculated assuming water only was added; savoury rice cooked with fat contains approximately 8.8g fat per 100g

No.	Food	Labelling information for Group 2 nutrients per 100g food: Sugars (actual weight) g	Saturates g	Fibre (Englyst) g	Sodium g	Additional nutrients and information per 100g food: Sodium mg	Starch (actual weight) g	Water g
Rice								
18L	**Brown rice**, *raw*	1.3	0.7	1.9	Tr	3	72.7	13.9
19L	*boiled*	0.5	0.3	0.8	Tr	1	28.7	66.0
20L	**Savoury rice**, *raw*	3.4	3.2	N	1.4	1440	67.1	7.0
21L	*cooked*	1.3	1.1	1.4	0.5	490	22.8	68.7
22L	**White rice**, easy cook, *raw*	Tr	0.9	0.4	Tr	4	78.0	11.4
23L	easy cook, *boiled*	Tr	0.3	0.1	Tr	1	28.1	68.0
24L	fried in lard/dripping	1.8	1.4	0.6	0.1	56	21.0	70.3
Pasta								
25L	**Macaroni**, *raw*	2.0	0.3	3.1[a]	Tr	11	66.9	9.7
26L	*boiled*	0.3	0.1	0.9[a]	Tr	1	16.5	78.1
27L	**Noodles**, egg, *raw*	1.7	2.3	2.9	0.2	180	63.5	9.1
28L	egg, *boiled*	0.2	0.1	0.6	Tr	15	11.6	84.3
29L	**Spaghetti**, white, *raw*	2.9	0.2	2.9	Tr	3	64.4	9.8
30L	white, *boiled*	0.4	0.1	1.2	Tr	Tr	19.7	73.8
31L	wholemeal, *raw*	3.4	0.4	8.4	0.1	130	56.8	10.5
32L	wholemeal, *boiled*	1.2	0.1	3.5	Tr	45	19.9	69.1

[a] Wholemeal macaroni contains 8.3g (raw) and 2.8g (boiled) Englyst fibre per 100g

Labelling information for Group 1 nutrients per 100g food

No.	Food	Description and main data sources	Edible proportion	Energy kJ	Energy kcal	Protein (N × 6.25) g	Carbohydrate (actual wt.) g	Fat g
	Breads							
33L	**Brown bread**, *average*	Average of 2 types of brown bread, sliced and unsliced	1.00	919	217	9.3	40.4	2.0
34L	*toasted*	Calculated using 22% weight loss	1.00	1150	271	11.4	51.7	2.1
35L	**Chapatis**, *made with fat*[a]	6 samples	1.00	1373	327	8.9	44.0	12.8
36L	*made without fat*	Analysed and calculated values	1.00	850	200	8.0	39.8	1.0
37L	**Currant bread**	10 samples, 10 different shops	1.00	1226	291	8.3	47.3	7.6
38L	*toasted*	Calculated using 12% weight loss	1.00	1374	326	9.3	53.0	8.5
39L	**Granary bread**	10 samples, 10 different shops	1.00	989	234	10.1	42.2	2.7
40L	**Hovis**, *average*	Average of 3 types of Hovis (wheatgerm) bread	1.00	893	211	10.4	37.8	2.0
41L	*toasted*	Calculated using 22% weight loss	1.00	1138	269	12.8	48.5	2.6
42L	**Malt bread**	10 samples, 5 brands	1.00	1150	271	9.1	53.3	2.4
43L	**Naan bread**	Recipe	1.00	1404	334	9.6	45.8	12.5
44L	**Papadums**, *fried in vegetable oil*	Calculated from raw using weighed fat uptake	1.00	1526	364	17.5	35.5	16.9
45L	**Pitta bread**, white	10 samples, 4 brands	1.00	1114	262	10.1	52.8	1.2
46L	**Rye bread**	15 samples, different shops; literature sources	1.00	927	219	9.1	41.7	1.7
47L	**Vitbe**, *average*	Average of 3 types of Vitbe (wheatgerm) bread	1.00	968	229	10.6	39.6	3.1

[a] Puris (deep fried chapatis) contain 19.1g water, 7.0g protein, 25.0g fat and 39.4g carbohydrate per 100g

No.	Food	Sugars (actual weight) g	Saturates g	Fibre (Englyst) g	Sodium g	Sodium mg	Starch (actual weight) g	Water g
		Labelling information for Group 2 nutrients per 100g food				Additional nutrients and information per 100g food		
	Breads							
33L	**Brown bread**, *average*	2.9	0.4	3.5	0.5	540	37.5	39.5
34L	*toasted*	4.3	0.4	4.5	0.7	690	47.4	24.4
35L	**Chapatis**, *made with fat*	1.7	N	N	0.1	130	42.3	28.5
36L	*made without fat*	1.5	0.1	N	0.1	120	38.3	45.8
37L	**Currant bread**	14.3	1.6	N	0.3	290	33.0	29.4
38L	*toasted*	16.0	1.8	N	0.3	330	37.0	25.9
39L	**Granary bread**	2.1	0.5	4.3	0.6	580	40.1	35.4
40L	**Hovis**, *average*	1.7	0.3	3.3	0.6	600	36.1	40.3
41L	*toasted*	2.2	0.4	4.2	0.8	770	46.3	23.5
42L	**Malt bread**	25.4	0.3	N	0.3	280	27.9	25.8
43L	**Naan bread**	5.3	N	1.9	0.4	380	40.5	28.8
44L	**Papadums**, *fried in vegetable oil*	Tr	1.7	N	2.4	2420	35.5	10.3
45L	**Pitta bread**, white	2.3	0.2	2.2[a]	0.5	520[a]	50.5	32.7
46L	**Rye bread**	1.7	0.3	4.4[b]	0.6	580	40.0	37.4
47L	**Vitbe**, *average*	2.9	0.6	3.3	0.6	550	36.7	37.5

[a] Wholemeal pitta bread contains 5.2g Englyst fibre and 460mg sodium per 100g

[b] Pumpernickel contains approximately 7.5g Englyst fibre per 100g

Labelling information for Group 1 nutrients per 100g food

No.	Food	Description and main data sources	Edible proportion	Energy kJ	Energy kcal	Protein (N × 6.25) g	Carbohydrate (actual wt.) g	Fat g
Breads								
48L	**White bread**, *average*	Weighted average of 5 main types of white bread	1.00	992	234	9.2	45.0	1.9
49L	*sliced*	42 samples, 6 batches	1.00	915	216	8.3	42.7	1.3
50L	*fried in blended oil*	Calculated from fried in lard	1.00	2089	501	8.6	44.2	32.2[a]
51L	*fried in lard*	Calculated on white sliced bread using analysed fat and water changes	1.00	2089	501	8.6	44.2	32.2[a]
52L	*toasted*	Calculated using water loss of 18%	1.00	1115	263	10.1	52.0	1.6
53L	French stick	10 samples, 10 different shops	1.00	1135	268	10.5	50.4	2.7
54L	'with added fibre'	Manufacturer's data for Mighty White (Allied Bakeries) and Champion (British Bakeries)	1.00	965	228	8.3	45.2	1.5
55L	'with added fibre', *toasted*	Calculated using water loss of 16%	1.00	1149	271	9.9	53.8	1.8
56L	**Wholemeal bread**, *average*	Average of 3 types of wholemeal bread	1.00	905	214	9.9	37.9	2.5
57L	*toasted*	Calculated using water loss of 14.6%	1.00	1059	250	11.6	44.4	2.9
Rolls								
58L	**Brown rolls**, *crusty*	12 samples of 6 rolls, different shops	1.00	1076	254	11.3	45.9	2.8
59L	*soft*	14 samples of 6 rolls, different shops	1.00	1128	267	10.9	47.2	3.8
60L	**Croissants**	Recipe	1.00	1496	358	9.0	34.8	20.3
61L	**Hamburger buns**	5 packets of 6 buns including frozen	1.00	1112	263	10.0	44.5	5.0
62L	**White rolls**, *crusty*	14 samples of 6 rolls, different shops	1.00	1182	279	12.0	52.5	2.3
63L	*soft*	14 samples of 6 rolls, different shops	1.00	1126	266	10.1	47.0	4.2
64L	**Wholemeal rolls**	2 samples of 6 rolls, different shops	1.00	1008	238	9.1	43.9	2.9

[a] The fat content depends on the conditions of frying; thin slices pick up proportionately more fat than thick ones

No.	Food	Labelling information for Group 2 nutrients per 100g food				Additional nutrients and information per 100g food		
		Sugars (actual weight) g	Saturates g	Fibre (Englyst) g	Sodium g	Sodium mg	Starch (actual weight) g	Water g
Breads								
48L	**White bread**, *average*	2.5	0.4	1.5	0.5	520	42.5	37.3
49L	*sliced*	2.9	0.3	1.5	0.5	530	39.8	40.4
50L	*fried in blended oil*	3.0	2.8	1.6	0.6	550	41.2	7.4
51L	*fried in lard*	3.0	12.5	1.6	0.6	550	41.2	7.4
52L	*toasted*	3.5	0.4	1.8	0.7	650	48.5	27.3
53L	French stick	1.8	0.6	1.5	0.6	570	48.6	29.2
54L	'with added fibre'	3.1	0.4	3.1	0.5	450	42.1	40.0
55L	'with added fibre', *toasted*	3.7	0.5	3.7	0.5	540	50.1	26.2
56L	**Wholemeal bread**, *average*	1.7	0.5	5.8	0.6	550	36.2	38.3
57L	*toasted*	2.0	0.6	5.9	0.6	640	42.4	27.8
Rolls								
58L	**Brown rolls**, *crusty*	1.8	0.6	3.5	0.6	570	44.1	30.5
59L	*soft*	2.4	0.9	3.5	0.6	560	44.8	31.6
60L	**Croissants**	1.0	6.5	1.6	0.4	390	33.8	31.1
61L	**Hamburger buns**	2.1	1.1	1.5	0.6	550	42.4	32.9
62L	**White rolls**, *crusty*	2.1	0.5	1.5	0.6	640	50.4	26.4
63L	*soft*	2.1	1.0	1.5	0.6	560	44.9	32.7
64L	**Wholemeal rolls**	1.4	0.7	5.9	0.5	460	42.5	31.2

Labelling information for Group 1 nutrients per 100g food

No.	Food	Description and main data sources	Edible proportion	Energy kJ	Energy kcal	Protein (N × 6.25) g	Carbohydrate (actual wt.) g	Fat g
	Breakfast cereals							
65L	**All-Bran**	Analysis and manufacturer's data (Kelloggs)	1.00	1098	259	13.9	43.3	3.4
66L	**Bran Flakes**	Manufacturer's data (Kelloggs)	1.00	1349	318	11.2	64.0	1.9
67L	**Coco Pops**	Manufacturer's data (Kelloggs)	1.00	1620	381	5.6	87.5	1.0
68L	**Common Sense Oat Bran Flakes**	Manufacturer's data (Kelloggs)	1.00	1494	353	11.0	68.2	4.0
69L	**Corn Flakes**	Analysis and manufacturer's data (Kelloggs)	1.00	1496	352	7.9	78.6	0.7
70L	**Crunchy Nut Corn Flakes**	Manufacturer's data (Kelloggs)	1.00	1669	394	7.4	82.1	4.0
71L	**Frosties**	Manufacturer's data (Kelloggs)	1.00	1588	374	5.3	87.0	0.5
72L	**Fruit 'n Fibre**	Manufacturer's data (Kelloggs)	1.00	1474	348	9.9	66.6	4.7
73L	**Muesli**, *Swiss style*[a]	Analysis and manufacturers' data (Kelloggs, Weetabix)	1.00	1526	361	9.8	67.1	5.9
74L	*with no added sugar*	Analysis and manufacturers' data (Kelloggs, Weetabix)	1.00	1521	360	10.5	62.0	7.8
75L	**Oat and Wheat Bran**	Manufacturer's data (Weetabix)	1.00	1371	324	10.6	62.4	3.5
76L	**Porridge**, *made with water*	Recipe. Ref. Wiles *et al.* (1980)	1.00	207	49	1.6	8.2	1.1
77L	*made with whole milk*	Recipe	1.00	486	116	4.8	12.7	5.1
78L	**Puffed Wheat**	Analytical and literature sources	1.00	1349	318	15.3	61.2	1.3

[a] Muesli composition is very variable

No.	Food	Labelling information for Group 2 nutrients per 100g food				Additional nutrients and information per 100g food		
		Sugars (actual weight) g	Saturates g	Fibre (Englyst) g	Sodium g	Sodium mg	Starch (actual weight) g	Water g
	Breakfast cereals							
65L	**All-Bran**	18.2	0.6	24.5	0.9	900	25.1	3.0
66L	**Bran Flakes**	18.0	0.4	13.0	1.0	1000	46.0	3.0
67L	**Coco Pops**	36.5	0.4	0.6	0.8	800	51.0	3.0
68L	**Common Sense Oat Bran Flakes**	16.2	0.7	10.0	0.9	900	52.0	3.0
69L	**Corn Flakes**	8.0	0.1	0.9	1.1	1110	70.6	3.0
70L	**Crunchy Nut Corn Flakes**	34.6	0.8	0.8	0.8	770	47.5	3.0
71L	**Frosties**	39.9	0.1	0.6	0.8	800	47.1	3.0
72L	**Fruit 'n Fibre**	23.2	2.5	7.0	0.7	700	43.4	5.7
73L	**Muesli**, *Swiss style*	25.3	0.8	6.4	0.4	380	41.8	7.2
74L	*with no added sugar*	15.3	1.5	7.6	Tr	47	46.7	7.6
75L	**Oat and Wheat Bran**	16.0	0.6	17.9	0.6	600	46.4	2.6
76L	**Porridge**, *made with water*	Tr	0.2	0.8	0.6	560	8.2	87.4
77L	*made with whole milk*	4.5	2.7	0.8	0.6	620	8.2	74.8
78L	**Puffed Wheat**	0.3	0.2	5.6	Tr	4	60.9	2.5

Labelling information for Group 1 nutrients per 100g food

No.	Food	Description and main data sources	Edible proportion	Energy		Protein (N × 6.25)	Carbohydrate (actual wt.)	Fat
				kJ	kcal	g	g	g
	Breakfast cereals							
79L	**Raisin Splitz**	Manufacturer's data (Kelloggs)	1.00	1427	336	9.6	70.0	2.0
80L	**Ready Brek**	6 packets of the same brand (Weetabix)	1.00	1557	369	12.2	62.4	7.8
81L	**Rice Krispies**	Analysis and manufacturer's data (Kelloggs)	1.00	1538	362	6.4	82.1	0.9
82L	**Ricicles**	Manufacturer's data (Kelloggs)	1.00	1605	378	4.5	88.8	0.5
83L	**Shredded Wheat**	6 packets of the same brand (Nabisco)	1.00	1361	321	11.3	62.2	3.0
84L	**Shreddies**	10 samples (Nabisco)	1.00	1399	330	10.8	68.2	1.5
85L	**Smacks**	Manufacturer's data (Kelloggs)	1.00	1631	384	8.0	83.6	2.0
86L	**Special K**	Analysis and manufacturer's data (Kelloggs)	1.00	1574	371	15.4	75.0	1.0
87L	**Start**	Manufacturer's data (Kelloggs)	1.00	1484	350	7.9	75.7	1.7
88L	**Sugar Puffs**	6 packets of the same brand (Quaker)	1.00	1490	351	6.3	79.6	0.8
89L	**Sultana Bran**	Manufacturer's data (Kelloggs)	1.00	1300	306	9.3	63.7	1.6
90L	**Weetabix**	Manufacturer's data (Weetabix)	1.00	1472	347	11.9	68.8	2.7
91L	**Weetaflake**	Manufacturer's data (Weetabix)	1.00	1513	357	9.9	73.0	2.8
92L	**Weetos**	Manufacturer's data (Weetabix)	1.00	1565	369	6.5	79.7	2.7

		Labelling information for Group 2 nutrients per 100g food				Additional nutrients and information per 100g food		
No.	Food	Sugars (actual weight) g	Saturates g	Fibre (Englyst) g	Sodium g	Sodium mg	Starch (actual weight) g	Water g
	Breakfast cereals							
79L	**Raisin Splitz**	18.0	0.4	8.0	Tr	10	52.0	9.0
80L	**Ready Brek**	1.6[a]	1.2	7.2	Tr	12	60.8	8.6
81L	**Rice Krispies**	10.2	0.3	0.7	1.3	1260	71.9	3.0
82L	**Ricicles**	39.9	0.2	0.4	0.8	800	48.9	3.0
83L	**Shredded Wheat**	0.8	0.4	9.8	Tr	8	61.4	7.6
84L	**Shreddies**	10.1	0.2	9.5	0.6	550	58.1	4.0
85L	**Smacks**	47.6	0.4	3.0	Tr	20	36.0	3.0
86L	**Special K**	16.4	0.3	2.0	1.0	1000	58.6	3.0
87L	**Start**	27.9	0.3	5.7	0.5	500	47.8	3.0
88L	**Sugar Puffs**	54.1	0.1	3.2	Tr	9	25.5	1.8
89L	**Sultana Bran**	28.1	0.4	10.0	0.7	700	35.6	7.0
90L	**Weetabix**	4.7	0.4	9.7	0.3	270	64.1	5.6
91L	**Weetaflake**	19.4	0.4	8.8	0.7	660	53.6	3.6
92L	**Weetos**	31.6	0.6	5.3	0.3	300	48.1	4.4

[a] Flavoured instant oat varieties contain approximately 8.1g total sugars per 100g

Labelling information for Group 1 nutrients per 100g food

No.	Food	Description and main data sources	Edible proportion	Energy		Protein (N × 6.25)	Carbohydrate (actual wt.)	Fat
				kJ	kcal	g	g	g
Biscuits								
93L	**Chocolate biscuits**, full coated	7 different kinds	1.00	2201	526	6.3	63.1	27.6
94L	**Cream crackers**	6 packets	1.00	1836	437	10.4	62.1	16.3
95L	**Crispbread**, rye	Analytical and literature sources	1.00	1344	317	10.1	64.4	2.1
96L	**Digestive biscuits**, chocolate	10 packets, 5 plain chocolate, 5 milk chocolate	1.00	2063	493	7.3	61.6	24.1
97L	plain	10 samples, 3 brands	1.00	1962	468	6.9	63.0	20.9
98L	**Flapjacks**	Recipe	1.00	2023	484	4.8	56.3	26.6
99L	**Gingernut biscuits**	10 packets, 6 brands	1.00	1917	456	6.1	73.6	15.2
100L	**Homemade biscuits**, *creaming method*	Recipe	1.00	1939	463	6.7	59.7	21.9
101L	**Jaffa cakes**	Recipe	1.00	1553	369	3.6	64.9	10.5
102L	**Oatcakes**, *retail*	6 packets, 4 brands	1.00	1837	438	10.7	57.5	18.3
103L	**Sandwich biscuits**	10 packets, custard creams and similar types	1.00	2145	512	5.4	64.4	25.9
104L	**Semi-sweet biscuits**	10 packets, Osborne, Rich Tea, Marie	1.00	1911	455	7.4	68.9	16.6
105L	**Short-sweet biscuits**	10 packets, shortcake and Lincoln	1.00	1961	468	6.8	57.6	23.4
106L	**Shortbread**	Recipe	1.00	2076	496	6.5	58.8	26.1
107L	**Wafer biscuits**, filled	9 packets, assorted	1.00	2247	538	5.1	62.0	29.9
108L	**Wholemeal crackers**	Farmhouse-type, recipe	1.00	1720	408	11.0	65.6	11.3

No.	Food	Sugars (actual weight) g	Saturates g	Fibre (Englyst) g	Sodium g	Sodium mg	Starch (actual weight) g	Water g
		Labelling information for Group 2 nutrients per 100g food				**Additional nutrients and information per 100g food**		
Biscuits								
93L	**Chocolate biscuits**, full coated	41.3	16.7	2.1	0.2	160	21.8	2.2
94L	**Cream crackers**	Tr	N	2.2	0.6	610	62.1	4.3
95L	**Crispbread**, rye	3.1	0.3	11.7[a,b]	0.2	220[a]	61.3	6.4
96L	**Digestive biscuits**, chocolate	27.1	12.2	2.2	0.5	450	34.5	2.5
97L	plain	13.0	8.6	2.2	0.6	600	50.0	2.5
98L	**Flapjacks**	33.6	7.6	2.7	0.3	280	22.7	6.4
99L	**Gingernut biscuits**	34.2	7.2	1.4	0.3	330	39.4	3.4
100L	**Homemade biscuits**, *creaming method*	25.5	6.6	1.5	0.2	220	34.2	9.0
101L	**Jaffa cakes**	55.3	N	N	0.1	130	9.6	18.0
102L	**Oatcakes**, *retail*	3.0	3.9	N	1.2	1230	54.5	5.5
103L	**Sandwich biscuits**	28.9	14.5	N	0.2	220	35.5	2.6
104L	**Semi-sweet biscuits**	21.2	8.0	1.7	0.4	410	47.7	2.5
105L	**Short-sweet biscuits**	23.0	11.7	1.5	0.4	360	34.6	2.6
106L	**Shortbread**	16.2	17.3	1.9	0.2	230	42.6	5.8
107L	**Wafer biscuits**, filled	42.6	18.6	N	0.1	70	19.4	2.3
108L	**Wholemeal crackers**	1.5	N	4.4	0.7	700	64.1	4.4

[a] Cracotte type crispbread contains 3.5g Englyst fibre and 640mg sodium per 100g

[b] High fibre varieties contain approximately 17.9g Englyst fibre per 100g

Labelling information for Group 1 nutrients per 100g food

No.	Food	Description and main data sources	Edible proportion	Energy		Protein (N × 6.25)	Carbohydrate (actual wt.)	Fat
				kJ	kcal	g	g	g
Cakes								
109L	**Battenburg cake**	Recipe. Ref. Wiles *et al.* (1980)	1.00	1555	371	6.4	47.0	17.5
110L	**Cake mix**, *made up*	Recipe; made as packet directions	1.00	1049	248	5.6	48.9	3.3
111L	**Crispie cakes**	Chocolate-coated; recipe	1.00	1945	463	5.6	68.3	18.6
112L	**Fancy iced cakes**, individual	10 different types	1.00	1729	411	4.1	65.2	14.9
113L	**Fruit cake**, plain, *retail*	10 cakes, 4 brands	1.00	1518	361	5.6	55.6	12.9
114L	rich	Recipe	1.00	1454	345	3.9	57.7	11.0
115L	rich, iced	Coated with marzipan and Royal icing; recipe	1.00	1520	361	4.4	60.2	11.4
116L	wholemeal	Recipe	1.00	1535	366	6.3	49.8	15.7
117L	**Gateau**	Recipe. Ref. Wiles *et al.* (1980)	1.00	1414	338	5.8	40.8	16.8
118L	**Madeira cake**	10 cakes, 4 brands	1.00	1656	395	5.9	54.7	16.9
119L	**Sponge cake**	Basic recipe, creaming method	1.00	1920	460	6.6	49.1	26.3
120L	*fatless*	Basic recipe, whisking method	1.00	1241	294	10.3	49.4	6.1
121L	*jam filled*	10 cakes, 3 brands; sandwich and Swiss roll	1.00	1297	307	4.6	61.0	4.9
122L	*with butter icing*	Recipe. Ref. Wiles *et al.* (1980)	1.00	2047	491	4.6	49.2	30.6
123L	**Swiss rolls**, chocolate, individual	10 samples, 5 brands, 4 bakeries	1.00	1430	340	4.7	54.8	11.3

No.	Food	Sugars (actual weight) g	Saturates g	Fibre (Englyst) g	Sodium g	Sodium mg	Starch (actual weight) g	Water g
		Labelling information for Group 2 nutrients per 100g food				**Additional nutrients and information per 100g food**		
Cakes								
109L	**Battenburg cake**	32.4	4.7	N	0.4	440	14.6	25.3
110L	**Cake mix**, *made up*	26.9	1.4	N	0.4	370	22.0	31.5
111L	**Crispie cakes**	38.8	10.7	0.3	0.5	450	29.5	1.6
112L	**Fancy iced cakes**, individual	51.7	9.3	N	0.3	250	13.5	12.7
113L	**Fruit cake**, plain, *retail*	42.1	5.8	N	0.3	250	13.5	19.5
114L	rich	47.5	3.4	1.7	0.2	200	10.2	17.6
115L	rich, iced	53.4	2.6	1.7	0.1	140	6.8	15.7
116L	wholemeal	28.4	4.8	2.4	0.3	310	21.4	21.5
117L	**Gateau**	30.8	9.5	0.4	0.1	56	10.0	35.1
118L	**Madeira cake**	34.8	8.8	0.9	0.4	380	19.9	20.2
119L	**Sponge cake**	29.1	8.0	0.9	0.4	350	20.0	15.2
120L	*fatless*	29.3	1.7	0.9	0.1	82	20.1	31.5
121L	*jam filled*	46.0	1.6	1.8	0.4	420	15.0	24.5
122L	*with butter icing*	35.2	9.4	0.6	0.4	360	14.0	13.0
123L	**Swiss rolls**, chocolate, individual	40.0	N	N	0.4	350	14.8	17.5

Labelling information for Group 1 nutrients per 100g food

No.	Food	Description and main data sources	Edible proportion	Energy kJ	Energy kcal	Protein (N × 6.25) g	Carbohydrate (actual wt.) g	Fat g
Pastry								
124L	**Flaky pastry**, *raw*	Recipe	1.00	1753	422	4.6	31.7	30.7
125L	*cooked*	Recipe	1.00	2317	557	6.1	41.8	40.6
126L	**Shortcrust pastry**, *raw*	Recipe	1.00	1860	446	6.2	42.5	27.9
127L	*cooked*	Recipe	1.00	2159	518	7.2	49.5	32.3
128L	**Wholemeal pastry**, *raw*	Recipe. Ref. Wiles *et al.* (1980)	1.00	1787	429	8.3	35.0	28.4
129L	*cooked*	Recipe. Ref. Wiles *et al.* (1980)	1.00	2071	497	9.5	40.7	32.9
Buns and pastries								
130L	**Chelsea buns**	Recipe. Ref. Wiles *et al.* (1980)	1.00	1543	367	8.4	52.3	13.8
131L	**Cream horns**	Recipe. Ref. Wiles *et al.* (1980)	1.00	1799	434	4.1	23.8	35.8
132L	**Crumpets**, *toasted*	Calculated using 11% weight loss	1.00	834	197	7.4	39.5	1.0
133L	**Currant buns**	10 samples, 5 brands, 5 bakeries	1.00	1257	298	8.4	49.2	7.5
134L	**Custard tarts**, individual	10 samples, 2 brands, 8 bakeries	1.00	1154	276	6.3	30.0	14.5
135L	**Danish pastries**	10 samples, different shops	1.00	1581	377	6.3	48.4	17.6
136L	**Doughnuts**, jam	10 samples, different shops	1.00	1419	338	6.3	45.6	14.5
137L	ring	10 samples, different shops	1.00	1661	397	6.7	43.8	21.7
138L	**Eccles cake**	Recipe. Ref. Wiles *et al.* (1980)	1.00	2021	483	4.3	57.1	26.4
139L	**Eclairs**, *frozen*	10 samples of the same brand (Birds Eye)	1.00	1642	395	6.1	23.9	30.6

No.	Food	Labelling information for Group 2 nutrients per 100g food				Additional nutrients and information per 100g food		
		Sugars (actual weight) g	Saturates g	Fibre (Englyst) g	Sodium g	Sodium mg	Starch (actual weight) g	Water g
Pastry								
124L	**Flaky pastry**, *raw*	0.7	11.1	1.4	0.4	350	31.0	30.1
125L	*cooked*	0.9	14.7	1.8	0.5	460	40.9	7.7
126L	**Shortcrust pastry**, *raw*	0.9	10.1	1.9	0.4	410	41.6	20.0
127L	*cooked*	1.1	11.7	2.2	0.5	480	48.4	7.2
128L	**Wholemeal pastry**, *raw*	1.2	10.2	5.4	0.4	360	33.8	20.0
129L	*cooked*	1.5	11.8	6.3	0.4	410	39.2	7.4
Buns and pastries								
130L	**Chelsea buns**	20.8	4.2	1.7	0.3	330	31.5	20.1
131L	**Cream horns**	6.0	16.7	0.9	0.2	200	17.8	34.4
132L	**Crumpets**, *toasted*	1.8	0.1	2.0	0.8	810	37.7	46.5
133L	**Currant buns**	15.0	N	N	0.2	230	34.2	27.7
134L	**Custard tarts**, individual	12.2	5.6	1.2	0.1	130	17.8	44.7
135L	**Danish pastries**	27.7	5.6	1.6	0.2	190	20.7	21.6
136L	**Doughnuts**, jam	18.3	4.3	N	0.2	180	27.3	26.9
137L	ring	14.8	6.3	N	0.2	230	29.0	23.8
138L	**Eccles cake**	40.6	10.1	1.6	0.2	240	16.5	4.2
139L	**Eclairs**, *frozen*	6.2	16.1	0.8	0.1	73	17.7	38.7

Labelling information for Group 1 nutrients per 100g food

No.	Food	Description and main data sources	Edible proportion	Energy kJ	Energy kcal	Protein (N × 6.25) g	Carbohydrate (actual wt.) g	Fat g
Buns and pastries								
140L	**Greek pastries**	4 assorted samples, baclava, tangos, tsamika, shredded type	1.00	1346	322	5.1	37.1	17.0
141L	**Hot cross buns**	Recipe	1.00	1314	311	7.9	54.6	6.8
142L	**Jam tarts**	Recipe	1.00	1617	385	3.6	59.1	14.9
143L	*retail*	10 samples, 6 brands, 4 bakeries	1.00	1559	371	3.3	60.1	13.0
144L	**Mince pies**, individual	Recipe	1.00	1790	427	4.7	56.2	20.4
145L	**Scones**, fruit	10 samples, 2 brands, 8 bakeries	1.00	1332	316	8.0	49.0	9.8
146L	plain	Recipe	1.00	1519	362	7.7	49.9	14.6
147L	wholemeal	Recipe. Ref. Wiles *et al.* (1980)	1.00	1359	324	9.3	39.3	14.4
148L	**Scotch pancakes**	Drop scones; recipe	1.00	1218	290	6.2	40.0	11.7
149L	**Teacakes**, *toasted*	Calculated using weight loss of 10%	1.00	1399	332	9.8	54.4	8.3
Puddings								
150L	**Blackcurrant pie**, *pastry top and bottom*	Recipe. Ref. Wiles *et al.* (1980)	1.00	1096	262	3.4	32.1	13.3
151L	**Bread pudding**	Recipe	1.00	1265	300	6.1	47.4	9.6
152L	**Christmas pudding**	Recipe	1.00	1251	297	4.9	47.6	9.7
153L	*retail*	10 samples, 4 brands	1.00	1431	340	3.3	55.2	11.8
154L	**Crumble**, fruit	Recipe. Apple, gooseberry, plum, rhubarb	1.00	837	199	2.2	32.0	6.9
155L	fruit, wholemeal	Recipe. Apple, gooseberry, plum, rhubarb	1.00	820	195	2.8	30.0	7.1

No.	Food	Labelling information for Group 2 nutrients per 100g food				Additional nutrients and information per 100g food		
		Sugars (actual weight) g	Saturates g	Fibre (Englyst) g	Sodium g	Sodium mg	Starch (actual weight) g	Water g
	Buns and pastries							
140L	**Greek pastries**	17.5	N	N	0.3	310	19.6	17.5
141L	**Hot cross buns**	22.7	2.1	1.7	0.1	120	31.9	25.2
142L	**Jam tarts**	36.8	5.1	1.6	0.2	230	22.3	19.6
143L	*retail*	35.2	4.8	N	0.1	130	24.9	14.4
144L	**Mince pies**, individual	28.1	7.4	2.1	0.3	310	28.1	12.0
145L	**Scones**, fruit	16.3	3.3	N	0.7	710	32.7	25.3
146L	plain	6.4	4.9	1.9	0.8	770	43.5	22.9
147L	wholemeal	5.6	4.8	5.2	0.7	730	33.7	26.9
148L	**Scotch pancakes**	8.4	4.1	1.4	0.4	430	31.6	39.1
149L	**Teacakes**, *toasted*	16.3	N	N	0.3	300	38.1	18.6
	Puddings							
150L	**Blackcurrant pie**, *pastry top and bottom*	12.1	4.8	2.6[a]	0.2	200	20.0	42.3
151L	**Bread pudding**	32.3	5.9	1.2	0.3	310	15.1	29.3
152L	**Christmas pudding**	33.8	4.5	1.3	0.2	200	13.8	30.4
153L	*retail*	46.0	6.1	1.7	0.2	170	9.2	23.6
154L	**Crumble**, fruit	20.5	2.1	1.7	0.1	68	11.5	54.8
155L	fruit, wholemeal	20.6	2.1	2.7	0.1	68	9.4	54.8

[a] Blackcurrant pie made with wholemeal pastry contains 4.3g Englyst fibre per 100g

Labelling information for Group 1 nutrients per 100g food

No.	Food	Description and main data sources	Edible proportion	Energy kJ	Energy kcal	Protein (N × 6.25) g	Carbohydrate (actual wt.) g	Fat g
Puddings								
156L	**Fruit pie**, *one crust*	Recipe. Apple, gooseberry, plum, rhubarb	1.00	785	187	2.2	26.8	7.9
157L	*pastry top and bottom*	Recipe. Ref. Wiles *et al.* (1980)	1.00	1084	259	3.3	31.5	13.3
158L	individual	10 pies, as purchased, 3 brands; apple, blackcurrant, blackberry, apricot	1.00	1560	372	4.7	53.3	15.5
159L	wholemeal, *one crust*	Recipe. Ref. Wiles *et al.* (1980). Apple, gooseberry, plum, rhubarb	1.00	772	184	2.8	25.0	8.1
160L	wholemeal, *pastry top and bottom*	Recipe. Ref. Wiles *et al.* (1980). Apple, gooseberry, plum, rhubarb	1.00	1051	251	4.3	27.9	13.6
161L	**Lemon meringue pie**	Recipe	1.00	1340	320	4.7	42.8	14.4
162L	**Pancakes**, sweet, *made with whole milk*	Recipe	1.00	1254	300	6.1	32.4	16.2
163L	**Pie**, *with pie filling*	Recipe	1.00	1140	273	3.4	32.1	14.5
164L	**Sponge pudding**	Recipe	1.00	1419	339	6.1	41.9	16.3
165L	**Treacle tart**	Recipe	1.00	1550	369	4.0	56.5	14.1
Savouries								
166L	**Cauliflower cheese**	Recipe	1.00	439	105	5.9	4.9	6.9
167L	**Dumplings**	Recipe	1.00	861	206	3.0	22.2	11.7
168L	**Macaroni cheese**	Recipe	1.00	738	177	7.4	12.5	10.8
169L	**Pancakes**, savoury, *made with whole milk*	Recipe	1.00	1130	271	6.5	21.9	17.5

No.	Food	Labelling information for Group 2 nutrients per 100g food: Sugars (actual weight) g	Saturates g	Fibre (Englyst) g	Sodium g	Additional nutrients and information per 100g food: Sodium mg	Starch (actual weight) g	Water g
	Puddings							
156L	**Fruit pie**, *one crust*	15.0	2.9	1.7	0.1	120	11.8	59.0
157L	*pastry top and bottom*	11.5	4.8	1.8	0.2	200	20.0	47.9
158L	individual	29.8	N	N	0.2	210	23.5	22.9
159L	wholemeal, *one crust*	15.3	2.9	2.7	0.1	100	9.7	58.6
160L	wholemeal, *pastry top and bottom*	11.6	4.9	3.5	0.2	170	16.3	47.9
161L	**Lemon meringue pie**	23.6	5.0	0.7	0.2	200	19.2	35.2
162L	**Pancakes**, sweet, *made with whole milk*	15.3	7.1	0.8	0.1	53	17.1	43.4
163L	**Pie**, *with pie filling*	8.0	5.3	1.5	0.2	240	24.1	47.5
164L	**Sponge pudding**	17.9	5.1	1.1	0.3	310	24.0	32.8
165L	**Treacle tart**	32.1	5.1	1.1	0.4	360	24.4	21.4
	Savouries							
166L	**Cauliflower cheese**	3.0	3.4	1.3	0.2	200	1.9	78.6
167L	**Dumplings**	0.4	6.4	0.9	0.4	400	21.8	60.5
168L	**Macaroni cheese**	2.8	5.6	0.5	0.3	310	9.7	67.1
169L	**Pancakes**, savoury, *made with whole milk*	3.5	7.7	0.8	0.2	150	18.4	51.9

Labelling information for Group 1 nutrients per 100g food

No.	Food	Description and main data sources	Edible proportion	Energy		Protein (N × 6.25)	Carbohydrate (actual wt.)	Fat
				kJ	kcal	g	g	g
	Savouries							
170L	**Pizza**	Cheese and tomato, recipe	1.00	976	233	9.1	22.6	11.8
171L	*frozen*	10 samples, 2 brands, cheese and tomato	1.00	1049	250	8.2	30.2	10.7
172L	**Ravioli**, *canned in tomato sauce*	10 samples, 4 brands	1.00	301	71	3.3	9.6	2.2
173L	**Risotto**, *plain*	Recipe	1.00	932	222	3.2	31.4	9.3
174L	**Samosas**, meat	Recipe	1.00	2443	591	5.3	16.3	56.1
175L	vegetable	Recipe	1.00	1951	471	3.3	20.5[a]	41.8
176L	**Spaghetti**, *canned in tomato sauce*	10 samples, 3 brands	1.00	272	64	2.1	13.0	0.4
177L	**Stuffing**, sage and onion	Recipe	1.00	959	230	5.4	18.8	14.8
178L	**Stuffing mix**	10 samples, 4 brands; assorted flavours	1.00	1405	332	9.9	61.4	5.2
179L	*made up with water*	Calculated from No. 178; made up and cooked according to packet directions	1.00	404	96	2.8	17.7	1.5
180L	**Yorkshire pudding**	Recipe	1.00	864	206	6.8	22.5	9.9

[a] Including oligosaccharides

No.	Food	Sugars (actual weight) g	Saturates g	Fibre (Englyst) g	Sodium g	Sodium mg	Starch (actual weight) g	Water g
		Labelling information for Group 2 nutrients per 100g food				**Additional nutrients and information per 100g food**		
Savouries								
170L	**Pizza**	2.1	5.5	1.5	0.6	570	20.5	51.7
171L	*frozen*	6.6	4.3	1.5	0.5	540	23.6	49.3
172L	**Ravioli**, *canned in tomato sauce*	2.2	0.8	0.9	0.5	490	7.4	79.9
173L	**Risotto**, *plain*	1.2	2.8	0.4	0.4	410	30.2	55.1
174L	**Samosas**, meat	1.0	7.8	1.2	Tr	33	15.3	20.4
175L	vegetable	1.9[a]	5.2	1.8	0.2	200	18.3	31.5
176L	**Spaghetti**, *canned in tomato sauce*	5.2	0.1	0.7[b]	0.4	420	7.8	81.9
177L	**Stuffing**, sage and onion	5.5	4.5	1.7	0.4	420	13.3	56.5
178L	**Stuffing mix**	4.3	2.4	4.7	1.5	1460	57.1	5.9
179L	*made up with water*	1.3	0.8	1.3	0.4	420	16.4	76.4
180L	**Yorkshire pudding**	3.4	5.3	0.9	0.6	590	19.1	57.4

[a] Not including oligosaccharides

[b] Wholemeal types contain 2.0g Englyst fibre per 100g

Labelling information for Group 1 nutrients per 100g food

No.	Food	Description and main data sources	Edible proportion	Energy kJ	Energy kcal	Protein (N × 6.25) g	Carbohydrate (actual wt.) g	Fat g
181L	**Skimmed milk**, *average*	Weighted average of pasteurised, sterilised and UHT	1.00	141	33	3.3	4.8	0.1
182L	pasteurised	10 samples	1.00	141	33	3.3	4.8	0.1
183L	*fortified plus SMP*	10 samples, own label and Vitapint	1.00	165	39	3.8	5.7	0.1
184L	UHT, *fortified*	9 samples	1.00	147	35	3.4	4.8	0.2
185L	**Semi-skimmed milk**, *average*	Weighted average of pasteurised and UHT	1.00	197	47	3.3	4.8	1.6
186L	pasteurised	10 samples	1.00	197	47	3.3	4.8	1.6
187L	*fortified plus SMP*	10 samples, own label and Vitapint	1.00	216	51	3.7	5.5	1.6
188L	UHT	10 samples	1.00	197	47	3.3	4.6	1.7
189L	**Whole milk**, *average*	Weighted average of pasteurised, sterilised and UHT	1.00	275	66	3.1	4.6	3.9
190L	pasteurised[a]	186 samples, bottles and cartons. Fat from Milk Marketing Board	1.00	275	66	3.1	4.6	3.9
191L	*summer*	Selected nutrients only	1.00	275	66	3.1	4.6	3.9
192L	*winter*	Selected nutrients only	1.00	275	66	3.1	4.6	3.9
193L	sterilised	10 samples, 2 brands, polybottles	1.00	275	66	3.4	4.3	3.9
194L	**Channel Island milk**, whole, pasteurised	Samples from dairy and retail outlets. Fat from Milk Marketing Board	1.00	328	79	3.6	4.6	5.1
195L	*summer*	Selected nutrients only	1.00	328	79	3.6	4.6	5.1
196L	*winter*	Selected nutrients only	1.00	328	79	3.6	4.6	5.1
197L	semi-skimmed, UHT	10 samples	1.00	199	47	3.6	4.6	1.6

[a] All the values for pasteurised milk are equally applicable to unpasteurised milk

No.	Food	Labelling information for Group 2 nutrients per 100g food				Additional nutrients and information per 100g food		
		Sugars (actual weight) g	Saturates g	Fibre (Englyst) g	Sodium g	Sodium mg	Starch (actual weight) g	Water g
181L	**Skimmed milk**, *average*	4.8	0.1	0	0.1	54	0	91.1
182L	pasteurised	4.8	0.1	0	0.1	55	0	91.1
183L	*fortified plus SMP*	5.7	0.1	0	0.1	61	0	89.3
184L	UHT, *fortified*	4.8	0.1	0	0.1	54	0	90.9
185L	**Semi-skimmed milk**, *average*	4.8	1.0	0	0.1	55	0	89.8
186L	pasteurised	4.8	1.0	0	0.1	55	0	89.8
187L	*fortified plus SMP*	5.5	1.0	0	0.1	59	0	88.4
188L	UHT	4.6	1.1	0	0.1	50	0	89.7
189L	**Whole milk**, *average*	4.6	2.4	0	0.1	55	0	87.8
190L	pasteurised	4.6	2.4	0	0.1	55	0	87.8
191L	*summer*	4.6	2.4	0	0.1	55	0	87.8
192L	*winter*	4.6	2.5	0	0.1	55	0	87.8
193L	sterilised	4.3	2.4	0	0.1	57	0	87.6
194L	**Channel Island milk**, whole, pasteurised	4.6	3.3	0	0.1	54	0	86.4
195L	*summer*	4.6	3.2	0	0.1	54	0	86.4
196L	*winter*	4.6	3.3	0	0.1	54	0	86.4
197L	semi-skimmed, UHT	4.6	1.0	0	0.1	55	0	89.4

Labelling information for Group 1 nutrients per 100g food

No.	Food	Description and main data sources	Edible proportion	Energy kJ	Energy kcal	Protein (N × 6.25) g	Carbohydrate (actual wt.) g	Fat g
198L	**Condensed milk**, skimmed, *sweetened*	10 cans (Fussells)	1.00	1145	269	9.8	57.1	0.2
199L	whole, *sweetened*	10 cans, 2 brands	1.00	1414	336	8.3	52.9	10.1
200L	**Dried skimmed milk**	20 samples, 7 brands, fortified	1.00	1484	349	35.6	50.4	0.6
201L	*with vegetable fat*	12 samples, 5 brands, fortified	1.00	2041	488	23.1	40.6	25.9
202L	**Evaporated milk**, whole	12 samples, Ideal, Carnation and own brands	1.00	627	150	8.3	8.1	9.4
203L	**Flavoured milk**	32 samples in polybottles; mixed flavours, sterilised; skimmed and whole milk	1.00	287	68	3.5	10.1[a]	1.5
204L	**Goats milk**, pasteurised	20 samples from one herd and literature sources	1.00	254	61	3.1	4.2	3.5
205L	**Human milk**, colostrum	Literature sources	1.00	236	56	1.9	6.3	2.6
206L	transitional	Mixed sample, 15 mothers at 10th day post partum and literature sources	1.00	273	65	1.4	6.6	3.7
207L	mature	Department of Health and literature sources	1.00	291	70	1.3	6.9	4.1
208L	**Sheeps milk**, *raw*	30 samples from 2 herds and literature sources	1.00	395	95	5.3	4.9	6.0
209L	**Soya milk**, plain	6 samples, 4 brands	1.00	140	34	3.3	0.8	1.9
210L	flavoured	4 brands, assorted flavours	1.00	175	42	3.1	3.5	1.7

[a] Including oligosaccharides from the glucose syrup/maltodextrins in the product

No.	Food	Labelling information for Group 2 nutrients per 100g food				Additional nutrients and information per 100g food		
		Sugars (actual weight) g	Saturates g	Fibre (Englyst) g	Sodium g	Sodium mg	Starch (actual weight) g	Water g
198L	**Condensed milk**, skimmed, *sweetened*	57.1	0.1	0	0.2	150	0	29.7
199L	whole, *sweetened*	52.9	6.3	0	0.1	140	0	25.9
200L	**Dried skimmed milk**	50.4	0.4	0	0.6	550	0	3.0
201L	*with vegetable fat*	40.6	16.8	0	0.4	440	0	2.0
202L	**Evaporated milk**, whole	8.1	5.9	0	0.2	180	0	69.1
203L	**Flavoured milk**	9.0[a]	0.9	0	0.1	61	Tr	85.4
204L	**Goats milk**, pasteurised	4.2	2.3	0	Tr	42	0	88.9
205L	**Human milk**, colostrum	6.3	1.1	0	Tr	47	0	88.2
206L	transitional	6.6	1.5	0	Tr	30	0	87.4
207L	mature	6.9	1.8	0	Tr	15	0	87.1
208L	**Sheeps milk**, *raw*	4.9	3.8	0	Tr	44	0	83.0
209L	**Soya milk**, plain	0.8	0.3	Tr	Tr	32	0	89.7
210L	flavoured	3.5	0.2	Tr	0.1	61	0	89.4

[a] Not including oligosaccharides from the glucose syrup/maltodextrins in the product

Labelling information for Group 1 nutrients per 100g food

No.	Food	Description and main data sources	Edible proportion	Energy kJ	Energy kcal	Protein (N × 6.25) g	Carbohydrate (actual wt.) g	Fat g
Fresh creams (pasteurised)								
211L	**Half**	10 samples, 5 brands	1.00	611	148	2.9	4.1	13.3
212L	**Single**	10 samples, 5 brands	1.00	817	198	2.6	3.9	19.1
213L	**Soured**	8 samples, 4 brands	1.00	845	205	2.8	3.6	19.9
214L	**Whipping**	10 samples, 6 brands	1.00	1537	373	1.9	3.0	39.3
215L	**Double**	12 samples, 5 brands	1.00	1849	449	1.7	2.6	48.0
216L	**Clotted**	17 samples, 3 brands	1.00	2414	587	1.6	2.2	63.5
Sterilised creams								
217L	**Sterilised**, canned	13 cans, 6 brands	1.00	985	239	2.4	3.5	23.9
UHT creams								
218L	**Canned spray**	8 samples (Anchor)	1.00	1272	309	1.9	3.3	32.0
Imitation creams								
219L	**Dessert Top**	Manufacturer's data (Nestlés)	1.00	1203	292	2.4	5.7	28.8
220L	**Dream Topping**, *made up with whole milk*	Recipe	1.00	756	182	3.7	11.4	13.5
221L	*made up with semi-skimmed milk*	Recipe	1.00	693	167	3.8	11.5	11.7
222L	**Elmlea**, single	Analysis and manufacturer's data (Van den Berghs)	1.00	785	190	3.1	3.9	18.0
223L	whipping	Analysis and manufacturer's data (Van den Berghs)	1.00	1313	319	2.4	3.0	33.0
224L	double	Analysis and manufacturer's data (Van den Berghs)	1.00	1868	454	2.4	3.0	48.0
225L	**Tip Top**	Manufacturer's data (Nestlés)	1.00	462	111	4.9	8.1	6.5

No.	Food	Labelling information for Group 2 nutrients per 100g food				Additional nutrients and information per 100g food		
		Sugars (actual weight) g	Saturates g	Fibre (Englyst) g	Sodium g	Sodium mg	Starch (actual weight) g	Water g
	Fresh creams (pasteurised)							
211L	**Half**	4.1	8.3	0	Tr	49	0	78.9
212L	**Single**	3.9	11.9	0	Tr	49	0	73.7
213L	**Soured**	3.6	12.5	0	Tr	41	0	72.5
214L	**Whipping**	3.0	24.6	0	Tr	40	0	55.4
215L	**Double**	2.6	30.0	0	Tr	37	0	47.5
216L	**Clotted**	2.2	39.7	0	Tr	18	0	32.2
	Sterilised creams							
217L	**Sterilised**, canned	3.5	14.9	0	0.1	53	0	69.2
	UHT creams							
218L	**Canned spray**	3.3	20.0	0	Tr	33	0	58.4
	Imitation creams							
219L	**Dessert Top**	N	27.0	Tr[a]	0.1	50	Tr	N
220L	**Dream Topping**, *made up with whole milk*	9.5	11.7	Tr	0.1	70	1.9	69.9
221L	*made up with semi-skimmed milk*	9.6	10.5	Tr	0.1	70	1.9	71.5
222L	**Elmlea**, single	3.9	14.0	0.3[a]	Tr	40	0	N
223L	whipping	3.0	28.0	0.1[a]	Tr	31	0	N
224L	double	3.0	29.0	0.1[a]	Tr	31	0	N
225L	**Tip Top**	N	5.8	Tr	0.1	90	N	N

[a] Carob and guar gums are added as thickeners

Labelling information for Group 1 nutrients per 100g food

No.	Food	Description and main data sources	Edible proportion	Energy kJ	Energy kcal	Protein (N × 6.25) g	Carbohydrate (actual wt.) g	Fat g
Cheeses								
226L	**Brie**	10 samples	1.00	1317	318	18.9	Tr	26.9
227L	**Camembert**	10 samples	1.00	1224	295	20.4	Tr	23.7
228L	**Cheddar**, *average*	Weighted average from 5 countries	1.00	1700	410	25.0	0.1	34.4
229L	vegetarian	10 samples	1.00	1751	423	25.3	Tr	35.7
230L	**Cheddar-type**, *reduced fat*	10 samples, Tendale	1.00	1080	259	30.9	Tr	15.0
231L	**Cheese spread**, plain	10 samples, 3 brands	1.00	1139	275	13.2	4.2	22.8[a]
232L	**Cottage cheese**, plain	10-19 samples	1.00	408	97	13.5	2.0	3.9
233L	*with additions*	10 samples, mixed, e.g. with pineapple, Cheddar cheese	1.00	396	94	12.5	2.5	3.8
234L	reduced fat	6 samples, different brands	1.00	326	77	13.0	3.1	1.4
235L	**Cream cheese**	3 samples	1.00	1807	439	3.1	Tr	47.4
236L	**Danish blue**	10 samples	1.00	1430	345	19.7	Tr	29.6
237L	**Edam**	10 samples	1.00	1373	331	25.5	Tr	25.4
238L	**Feta**	18 samples, made from sheeps and goats milk	1.00	1031	249	15.3	1.4	20.2
239L	**Fromage frais**, fruit	11 samples, 4 brands, mixed flavours	1.00	551	131	6.6	13.2	5.8
240L	plain	12 samples, 3 brands	1.00	467	112	6.6	5.4	7.1
241L	very low fat	10 samples, 4 brands, plain and fruit	1.00	247	58	7.6	6.5	0.2

[a] Reduced fat varieties contain approximately 9.0g fat per 100g

No.	Food	Labelling information for Group 2 nutrients per 100g food: Sugars (actual weight) g	Saturates g	Fibre (Englyst) g	Sodium g	Additional nutrients and information per 100g food: Sodium mg	Starch (actual weight) g	Water g
	Cheeses							
226L	**Brie**	Tr	16.8	0	0.7	700	0	48.6
227L	**Camembert**	Tr	14.8	0	0.7	650	0	50.7
228L	**Cheddar**, *average*	0.1	21.7	0	0.7	670	0	36.0
229L	vegetarian	Tr	22.5	0	0.7	670	0	33.9
230L	**Cheddar-type**, *reduced fat*	Tr	9.4	0	0.7	670	0	47.1
231L	**Cheese spread**, plain	4.2	14.3	0	1.1	1060	0	53.3
232L	**Cottage cheese**, plain	2.0	2.4	0	0.4	380	0	79.1
233L	*with additions*	2.5	2.4	Tr	0.4	360	0	76.9
234L	reduced fat	3.1	0.9	0	0.4	380	0	80.2
235L	**Cream cheese**	Tr	29.7	0	0.3	300	0	45.5
236L	**Danish blue**	Tr	18.5	0	1.3	1260	0	45.3
237L	**Edam**	Tr	15.9	0	1.0	1020	0	43.8
238L	**Feta**	1.4	13.7	0	1.4	1440	0	56.5
239L	**Fromage frais**, fruit	13.2	3.6	Tr	Tr	35	0	71.9
240L	plain	5.4	4.4	0	Tr	31	0	77.9
241L	very low fat	6.5	0.1	Tr	Tr	33	Tr	83.7

Labelling information for Group 1 nutrients per 100g food

No.	Food	Description and main data sources	Edible proportion	Energy kJ	Energy kcal	Protein (N × 6.25) g	Carbohydrate (actual wt.) g	Fat g
Cheeses								
242L	**Full fat soft cheese**	e.g. Philadelphia-type. Manufacturer's data plus calculation	1.00	1290	313	8.4	Tr	31.0
243L	**Gouda**	10 samples	1.00	1547	373	23.5	Tr	31.0
244L	**Hard cheese**, *average*	Average of Cheddar, Derby, Double Gloucester and Leicester	1.00	1671	403	24.2	0.1	34.0
245L	**Lymeswold**	Mild blue full fat soft cheese, 10 samples	1.00	1751	424	15.3	Tr	40.3
246L	**Medium fat soft cheese**	e.g. Philadelphia light, 5 samples, 3 brands	1.00	742	179	9.1	3.0	14.5
247L	**Parmesan**	10 samples, block and powdered	1.00	1866	449	38.6	Tr	32.7
248L	**Processed cheese**, plain	10 samples, blocks and slices	1.00	1361	328	20.4	0.9	27.0[a]
249L	**Stilton**, blue	10-13 samples	1.00	1694	409	22.3	0.1	35.5
250L	**White cheese**, *average*	Average of Caerphilly, Cheshire, Lancashire, Wensleydale	1.00	1549	374	22.9	0.1	31.3

[a] Reduced fat varieties contain approximately 9.5g fat per 100g

No.	Food	Labelling information for Group 2 nutrients per 100g food: Sugars (actual weight) g	Saturates g	Fibre (Englyst) g	Sodium g	Additional nutrients and information per 100g food: Sodium mg	Starch (actual weight) g	Water g
	Cheeses							
242L	**Full fat soft cheese**	Tr	19.4	0	0.3	330	0	58.0
243L	**Gouda**	Tr	19.4	0	0.9	910	0	40.1
244L	**Hard cheese**, *average*	0.1	21.3	0	0.6	620	0	37.2
245L	**Lymeswold**	Tr	25.2	0	0.6	560	0	41.0
246L	**Medium fat soft cheese**	3.0	9.1	0	N	N	0	69.5
247L	**Parmesan**	Tr	20.5	0	1.1	1090	0	18.4
248L	**Processed cheese**, plain	0.9	16.6	0	1.3	1320	0	45.7
249L	**Stilton**, blue	0.1	22.2	0	0.9	930	0	38.6
250L	**White cheese**, *average*	0.1	19.6	0	0.5	530	0	41.4

Labelling information for Group 1 nutrients per 100g food

No.	Food	Description and main data sources	Edible proportion	Energy kJ	Energy kcal	Protein (N × 6.25) g	Carbohydrate (actual wt.) g	Fat g
251L	**Drinking yogurt**	5 samples (Ambrosia), UHT	1.00	267	63	3.0	12.7	Tr[a]
252L	**Greek yogurt**, cows	5 samples, 3 brands, 'strained' variety	1.00	478	115	6.3	2.0	9.1[b]
253L	sheep	3 samples (Total), 'set' variety	1.00	442	106	4.3	5.4	7.5
254L	**Low calorie yogurt**	13 samples, 5 brands, assorted flavours	1.00	177	42	4.2	5.8	0.2
255L	**Low fat yogurt**, plain	10 samples, 5 brands	1.00	239	56	5.0	7.3	0.8
256L	flavoured	24 samples, 4 brands, assorted flavours	1.00	390	92	3.7	17.3	0.9
257L	fruit	26 samples, 9 brands, assorted flavours	1.00	386	91	4.0	17.2	0.7
258L	**Soya yogurt**	5 samples sweetened (Sojal)	1.00	314	75	5.5	3.8	4.2
259L	**Tzatziki**	Yogurt-based Greek starter. Recipe	1.00	278	67	3.7	2.0	4.9
260L	**Whole milk yogurt**, plain	22 samples, 2 brands	1.00	335	80	5.6	7.6	3.0
261L	fruit	10 samples, assorted flavours, 'thick and creamy' type	1.00	447	106	5.0	15.2	2.8

[a] The fat content is variable. Non-UHT varieties contain 0.3 - 2g fat per 100g

[b] 'Set' varieties contain approximately 4g fat per 100g

No.	Food	Labelling information for Group 2 nutrients per 100g food: Sugars (actual weight) g	Saturates g	Fibre (Englyst) g	Sodium g	Additional nutrients and information per 100g food: Sodium mg	Starch (actual weight) g	Water g
251L	**Drinking yogurt**	12.7	Tr	Tr	Tr	47	0	84.4
252L	**Greek yogurt**, cows	2.0	5.2	0	0.1	71	0	78.5
253L	sheep	5.4	4.8	0	0.2	150	0	80.9
254L	**Low calorie yogurt**	5.8	0.1	N	0.1	73	0	87.9
255L	**Low fat yogurt**, plain	7.3	0.5	N	0.1	83	0	84.9
256L	flavoured	17.3	0.5	N	0.1	65	0	77.9
257L	fruit	17.2	0.4	N	0.1	64	0	77.0
258L	**Soya yogurt**	3.8	0.6	N	N	N	Tr	82.4
259L	**Tzatziki**	1.7	2.9	0.2	0.4	370	0.3	85.8
260L	**Whole milk yogurt**, plain	7.6	1.7	N	0.1	80	0	81.9
261L	fruit	15.2[a]	1.5	N	0.1	82	0	73.1

[a] 'Real' fruit yogurts contain 10.4g total sugars per 100g

Labelling information for Group 1 nutrients per 100g food

No.	Food	Description and main data sources	Edible proportion	Energy kJ	Energy kcal	Protein (N × 6.25) g	Carbohydrate (actual wt.) g	Fat g
262L	**Arctic roll**	10 samples, 2 brands	1.00	851	202	4.1	31.6	6.6
263L	**Choc ice**	Plain and milk varieties; analysis and manufacturer's data (Birds Eye Wall's)	1.00	1161	278	3.4	26.8	17.5
264L	**Chocolate nut sundae**	Recipe	1.00	1171	280	3.1	32.5[a]	15.3
265L	**Cornetto**	Analysis and manufacturer's data (Birds Eye Wall's)	1.00	1094	261	3.7	32.6	12.9
266L	**Frozen ice cream desserts**	6 samples, different types eg Sonata, Viennetta	1.00	952	228	3.3	21.8	14.2
267L	**Ice cream**, dairy, vanilla	17 samples	1.00	820	196	3.5	23.4[a]	9.8
268L	flavoured	17 samples, assorted flavours	1.00	758	181	3.4	23.8[a]	8.0
269L	non-dairy, vanilla	11 samples, hard and soft scoop	1.00	745	178	3.1	21.8[a]	8.7
270L	flavoured	14 samples, hard and soft scoop assorted flavours	1.00	702	167	3.1	22.1[a]	7.4
271L	mixes	Prepared mix from ice cream parlour	1.00	767	183	4.1	23.8[a]	7.9
272L	**Ice cream wafers**	6 samples, 2 brands	1.00	1434	338	11.1	71.7	0.7
273L	**Sorbet**, lemon	Recipe	1.00	570	134	0.9	32.6	Tr

[a] Including oligosaccharides from the glucose syrup/maltodextrins in the product

No.	Food	Labelling information for Group 2 nutrients per 100g food				Additional nutrients and information per 100g food		
		Sugars (actual weight) g	Saturates g	Fibre (Englyst) g	Sodium g	Sodium mg	Starch (actual weight) g	Water g
262L	**Arctic roll**	24.3	3.1	Tr	0.2	150	7.3	51.3
263L	**Choc ice**	N	10.8	Tr	0.1	91	N	N
264L	**Chocolate nut sundae**	30.4[a]	8.3	0.1	0.2	150	0.4	46.0
265L	**Cornetto**	24.4	6.7[b]	N	0.1	91	8.2	N
266L	**Frozen ice cream desserts**	21.8	11.2	Tr	0.1	84	Tr	61.7
267L	**Ice cream**, dairy, vanilla	21.3[a]	6.4	Tr[c]	0.1	69	Tr	61.9
268L	flavoured	22.9[a]	5.2	Tr[c]	0.1	61	Tr	59.8
269L	non-dairy, vanilla	18.2[a]	4.4	Tr[c]	0.1	76	Tr	65.3
270L	flavoured	20.4[a]	3.7	Tr[c]	0.1	72	Tr	64.9
271L	mixes	20.7[a]	4.0	Tr[c]	0.1	59	Tr	63.4
272L	**Ice cream wafers**	1.1	N	N	0.1	93	70.6	2.8
273L	**Sorbet**, lemon	32.6	Tr	0	Tr	18	0	64.9

[a] Not including oligosaccharides from the glucose syrup/maltodextrins in the product

[b] Strawberry variety only

[c] Gums and cellulose derivatives are added as stabilisers

Labelling information for Group 1 nutrients per 100g food

No.	Food	Description and main data sources	Edible proportion	Energy kJ	Energy kcal	Protein (N × 6.25) g	Carbohydrate (actual wt.) g	Fat g
Puddings and chilled desserts								
274L	**Cheesecake**, *frozen*	10 samples, assorted flavours, fruit topping	1.00	1018	243	5.7	31.1	10.6
275L	**Creme caramel**	9 samples, 4 brands	1.00	466	110	2.9	19.7	2.2
276L	**Custard**, *made up with whole milk*	Recipe	1.00	491	117	3.6	15.5	4.5
277L	*made up with skimmed milk*	Recipe	1.00	335	79	3.8	15.7	0.1
278L	canned	10 samples, 3 brands	1.00	400	95	2.6	14.4	3.0
279L	**Instant dessert powder**	10 samples, 2 types, assorted flavours	1.00	1640	391	2.4	56.4	17.3
280L	*made up with whole milk*	Recipe	1.00	520	124	3.0	13.9	6.3
281L	*made up with skimmed milk*	Recipe	1.00	411	98	3.1	14.1	3.2
282L	**Jelly**, *made with water*	Recipe	1.00	270	64	1.3	14.6	0
283L	**Milk pudding**, *made with whole milk*	e.g. rice, sago, semolina, tapioca; recipe	1.00	543	129	3.9	18.7	4.3
284L	*made with skimmed milk*	e.g. rice, sago, semolina, tapioca; recipe	1.00	397	93	4.0	18.9	0.2
285L	**Mousse**, chocolate	10 samples, 4 brands, fresh	1.00	589	140	3.9	19.0	5.4
286L	fruit	8 samples, assorted flavours, fresh	1.00	582	139	4.4	17.4	5.7
287L	**Rice pudding**, canned	10 cans, 4 brands	1.00	371	88	3.3	13.1	2.5
288L	**Trifle**	Recipe	1.00	658	157	3.7	21.3	6.3
289L	*with fresh cream*	10 samples, individual and large	1.00	696	166	2.4	18.5	9.2

No.	Food	Labelling information for Group 2 nutrients per 100g food				Additional nutrients and information per 100g food		
		Sugars (actual weight) g	Saturates g	Fibre (Englyst) g	Sodium g	Sodium mg	Starch (actual weight) g	Water g
	Puddings and chilled desserts							
274L	**Cheesecake**, *frozen*	21.3	5.6	0.9	0.2	160	9.8	44.0
275L	**Creme caramel**	17.3	N	N	0.1	70	2.4	72.0
276L	**Custard**, *made up with whole milk*	10.9	2.8	Tr	0.1	81	4.6	75.5
277L	*made up with skimmed milk*	11.1	0.1	Tr	0.1	81	4.6	79.3
278L	canned	11.6	1.7	0.1	0.1	67	2.8	77.2
279L	**Instant dessert powder**	38.8	15.9	1.0	1.1	1100	17.6	1.0
280L	*made up with whole milk*	10.7	4.9	0.2	0.2	240	3.2	72.1
281L	*made up with skimmed milk*	10.9	2.9	0.2	0.2	240	3.2	74.9
282L	**Jelly**, *made with water*	14.6	0	0	Tr	5	0	84.0
283L	**Milk pudding**, *made with whole milk*	10.2	2.7	0.1	0.1	59	8.5	72.4
284L	*made with skimmed milk*	10.4	0.1	0.1	0.1	59	8.5	76.0
285L	**Mousse**, chocolate	16.8	N	N	0.1	67	2.2	67.3
286L	fruit	17.4	N	N	0.1	62	Tr	71.7
287L	**Rice pudding**, canned	7.8[a]	1.6	0.2	0.1	50	5.3	77.6
288L	**Trifle**	16.3	3.1	0.5	0.1	53	5.0	67.2
289L	*with fresh cream*	14.4	5.2	0.5	0.1	63	4.1	68.1

[a] Low calorie varieties contain approximately 3.0g total sugars per 100g

Labelling information for Group 1 nutrients per 100g food

No.	Food	Description and main data sources	Edible proportion	Energy kJ	Energy kcal	Protein (N × 6.25) g	Carbohydrate (actual wt.) g	Fat g
290L	**Eggs**, chicken, whole, *raw*[a]	Analysis of battery, deep litter and free range	1.00	614	148	12.6	Tr	10.8
291L	white, *raw*	34 eggs and literature sources	1.00	153	36	9.0	Tr	Tr
292L	yolk, *raw*	34 eggs and literature sources	1.00	1402	339	16.1	Tr	30.5
293L	chicken, *boiled*	10 eggs	1.00	614	148	12.6	Tr	10.8
294L	*fried in vegetable oil*	12 eggs, shallow fried	1.00	746	180	13.6	Tr	13.9
295L	*poached*[b]	10 eggs, no fat added	1.00	614	148	12.6	Tr	10.8
296L	*scrambled, with milk*	Recipe	1.00	1028	249	10.7	0.6	22.6
297L	duck, whole, *raw*	Analytical and literature sources. Ref. Posati and Orr (1976)	1.00	680	163	14.3	Tr	11.8
298L	**Egg fried rice**	Recipe	1.00	861	206	4.3	23.3	10.6
299L	**Meringue**	Recipe	1.00	1635	385	5.3	90.9	Tr
300L	*with cream*	Recipe. Ref. Wiles *et al.* (1980)	1.00	1579	378	3.3	38.2	23.6
301L	**Omelette**, plain	Recipe	1.00	792	191	10.9	Tr	16.4
302L	cheese	Recipe. Ref. Wiles *et al.* (1980)	1.00	1105	267	15.8	Tr	22.6
303L	**Quiche**, cheese and egg	Recipe. Ref. Wiles *et al.* (1980)	1.00	1304	313	12.6	15.8	22.2
304L	cheese and egg, wholemeal	Recipe	1.00	1278	307	13.3	13.1	22.4
305L	**Scotch eggs**, retail	10 samples, 8 brands	1.00	1039	250	12.0	11.9	17.1

[a] An average egg is composed of 11% shell, 58% white and 31% yolk

[b] Eggs poached with fat added contain 644 kJ , 155 kcal, 12.4g protein, Tr carbohydrate and 11.7g fat per 100g

No.	Food	Labelling information for Group 2 nutrients per 100g food				Additional nutrients and information per 100g food		
		Sugars (actual weight) g	Saturates g	Fibre (Englyst) g	Sodium g	Sodium mg	Starch (actual weight) g	Water g
290L	**Eggs**, chicken, whole, *raw*	Tr	3.1	0	0.1	140	0	75.1
291L	white, *raw*	Tr	Tr	0	0.2	190	0	88.3
292L	yolk, *raw*	Tr	8.7	0	0.1	50	0	51.0
293L	chicken, *boiled*	Tr	3.1	0	0.1	140	0	75.1
294L	*fried in vegetable oil*	Tr	4.0	0	0.2	160	0	70.1
295L	*poached*	Tr	3.1	0	0.1	140	0	75.1[a]
296L	*scrambled, with milk*	0.6	11.6	0	1.0	1030	0	62.4
297L	duck, whole, *raw*	Tr	2.9	0	0.1	120	0	70.6
298L	**Egg fried rice**	0.8	1.5	0.4	Tr	27	22.5	60.7
299L	**Meringue**	90.9	Tr	0	0.1	110	0	2.2
300L	*with cream*	38.2	14.7	0	0.1	70	0	34.1
301L	**Omelette**, plain	Tr	7.4	0	1.0	1030	0	69.0
302L	cheese	Tr	12.2	0	0.9	900	0	57.7
303L	**Quiche**, cheese and egg	1.5	10.3	0.6	0.3	340	14.3	46.7
304L	cheese and egg, wholemeal	1.6	10.4	1.9	0.3	340	11.5	46.7
305L	**Scotch eggs**, retail	Tr	4.3	N	0.7	670	11.9	54.0

[a] Eggs poached with fat added contain 74.4g water per 100g

Labelling information for Group 1 nutrients per 100g food

No.	Food	Description and main data sources	Edible proportion	Energy kJ	Energy kcal	Protein (N × 6.25) g	Carbohydrate (actual wt.) g	Fat g
	Spreading fats							
306L	**Butter**	Analysis and literature sources	1.00	3031	737	0.5	Tr	81.7[a,b]
307L	**Dairy/fat spread**	6 samples, Krona, Clover and Golden Churn	1.00	2723	662	0.4	Tr	73.4
308L	**Low-fat spread**	4 samples, Gold, Delight, Outline and own brand	1.00	1604	389	5.7	0.5	40.5
309L	**Margarine**	Mixed sample	1.00	3040	739	0.2	1.0	81.6
310L	hard, *animal and vegetable fat*	10 samples, 2 brands and estimation from No. 309	1.00	3040	739	0.2	1.0	81.6
311L	hard, *vegetable fat only*	4 samples of the same brand and estimation from No. 309	1.00	3040	739	0.2	1.0	81.6
312L	soft, *animal and vegetable fat*	16 samples, 3 brands and estimation from No. 309	1.00	3040	739	0.2	1.0	81.6
313L	soft, *vegetable fat only*	8 samples, 3 brands and estimation from No. 309	1.00	3040	739	0.2	1.0	81.6
314L	polyunsaturated	18 samples, 3 brands and estimation from No. 309	1.00	3040	739	0.2	1.0	81.6
315L	**Very low fat spread**	i.e. Gold Lowest, manufacturer's data (St Ivel)	1.00	1121	271	8.1	3.4	25.0
	Animal fats							
316L	**Compound cooking fat**	7 samples	1.00	3674	894	Tr	Tr	99.3
317L	**Dripping**, beef	Analysed as purchased	1.00	3663	891	Tr	Tr	99.0
318L	**Lard**	Analysed as purchased	1.00	3663	891	Tr	Tr	99.0
319L	**Suet**, *shredded*	6 samples of the same brand	1.00	3395	824	Tr	11.0	86.7

[a] Unsalted butter contains 82.7g fat per 100g

[b] 'Half-fat' butter spreads, e.g. Half-fat Anchor, Kerrygold light, contain 39-40g fat per 100g

No.	Food	Labelling information for Group 2 nutrients per 100g food				Additional nutrients and information per 100g food		
		Sugars (actual weight) g	Saturates g	Fibre (Englyst) g	Sodium g	Sodium mg	Starch (actual weight) g	Water g
Spreading fats								
306L	**Butter**	Tr	54.0	0	0.8	750[a]	0	15.6[a]
307L	**Dairy/fat spread**	Tr	28.1	0	0.8	760	0	22.0
308L	**Low-fat spread**	0.5	11.2	0	0.7	650	0	49.9
309L	**Margarine**	1.0	N	0	0.8	800	0	16.0
310L	hard, *animal and vegetable fat*	1.0	30.4	0	0.8	800	0	16.0
311L	hard, *vegetable fat only*	1.0	35.9	0	0.8	800	0	16.0
312L	soft, *animal and vegetable fat*	1.0	26.9	0	0.8	800	0	16.0
313L	soft, *vegetable fat only*	1.0	25.0	0	0.8	800	0	16.0
314L	polyunsaturated	1.0	16.2	0	0.8	800	0	16.0
315L	**Very low fat spread**	3.4	6.5	0	1.1	1050	Tr	N
Animal fats								
316L	**Compound cooking fat**	Tr	38.1	0	Tr	Tr	0	Tr
317L	**Dripping**, beef	Tr	54.8	0	Tr	5	0	1.0
318L	**Lard**	Tr	40.8	0	Tr	2	0	1.0
319L	**Suet**, *shredded*	0.2	48.0	0.5	Tr	Tr	10.8	1.5

[a] Unsalted butter contains 11mg sodium and 15.7g water per 100g

Labelling information for Group 1 nutrients per 100g food

No.	Food	Description and main data sources	Edible proportion	Energy kJ	Energy kcal	Protein (N × 6.25) g	Carbohydrate (actual wt.) g	Fat g
Oils								
320L	**Coconut oil**	Literature sources and estimation from No. 333	1.00	3696	899	Tr	0	99.9
321L	**Cod liver oil**	3 samples	1.00	3696	899	Tr	0	99.9
322L	**Corn oil**	Literature sources and estimation from No. 333; maize oil	1.00	3696	899	Tr	0	99.9
323L	**Cottonseed oil**	Literature sources and estimation from No. 333	1.00	3696	899	Tr	0	99.9
324L	**Olive oil**	Ref. Pellet and Shadarevian (1970)	1.00	3696	899	Tr	0	99.9
325L	**Palm oil**	Literature sources and estimation from No. 333; refined oil	1.00	3696	899	Tr	0	99.9
326L	**Peanut oil**	Literature sources and estimation from No. 333	1.00	3696	899	Tr	0	99.9
327L	**Rapeseed oil**, high erucic acid	Literature sources and estimation from No. 333	1.00	3696	899	Tr	0	99.9
328L	low erucic acid	Literature sources and estimation from No. 333	1.00	3696	899	Tr	0	99.9
329L	**Safflower oil**	Literature sources and estimation from No. 333	1.00	3696	899	Tr	0	99.9
330L	**Sesame oil**	Ref. Wu Leung *et al.* (1972)	1.00	3692	898	0.2	0	99.7
331L	**Soya oil**	Literature sources and estimation from No. 333	1.00	3696	899	Tr	0	99.9
332L	**Sunflowerseed oil**	Literature sources and estimation from No. 333	1.00	3696	899	Tr	0	99.9
333L	**Vegetable oil**, blended, *average*	All kinds	1.00	3696	899	Tr	0	99.9
334L	**Wheatgerm oil**	Literature sources and estimation from No. 333	1.00	3696	899	Tr	0	99.9
Ghee								
335L	**Ghee**, butter	5 assorted samples	1.00	3693	898	Tr	Tr	99.8
336L	palm	5 samples of the same brand	1.00	3689	897	Tr	Tr	99.7
337L	vegetable	5 samples, 2 different types	1.00	3693	898	Tr	Tr	99.8

No.	Food	Labelling information for Group 2 nutrients per 100g food				Additional nutrients and information per 100g food		
		Sugars (actual weight) g	Saturates g	Fibre (Englyst) g	Sodium g	Sodium mg	Starch (actual weight) g	Water g
Oils								
320L	**Coconut oil**	0	85.2	0	Tr	Tr	0	Tr
321L	**Cod liver oil**	0	N	0	Tr	Tr	0	Tr
322L	**Corn oil**	0	12.7	0	Tr	Tr	0	Tr
323L	**Cottonseed oil**	0	25.6	0	Tr	Tr	0	Tr
324L	**Olive oil**	0	14.0	0	Tr	Tr	0	Tr
325L	**Palm oil**	0	45.3	0	Tr	Tr	0	Tr
326L	**Peanut oil**	0	18.8	0	Tr	Tr	0	Tr
327L	**Rapeseed oil**, high erucic acid	0	5.3	0	Tr	Tr	0	Tr
328L	low erucic acid	0	6.6	0	Tr	Tr	0	Tr
329L	**Safflower oil**	0	10.2	0	Tr	Tr	0	Tr
330L	**Sesame oil**	0	14.2	0	Tr	2	0	0.1
331L	**Soya oil**	0	14.5	0	Tr	Tr	0	Tr
332L	**Sunflowerseed oil**	0	11.9	0	Tr	Tr	0	Tr
333L	**Vegetable oil**, blended, *average*	0	10.4[a]	0	Tr	Tr	0	Tr
334L	**Wheatgerm oil**	0	18.8	0	Tr	Tr	0	Tr
Ghee								
335L	**Ghee**, butter	Tr	66.0	0	Tr	2	0	0.1
336L	palm	Tr	47.0	0	Tr	1	0	0.1
337L	vegetable	Tr	N[a]	0	Tr	1	0	0.1

[a] The fatty acid profile will depend on the blend of oils used

Labelling information for Group 1 nutrients per 100g food

No.	Food	Description and main data sources	Edible proportion	Energy kJ	Energy kcal	Protein (N × 6.25) g	Carbohydrate (actual wt.) g	Fat g
	Bacon							
338L	fat only, *raw, average*	Fat from five different cuts	1.00	3075	747	4.8	0	80.9
339L	*cooked, average*	Fat from five different cuts	1.00	2852	692	9.3	0	72.8
340L	lean only, *raw, average*	Lean from five different cuts	1.00	617	147	20.2	0	7.4
341L	**Collar joint**, lean and fat, *raw*	12 samples, boneless, 70% lean	0.91	1318	318	14.6	0	28.9
342L	*boiled*	12 samples, 73% lean; soaked for 16 hours before cooking	1.00	1346	325	20.4	0	27.0
343L	lean only, *boiled*	12 samples; soaked for 16 hours before cooking	1.00	801	191	26.0	0	9.7
344L	**Gammon joint**, lean and fat, *raw*	12 samples, boneless, 80% lean	0.93	976	235	17.6	0	18.3
345L	*boiled*	12 samples 80% lean; soaked for 16 hours before cooking	1.00	1119	269	24.7	0	18.9
346L	lean only, *boiled*	12 samples; soaked for 16 hours before cooking	1.00	703	167	29.4	0	5.5
347L	**Gammon rasher**, lean and fat, *grilled*	24 samples, 88% lean; rind removed before cooking	1.00	953	228	29.5	0	12.2
348L	lean only, *grilled*	24 samples; rind removed before cooking	1.00	726	172	31.4	0	5.2

No.	Food	Labelling information for Group 2 nutrients per 100g food				Additional nutrients and information per 100g food		
		Sugars (actual weight) g	Saturates g	Fibre (Englyst) g	Sodium g	Sodium mg	Starch (actual weight) g	Water g
	Bacon							
338L	fat only, *raw, average*	0	31.5	0	0.6	560	0	12.8
339L	*cooked, average*	0	28.5	0	1.0	990	0	13.8
340L	lean only, *raw, average*	0[a]	2.7	0	1.9	1870[a]	0	67.0
341L	**Collar joint**, lean and fat, *raw*	0	11.2	0	1.7	1690	0	51.3
342L	*boiled*	0	10.6	0	1.1	1100	0	49.0
343L	lean only, *boiled*	0	3.6	0	1.4	1350	0	60.8
344L	**Gammon joint**, lean and fat, *raw*	0	7.1	0	1.2	1180	0	60.8
345L	*boiled*	0	7.4	0	1.0	960	0	53.9
346L	lean only, *boiled*	0	2.1	0	1.1	1110	0	62.7
347L	**Gammon rasher**, lean and fat, *grilled*	0	4.8	0	2.1	2140	0	52.1
348L	lean only, *grilled*	0	1.9	0	2.2	2210	0	57.0

[a] Sweetcure bacon lean contains 0.5g sugars and 1200mg sodium per 100g

Labelling information for Group 1 nutrients per 100g food

No.	Food	Description and main data sources	Edible proportion	Energy kJ	Energy kcal	Protein (N × 6.25) g	Carbohydrate (actual wt.) g	Fat g
Bacon								
349L	**Rasher**, lean and fat, *raw, back*	36 samples, 59% lean; rind removed	0.94	1766	428	14.2	0	41.2
350L	*raw, middle*	36 samples, 59% lean; rind removed	0.91	1755	425	14.2	0	40.9
351L	*-, streaky*	36 samples, 61% lean; rind removed	0.86	1710	414	14.6	0	39.5
352L	lean only, *fried, average*	Average of back, middle and streaky	1.00	1383	332	32.8	0	22.3
353L	lean and fat, *fried, back*	36 samples, 68% lean; rind removed before cooking	1.00	1926	465	24.9	0	40.6
354L	*fried, middle*	36 samples, 64% lean; rind removed before cooking	1.00	1975	477	24.1	0	42.3
355L	*-, streaky*	36 samples, 60% lean; rind removed before cooking	1.00	2050	496	23.1	0	44.8
356L	lean only, *grilled, average*	Average of back, middle and streaky	1.00	1218	292	30.5	0	18.9
357L	lean and fat, *grilled, back*	36 samples, 72% lean; rind removed before cooking	1.00	1681	405	25.3	0	33.8
358L	*grilled, middle*	36 samples, 70% lean; rind removed before cooking	1.00	1722	416	24.9	0	35.1
359L	*-, streaky*	36 samples, 69% lean; rind removed before cooking	1.00	1749	422	24.5	0	36.0
360L	**Ham**, canned	12 samples, 10 brands	1.00	501	120	18.4	0	5.1

No.	Food	Labelling information for Group 2 nutrients per 100g food				Additional nutrients and information per 100g food		
		Sugars (actual weight) g	Saturates g	Fibre (Englyst) g	Sodium g	Sodium mg	Starch (actual weight) g	Water g
Bacon								
349L	**Rasher**, lean and fat, *raw, back*	0	16.2	0	1.5	1470	0	40.5
350L	*raw, middle*	0	15.9	0	1.5	1470	0	40.8
351L	*-, streaky*	0	15.4	0	1.5	1500	0	41.8
352L	lean only, *fried, average*	0	8.3	0	2.3	2280	0	39.2
353L	lean and fat, *fried, back*	0	15.9	0	1.9	1910	0	29.7
354L	*fried, middle*	0	16.5	0	1.9	1870	0	28.7
355L	*-, streaky*	0	17.5	0	1.8	1820	0	27.5
356L	lean only, *grilled, average*	0	7.4	0	2.2	2240	0	46.0
357L	lean and fat, *grilled, back*	0	13.2	0	2.0	2020	0	36.0
358L	*grilled, middle*	0	13.8	0	2.0	2000	0	35.2
359L	*-, streaky*	0	14.1	0	2.0	1990	0	34.6
360L	**Ham**, canned	0	1.9	0	1.3	1250	0	72.5

Labelling information for Group 1 nutrients per 100g food

No.	Food	Description and main data sources	Edible proportion	Energy kJ	Energy kcal	Protein (N × 6.25) g	Carbohydrate (actual wt.) g	Fat g
Beef								
361L	fat only, *raw, average*	Fat from six different cuts	1.00	2625	637	8.8	0	66.9
362L	*cooked, average*	Fat from six different cuts	1.00	2526	613	11.9	0	62.8
363L	lean only, *raw, average*	Lean from six different cuts	1.00	515	123	20.3	0	4.6
364L	**Brisket**, lean and fat, *raw*	18 samples, boned and rolled, 77% lean	0.96	1044	252	16.8	0	20.5
365L	*boiled*	18 samples, boned and rolled, 77% lean; salt added	1.00	1354	326	27.6	0	23.9
366L	**Forerib**, lean and fat, *raw*	18 samples, with bone, 72% lean	0.76	1201	290	16.0	0	25.1
367L	*roast*	18 samples, 72% lean; cooked on the bone	1.00	1446	349	22.4	0	28.8
368L	lean only, *roast*	18 samples; cooked on the bone	1.00	941	225	27.9	0	12.6
369L	**Mince**, *raw*	18 samples	1.00	919	221	18.8	0	16.2
370L	*stewed*	18 samples; salt added	1.00	955	229	23.1	0	15.2
371L	**Rump steak**, lean and fat, *raw*	18 samples, 86% lean	0.97	821	197	18.9	0	13.5
372L	*fried*	18 samples, 87% lean	1.00	1026	246	28.6	0	14.6
373L	*grilled*	18 samples, 89% lean	1.00	912	218	27.3	0	12.1
374L	lean only, *fried*	18 samples	1.00	797	190	30.8	0	7.4
375L	*grilled*	18 samples	1.00	708	168	28.6	0	6.0

		Labelling information for Group 2 nutrients per 100g food				Additional nutrients and information per 100g food		
No.	Food	Sugars (actual weight) g	Saturates g	Fibre (Englyst) g	Sodium g	Sodium mg	Starch (actual weight) g	Water g
Beef								
361L	fat only, *raw, average*	0	28.6	0	Tr	33	0	24.0
362L	*cooked, average*	0	26.9	0	0.1	50	0	25.2
363L	lean only, *raw, average*	0	1.9	0	0.1	61	0	74.0
364L	**Brisket**, lean and fat, *raw*	0	8.1	0	0.1	68	0	62.2
365L	*boiled*	0	9.5	0	0.1	73	0	48.4
366L	**Forerib**, lean and fat, *raw*	0	10.7	0	Tr	48	0	57.4
367L	*roast*	0	12.3	0	0.1	51	0	48.4
368L	lean only, *roast*	0	5.2	0	0.1	56	0	59.1
369L	**Mince**, *raw*	0	6.9	0	0.1	86	0	64.5
370L	*stewed*	0	6.5	0	0.3	320	0	59.1
371L	**Rump steak**, lean and fat, *raw*	0	5.8	0	0.1	51	0	66.7
372L	*fried*	0	6.2	0	0.1	54	0	56.2
373L	*grilled*	0	5.2	0	0.1	55	0	59.3
374L	lean only, *fried*	0	3.1	0	0.1	57	0	61.1
375L	*grilled*	0	2.5	0	0.1	56	0	63.8

Labelling information for Group 1 nutrients per 100g food

No.	Food	Description and main data sources	Edible proportion	Energy kJ	Energy kcal	Protein (N × 6.25) g	Carbohydrate (actual wt.) g	Fat g
Beef								
376L	**Salted**, *fat removed, raw*	Ref. Wu Leung *et al.* (1968)	1.00	476	112	27.1	0	0.4
377L	*dried, raw*	Ref. Wu Leung *et al.* (1968)	1.00	997	235	55.4	0	1.5
378L	**Silverside**, lean and fat, *salted, boiled*	17 samples, 85% lean; soaked for 18 hours before cooking	1.00	1012	242	28.6	0	14.2
379L	lean only, *salted, boiled*	17 samples; soaked for 18 hours before cooking	1.00	730	173	32.3	0	4.9
380L	**Sirloin**, lean and fat, *raw*	18 samples, boneless, 72% lean	0.92	1126	272	16.6	0	22.8
381L	*roast*	18 samples, boneless, 80% lean	1.00	1182	284	23.6	0	21.1
382L	lean only, *roast*	18 samples, boneless	1.00	806	192	27.6	0	9.1
383L	**Stewing steak**, lean and fat, *raw*	18 samples, 85% lean	0.96	736	176	20.2	0	10.6
384L	*stewed*	18 samples, 92% lean; salt added	1.00	932	223	30.9	0	11.0
385L	**Topside**, lean and fat, *raw*	18 samples, 87% lean	0.95	748	179	19.6	0	11.2
386L	*roast*	18 samples, 88% lean	1.00	896	214	26.6	0	12.0
387L	lean only, *roast*	18 samples	1.00	659	156	29.2	0	4.4

		Labelling information for Group 2 nutrients per 100g food				Additional nutrients and information per 100g food		
No.	Food	Sugars (actual weight) g	Saturates g	Fibre (Englyst) g	Sodium g	Sodium mg	Starch (actual weight) g	Water g
Beef								
376L	**Salted**, *fat removed, raw*	0	N	0	N	N	0	50.6
377L	*dried, raw*	0	N	0	N	N	0	29.4
378L	**Silverside**, lean and fat, *salted, boiled*	0	6.2	0	0.9	910	0	54.5
379L	lean only, *salted, boiled*	0	2.0	0	1.0	1000	0	59.7
380L	**Sirloin**, lean and fat, *raw*	0	9.7	0	Tr	49	0	59.4
381L	*roast*	0	9.0	0	0.1	54	0	54.3
382L	lean only, *roast*	0	3.7	0	0.1	59	0	62.0
383L	**Stewing steak**, lean and fat, *raw*	0	4.5	0	0.1	72	0	68.7
384L	*stewed*	0	4.7	0	0.4	360	0	57.1
385L	**Topside**, lean and fat, *raw*	0	4.1	0	Tr	43	0	68.4
386L	*roast*	0	4.1	0	Tr	48	0	60.2
387L	lean only, *roast*	0	1.4	0	Tr	49	0	65.1

Labelling information for Group 1 nutrients per 100g food

No.	Food	Description and main data sources	Edible proportion	Energy kJ	Energy kcal	Protein (N × 6.25) g	Carbohydrate (actual wt.) g	Fat g
Lamb								
388L	fat only, *raw, average*	Fat from six different cuts	1.00	2762	671	6.2	0	71.8
389L	*cooked, average*	Fat from six different cuts	1.00	2538	616	11.3	0	63.4
390L	lean only, *raw, average*	Lean from six different cuts	1.00	679	162	20.8	0	8.8
391L	**Breast**, lean and fat, *raw*	15 samples, boneless, 59% lean	0.84	1564	378	16.7	0	34.6
392L	*roast*	15 samples, boneless, 60% lean	1.00	1697	410	19.1	0	37.1
393L	lean only, *roast*	15 samples, boneless	1.00	1049	252	25.6	0	16.6
394L	**Chops**, loin, lean and fat, *raw*	15 samples, 60% lean	0.84	1558	377	14.6	0	35.4
395L	*grilled*	15 samples, 70% lean	1.00	1473	355	23.5	0	29.0
396L	*grilled, weighed with bone*	Calculated from lean and fat, grilled	0.79	1147	277	18.3	0	22.6
397L	loin, lean only, *grilled*	15 samples	1.00	928	222	27.8	0	12.3
398L	*grilled, weighed with fat and bone*	Calculated from lean only, grilled	0.55	512	122	15.3	0	6.8

No.	Food	Labelling information for Group 2 nutrients per 100g food				Additional nutrients and information per 100g food		
		Sugars (actual weight) g	Saturates g	Fibre (Englyst) g	Sodium g	Sodium mg	Starch (actual weight) g	Water g
Lamb								
388L	fat only, *raw, average*	0	35.6	0	Tr	36	0	21.2
389L	*cooked, average*	0	31.5	0	0.1	56	0	24.6
390L	lean only, *raw, average*	0	4.2	0	0.1	88	0	70.1
391L	**Breast**, lean and fat, *raw*	0	17.7	0	0.1	100	0	48.3
392L	*roast*	0	18.4	0	0.1	73	0	43.6
393L	lean only, *roast*	0	7.9	0	0.1	86	0	57.8
394L	**Chops**, loin, lean and fat, *raw*	0	17.6	0	0.1	61	0	49.5
395L	*grilled*	0	14.4	0	0.1	72	0	46.6
396L	*grilled, weighed with bone*	0	11.2	0	0.1	56	0	36.3
397L	loin, lean only, *grilled*	0	5.9	0	0.1	75	0	58.9
398L	*grilled, weighed with fat and bone*	0	3.2	0	Tr	41	0	32.4

Labelling information for Group 1 nutrients per 100g food

No.	Food	Description and main data sources	Edible proportion	Energy kJ	Energy kcal	Protein (N × 6.25) g	Carbohydrate (actual wt.) g	Fat g
	Lamb							
399L	**Cutlets**, lean and fat, *raw*	15 samples, 59% lean	0.77	1593	386	14.7	0	36.3
400L	*grilled*	15 samples, 67% lean	1.00	1534	370	23.0	0	30.9
401L	*grilled, weighed with bone*	Calculated from lean and fat, grilled	0.68	1013	244	15.2	0	20.4
402L	lean only, *grilled*	15 samples	1.00	928	222	27.8	0	12.3
403L	*grilled, weighed with fat and bone*	Calculated from lean only, grilled	0.44	407	97	12.2	0	5.4
404L	**Leg**, lean and fat, *raw*	15 samples, 80% lean	0.77	996	240	17.9	0	18.7
405L	*roast*	15 samples, 82% lean	1.00	1106	266	26.1	0	17.9
406L	lean only, *roast*	15 samples	1.00	800	191	29.4	0	8.1
407L	**Scrag and neck**, lean and fat, *raw*	15 samples, 71% lean	0.61	1309	316	15.6	0	28.2
408L	*stewed*	15 samples, 84% lean	1.00	1216	292	25.6	0	21.1
409L	lean only, *stewed*	15 samples	1.00	1054	253	27.8	0	15.7
410L	*stewed, weighed with fat and bone*	Calculated from lean only, stewed	0.51	536	128	14.1	0	8.0
411L	**Shoulder**, lean and fat, *raw*	15 samples, 68% lean	0.79	1301	314	15.6	0	28.0
412L	*roast*	15 samples, 73% lean	1.00	1311	316	19.9	0	26.3
413L	lean only, *roast*	15 samples	1.00	819	196	23.8	0	11.2

No.	Food	Labelling information for Group 2 nutrients per 100g food				Additional nutrients and information per 100g food		
		Sugars (actual weight) g	Saturates g	Fibre (Englyst) g	Sodium g	Sodium mg	Starch (actual weight) g	Water g
Lamb								
399L	**Cutlets**, lean and fat, *raw*	0	18.0	0	0.1	60	0	48.7
400L	*grilled*	0	15.3	0	0.1	71	0	45.1
401L	*grilled, weighed with bone*	0	10.1	0	Tr	47	0	29.8
402L	lean only, *grilled*	0	5.9	0	0.1	75	0	58.9
403L	*grilled, weighed with fat and bone*	0	2.5	0	Tr	33	0	25.9
404L	**Leg**, lean and fat, *raw*	0	9.3	0	0.1	52	0	63.1
405L	*roast*	0	8.9	0	0.1	65	0	55.3
406L	lean only, *roast*	0	3.9	0	0.1	67	0	61.8
407L	**Scrag and neck**, lean and fat, *raw*	0	14.0	0	0.1	71	0	55.7
408L	*stewed*	0	10.5	0	0.2	240	0	52.6
409L	lean only, *stewed*	0	7.5	0	0.3	250	0	55.9
410L	*stewed, weighed with fat and bone*	0	3.8	0	0.1	130	0	28.5
411L	**Shoulder**, lean and fat, *raw*	0	13.9	0	0.1	66	0	56.1
412L	*roast*	0	13.1	0	0.1	61	0	53.6
413L	lean only, *roast*	0	5.4	0	0.1	65	0	64.8

Labelling information for Group 1 nutrients per 100g food

No.	Food	Description and main data sources	Edible proportion	Energy kJ	Energy kcal	Protein (N × 6.25) g	Carbohydrate (actual wt.) g	Fat g
	Pork							
414L	fat only, *raw, average*	Fat from three different cuts	1.00	2757	670	6.8	0	71.4
415L	*cooked, average*	Fat from three different cuts	1.00	2553	619	14.8	0	62.2
416L	lean only, *raw, average*	Lean from three different cuts	1.00	613	146	20.6	0	7.1
417L	**Belly rashers**, lean and fat, *raw*	15 samples, 56% lean	0.90	1574	381	15.3	0	35.5
418L	*grilled*	15 samples, 56% lean	1.00	1646	398	21.1	0	34.8
419L	**Chops**, loin, lean and fat, *raw*	15 samples, 65% lean; without kidney	0.84	1362	329	15.9	0	29.5
420L	*grilled*	15 samples, 75% lean; without kidney	1.00	1378	331	28.4	0	24.2
421L	*grilled, weighed with bone*	Calculated from lean and fat, grilled	0.78	1073	258	22.2	0	18.8
422L	loin, lean only, *grilled*	15 samples	1.00	945	226	32.3	0	10.7
423L	*grilled, weighed with fat and bone*	Calculated from lean only, grilled	0.59	558	133	19.1	0	6.3
424L	**Leg**, lean and fat, *raw*	15 samples, fillet end, 73% lean	0.85	1115	269	16.6	0	22.5
425L	*roast*	15 samples, fillet end, 76% lean	1.00	1190	286	26.9	0	19.8
426L	lean only, *roast*	15 samples, fillet end	1.00	777	185	30.7	0	6.9
427L	**Trotters and tails**, *salted, boiled*	23% trotters and 77% tails, boiled for 2 hours.	0.54	1162	280	19.8	0	22.3

No.	Food	Labelling information for Group 2 nutrients per 100g food				Additional nutrients and information per 100g food		
		Sugars (actual weight) g	Saturates g	Fibre (Englyst) g	Sodium g	Sodium mg	Starch (actual weight) g	Water g
Pork								
414L	fat only, *raw, average*	0	26.4	0	Tr	38	0	21.1
415L	*cooked, average*	0	23.0	0	0.1	79	0	20.9
416L	lean only, *raw, average*	0	2.5	0	0.1	76	0	71.5
417L	**Belly rashers**, lean and fat, *raw*	0	13.1	0	0.1	73	0	48.7
418L	*grilled*	0	12.9	0	0.1	95	0	43.0
419L	**Chops**, loin, lean and fat, *raw*	0	10.9	0	0.1	56	0	54.3
420L	*grilled*	0	9.0	0	0.1	84	0	46.3
421L	*grilled, weighed with bone*	0	6.9	0	0.1	66	0	36.1
422L	loin, lean only, *grilled*	0	3.8	0	0.1	84	0	56.1
423L	*grilled, weighed with fat and bone*	0	2.2	0	0.1	50	0	33.1
424L	**Leg**, lean and fat, *raw*	0	8.3	0	0.1	59	0	59.5
425L	*roast*	0	7.3	0	0.1	79	0	51.9
426L	lean only, *roast*	0	2.4	0	0.1	79	0	61.6
427L	**Trotters and tails**, *salted, boiled*	0	N	0	1.6	1615	0	53.5

Labelling information for Group 1 nutrients per 100g food

No.	Food	Description and main data sources	Edible proportion	Energy kJ	Energy kcal	Protein (N × 6.25) g	Carbohydrate (actual wt.) g	Fat g
Veal								
428L	**Cutlet**, *fried in vegetable oil*	Samples coated in egg and crumbs and fried	1.00	902	215	31.4	4.0	8.1
429L	**Fillet**, *raw*	Lean samples	1.00	459	109	21.1	0	2.7
430L	*roast*	Lean samples	1.00	963	230	31.6	0	11.5
431L	**Chicken**, *meat only, raw*	15 samples, light and dark meat from dressed carcase	0.44	508	121	20.5	0	4.3
432L	*meat and skin, raw*	15 samples, dressed carcase excluding waste	0.64	954	230	17.6	0	17.7
433L	*light meat, raw*	15 samples	0.23	489	116	21.8	0	3.2
434L	*dark meat, raw*	15 samples	0.21	528	126	19.1	0	5.5
435L	boiled, *meat only*	15 samples, light and dark meat	1.00	767	183	29.2	0	7.3
436L	*light meat*	15 samples	1.00	686	163	29.7	0	4.9
437L	*dark meat*	15 samples	1.00	853	204	28.6	0	9.9
438L	roast, *meat only*	15 samples, light and dark meat	1.00	621	148	24.8	0	5.4
439L	*meat and skin*	15 samples	1.00	902	216	22.6	0	14.0
440L	*light meat*	15 samples	1.00	599	142	26.5	0	4.0
441L	*dark meat*	15 samples	1.00	648	155	23.1	0	6.9
442L	wing quarter, roast, *meat only, weighed with bone*	Meat from whole wing quarter	0.50	311	74	12.4	0	2.7
443L	leg quarter, roast, *meat only, weighed with bone*	Meat from whole leg quarter	0.38	388	92	15.4	0	3.4
444L	breaded, *fried in vegetable oil*	4 samples, 4 brands; fried 8-12 minutes	1.00	1005	240	18.0	13.5	12.7

No.	Food	Sugars (actual weight) g	Saturates g	Fibre (Englyst) g	Sodium g	Sodium mg	Starch (actual weight) g	Water g
		Labelling information for Group 2 nutrients per 100g food				**Additional nutrients and information per 100g food**		
	Veal							
428L	**Cutlet**, *fried in vegetable oil*	0.1	0.8	0.1	0.1	110	3.9	54.6
429L	**Fillet**, *raw*	0	0.9	0	0.1	110	0	74.9
430L	*roast*	0	3.7	0	0.1	97	0	55.1
431L	**Chicken**, *meat only, raw*	0	1.4	0	0.1	81	0	74.4
432L	*meat and skin, raw*	0	5.9	0	0.1	70	0	64.4
433L	*light meat, raw*	0	1.0	0	0.1	72	0	74.4
434L	*dark meat, raw*	0	1.8	0	0.1	89	0	74.5
435L	boiled, *meat only*	0	2.4	0	0.1	82	0	63.4
436L	*light meat*	0	1.6	0	0.1	70	0	65.2
437L	*dark meat*	0	3.2	0	0.1	95	0	61.5
438L	roast, *meat only*	0	1.6	0	0.1	81	0	68.4
439L	*meat and skin*	0	4.2	0	0.1	72	0	61.9
440L	*light meat*	0	1.2	0	0.1	71	0	68.5
441L	*dark meat*	0	2.1	0	0.1	91	0	68.2
442L	wing quarter, roast, *meat only, weighed with bone*	0	0.8	0	Tr	41	0	34.2
443L	leg quarter, roast, *meat only, weighed with bone*	0	1.0	0	0.1	50	0	42.4
444L	breaded, *fried in vegetable oil*	0.8	2.1	0.7	0.4	420	12.7	53.2

Labelling information for Group 1 nutrients per 100g food

No.	Food	Description and main data sources	Edible proportion	Energy kJ	Energy kcal	Protein (N × 6.25) g	Carbohydrate (actual wt.) g	Fat g
445L	**Duck**, *meat only, raw*	9 samples, meat from dressed carcase	0.28	513	122	19.7	0	4.8
446L	*meat, fat and skin, raw*	9 samples, dressed carcase excluding waste	0.67	1772	430	11.3	0	42.7
447L	*roast, meat only*	11 samples	1.00	789	189	25.3	0	9.7
448L	*-, meat, fat and skin*	11 samples	1.00	1406	339	19.6	0	29.0
449L	**Goose**, *roast, meat only*	Meat from carcase	1.00	1327	319	29.3	0	22.4
450L	**Grouse**, *roast, meat only*	Meat from carcase	1.00	728	173	31.3	0	5.3
451L	*roast, weighed with bone*	Calculated from roast, meat only	0.66	480	114	20.6	0	3.5
452L	**Partridge**, *roast, meat only*	Meat from carcase	1.00	890	212	36.7	0	7.2
453L	*roast, weighed with bone*	Calculated from roast, meat only	0.60	533	127	22.0	0	4.3
454L	**Pheasant**, *roast, meat only*	Meat from carcase	1.00	892	213	32.2	0	9.3
455L	*roast, weighed with bone*	Calculated from roast, meat only	0.63	563	134	20.3	0	5.9
456L	**Pigeon**, *roast, meat only*	Meat from carcase	1.00	961	230	27.8	0	13.2
457L	*roast, weighed with bone*	Calculated from roast, meat only	0.44	422	101	12.2	0	5.8

No.	Food	Labelling information for Group 2 nutrients per 100g food: Sugars (actual weight) g	Saturates g	Fibre (Englyst) g	Sodium g	Additional nutrients and information per 100g food: Sodium mg	Starch (actual weight) g	Water g
445L	**Duck**, *meat only, raw*	0	1.3	0	0.1	110	0	75.0
446L	*meat, fat and skin, raw*	0	11.6	0	0.1	77	0	43.9
447L	*roast, meat only*	0	2.7	0	0.1	96	0	64.2
448L	*-, meat, fat and skin*	0	7.9	0	0.1	76	0	49.6
449L	**Goose**, *roast, meat only*	0	N	0	0.2	150	0	46.7
450L	**Grouse**, *roast, meat only*	0	1.2	0	0.1	96	0	61.6
451L	*roast, weighed with bone*	0	0.8	0	0.1	63	0	40.6
452L	**Partridge**, *roast, meat only*	0	1.9	0	0.1	100	0	54.5
453L	*roast, weighed with bone*	0	1.1	0	0.1	60	0	32.7
454L	**Pheasant**, *roast, meat only*	0	3.1	0	0.1	100	0	56.9
455L	*roast, weighed with bone*	0	2.0	0	0.1	66	0	35.8
456L	**Pigeon**, *roast, meat only*	0	N	0	0.1	110	0	57.2
457L	*roast, weighed with bone*	0	N	0	Tr	46	0	25.2

Labelling information for Group 1 nutrients per 100g food

No.	Food	Description and main data sources	Edible proportion	Energy		Protein (N × 6.25)	Carbohydrate (actual wt.)	Fat
				kJ	kcal	g	g	g
458L	**Turkey**, *meat only, raw*	5 samples, light and dark meat from dressed carcase	0.57	454	107	21.9	0	2.2
459L	*meat and skin, raw*	5 samples, dressed carcase excluding waste	0.70	606	145	20.6	0	6.9
460L	*light meat, raw*	5 samples	0.32	435	103	23.2	0	1.1
461L	*dark meat, raw*	5 samples	0.25	478	114	20.3	0	3.6
462L	roast, *meat only*	5 samples, light and dark meat	1.00	590	140	28.8	0	2.7
463L	*meat and skin*	5 samples	1.00	717	171	28.0	0	6.5
464L	*light meat*	5 samples	1.00	558	132	29.8	0	1.4
465L	*dark meat*	5 samples	1.00	624	148	27.8	0	4.1
466L	**Hare**, stewed, *meat only*	Meat from carcase	1.00	804	192	29.9	0	8.0
467L	stewed, *weighed with bone*	Calculated from stewed, *meat only*	0.73	585	139	21.8	0	5.8
468L	**Rabbit**, *meat only, raw*	9 samples, pieces of loin and leg	0.62	520	124	21.9	0	4.0
469L	stewed, *meat only*	Pieces of loin and leg	1.00	749	179	27.3	0	7.7
470L	-, *weighed with bone*	Calculated from stewed, *meat only*	0.64	381	91	13.9	0	3.9
471L	**Venison**, *roast*	Haunch, meat only	1.00	832	198	35.0	0	6.4

No.	Food	Labelling information for Group 2 nutrients per 100g food: Sugars (actual weight) g	Saturates g	Fibre (Englyst) g	Sodium g	Additional nutrients and information per 100g food: Sodium mg	Starch (actual weight) g	Water g
458L	**Turkey**, *meat only, raw*	0	0.7	0	0.1	54	0	75.5
459L	*meat and skin, raw*	0	2.2	0	Tr	49	0	72.0
460L	*light meat, raw*	0	0.3	0	Tr	43	0	75.2
461L	*dark meat, raw*	0	1.2	0	0.1	68	0	75.9
462L	roast, *meat only*	0	0.9	0	0.1	57	0	68.0
463L	*meat and skin*	0	2.1	0	0.1	52	0	65.0
464L	*light meat*	0	0.4	0	Tr	45	0	68.4
465L	*dark meat*	0	1.3	0	0.1	71	0	67.7
466L	**Hare**, stewed, *meat only*	0	N	0	Tr	40	0	60.7
467L	stewed, *weighed with bone*	0	N	0	Tr	29	0	44.3
468L	**Rabbit**, *meat only , raw*	0	1.6	0	0.1	67	0	74.6
469L	stewed, *meat only*	0	3.2	0	Tr	32	0	63.9
470L	-, *weighed with bone*	0	1.6	0	Tr	16	0	32.5
471L	**Venison**, *roast*	0	N	0	0.1	86	0	56.8

Labelling information for Group 1 nutrients per 100g food

No.	Food	Description and main data sources	Edible proportion	Energy kJ	Energy kcal	Protein (N × 6.25) g	Carbohydrate (actual wt.) g	Fat g
Offal								
472L	**Heart**, lamb, *raw*	12 samples; fat and valves removed	0.73	498	119	17.1	0	5.6
473L	ox, *raw*	18 samples; fat and valves removed	0.81	455	108	18.9	0	3.6
474L	*stewed*	18 samples; fat and valves removed before cooking	1.00	752	179	31.4	0	5.9
475L	pig, *raw*	Fat removed	N	391	93	17.1	0	2.7
476L	sheep, *roast*	Ventricles only	1.00	988	237	26.1	0	14.7
477L	**Kidney**, lamb, *raw*	19 samples; core removed	0.93	380	90	16.5	0	2.7
478L	*fried*	19 samples; core removed before cooking	1.00	651	155	24.6	0	6.3
479L	ox, *raw*	18 samples; core removed	0.82	363	86	15.7	0	2.6
480L	*stewed*	18 samples; core removed before cooking, salt added	1.00	720	172	25.6	0	7.7
481L	pig, *raw*	20 samples; core removed	0.90	377	90	16.3	0	2.7
482L	*stewed*	20 samples; core removed before cooking, salt added	1.00	641	153	24.4	0	6.1
483L	**Liver**, calf, *raw*	12 samples	1.00	641	153	20.1	1.7[a]	7.3
484L	*fried*	12 samples; coated in seasoned flour and fried	1.00	1058	253	26.9	6.6[b]	13.2
485L	chicken, *raw*	16 samples	1.00	566	135	19.1	0.5[a]	6.3
486L	*fried*	16 samples; coated in seasoned flour and fried	1.00	808	193	20.7	3.1[b]	10.9
487L	lamb, *raw*	33 samples	1.00	748	179	20.1	1.5[a]	10.3
488L	*fried*	18 samples; coated in seasoned flour and fried	1.00	967	232	22.9	3.5[b]	14.0
489L	ox, *raw*	33 samples	1.00	681	163	21.1	2.0[a]	7.8
490L	*stewed*	18 samples; coated in seasoned flour	1.00	829	198	24.8	3.3[b]	9.5
491L	pig, *raw*	33 samples	1.00	646	154	21.3	1.9[a]	6.8
492L	*stewed*	18 samples; coated in seasoned flour	1.00	791	189	25.6	3.3[b]	8.1

[a] As glycogen

[b] Including glycogen

No.	Food	Labelling information for Group 2 nutrients per 100g food				Additional nutrients and information per 100g food		
		Sugars (actual weight) g	Saturates g	Fibre (Englyst) g	Sodium g	Sodium mg	Starch (actual weight) g	Water g
Offal								
472L	**Heart**, lamb, *raw*	0	2.1	0	0.1	140	0	75.6
473L	ox, *raw*	0	1.7	0	0.1	95	0	76.3
474L	*stewed*	0	2.9	0	0.2	180	0	61.5
475L	pig, *raw*	0	N	0	0.1	80	0	79.2
476L	sheep, *roast*	0	N	0	0.2	150	0	57.3
477L	**Kidney**, lamb, *raw*	0	0.9	0	0.2	220	0	78.9
478L	*fried*	0	2.1	0	0.3	270	0	66.5
479L	ox, *raw*	0	1.1	0	0.2	180	0	79.8
480L	*stewed*	0	3.2	0	0.4	400	0	64.1
481L	pig, *raw*	0	0.9	0	0.2	190	0	78.8
482L	*stewed*	0	2.0	0	0.4	370	0	66.3
483L	**Liver**, calf, *raw*	0	2.2	0	0.1	93	1.7[a]	69.7
484L	*fried*	Tr	4.0	0.2	0.2	170	6.6[b]	52.6
485L	chicken, *raw*	0	2.0	0	0.1	85	0.5[a]	72.9
486L	*fried*	Tr	3.4	0.2	0.2	240	3.1[b]	64.2
487L	lamb, *raw*	0	2.9	0	0.1	76	1.5[a]	67.3
488L	*fried*	Tr	4.0	0.1	0.2	190	3.5[b]	58.4
489L	ox, *raw*	0	2.9	0	0.1	81	2.0[a]	68.6
490L	*stewed*	Tr	3.5	Tr	0.1	110	3.3[b]	62.6
491L	pig, *raw*	0	2.1	0	0.1	87	1.9[a]	69.5
492L	*stewed*	Tr	2.5	Tr	0.1	130	3.3[b]	62.1

[a] As glycogen

[b] Including glycogen

Labelling information for Group 1 nutrients per 100g food

No.	Food	Description and main data sources	Edible proportion	Energy kJ	Energy kcal	Protein (N × 6.25) g	Carbohydrate (actual wt.) g	Fat g
Offal								
493L	**Oxtail**, *stewed*	12 samples, lean only; salt added	1.00	1014	243	30.5	0	13.4
494L	*stewed, weighed with fat and bones*	Calculated from oxtail stewed	0.37	386	92	11.6	0	5.1
495L	**Sweetbread**, lamb, *raw*	12 samples	1.00	549	131	15.3	0	7.8
496L	*fried*	12 samples; soaked 2 hours, boiled for 1 hour then coated with egg and breadcrumbs and fried	1.00	957	229	19.4	5.1	14.6
497L	**Tongue**, lamb, *raw*	20 samples, fat and skin removed	0.57	800	193	15.3	0	14.6
498L	ox, pickled, *raw*	6 samples, fat and skin removed	0.60	914	220	15.7	0	17.5
499L	boiled	Fat and skin removed	1.00	1216	293	19.5	0	23.9
500L	sheep, *stewed*	Fat and skin removed	1.00	1197	289	18.2	0	24.0
501L	**Tripe**, *dressed*	18 samples; lime treated before purchase	1.00	252	60	9.4	0	2.5
502L	*dressed, stewed*	18 samples; lime treated before purchase, stewed in milk	1.00	418	100	14.8	0	4.5
Meat products								
503L	**Beefburgers**, *frozen, raw*	36 samples, 6 brands	1.00	1100	265	15.2	4.9	20.5
504L	*frozen, fried*	36 samples, 6 brands	1.00	1096	263	20.4	6.4	17.3
505L	**Black pudding**, *fried*	24 samples	1.00	1261	303	12.9	13.6	21.9
506L	**Brawn**	10 samples	1.00	636	153	12.4	0	11.5
507L	**Corned beef**, canned	18 samples	1.00	905	217	26.9	0	12.1
508L	**Cornish pastie**	18 pasties, average 62% pastry, 38% filling	1.00	1372	329	8.0	28.3	20.4

No.	Food	Labelling information for Group 2 nutrients per 100g food				Additional nutrients and information per 100g food		
		Sugars (actual weight) g	Saturates g	Fibre (Englyst) g	Sodium g	Sodium mg	Starch (actual weight) g	Water g
Offal								
493L	**Oxtail**, *stewed*	0	N	0	0.2	190	0	53.9
494L	*stewed, weighed with fat and bones*	0	N	0	0.1	72	0	20.5
495L	**Sweetbread**, lamb, *raw*	0	3.0	0	0.1	75	0	75.5
496L	*fried*	0.2	5.5	0.1	0.2	210	4.9	59.9
497L	**Tongue**, lamb, *raw*	0	N	0	0.4	420	0	67.9
498L	ox, pickled, *raw*	0	N	0	1.2	1210	0	62.4
499L	boiled	0	N	0	1.0	1000	0	48.6
500L	sheep, *stewed*	0	N	0	0.1	80	0	56.9
501L	**Tripe**, *dressed*	0	1.1	0	Tr	46	0	88.1
502L	*dressed, stewed*	Tr	2.4	0	0.1	73	0	78.5
Meat products								
503L	**Beefburgers**, *frozen, raw*	1.1	9.5	N	0.6	600	3.8	56.3
504L	*frozen, fried*	1.3	8.0	N	0.9	880	5.1	53.0
505L	**Black pudding**, *fried*	Tr	8.5	N	1.2	1210	13.6	44.0
506L	**Brawn**	0	N	0	0.8	750	0	72.0
507L	**Corned beef**, canned	0	6.3	0	1.0	950	0	58.5
508L	**Cornish pastie**	1.1	7.4	0.9	0.6	590	27.2	39.2

Labelling information for Group 1 nutrients per 100g food

No.	Food	Description and main data sources	Edible proportion	Energy kJ	Energy kcal	Protein (N × 6.25) g	Carbohydrate (actual wt.) g	Fat g
	Meat products							
509L	**Faggots**	38 samples	1.00	1110	267	11.1	13.9	18.5
510L	**Frankfurters**	12 samples, cans and packets, 6 brands	1.00	1132	274	9.5	2.7	25.0
511L	**Grillsteaks**, *grilled*	10 samples; beef based; grilled 15-20 minutes	1.00	1265	305	21.9	0.5	23.9
512L	**Haggis**, *boiled*	8 samples	1.00	1282	308	10.7	17.5	21.7
513L	**Ham and pork**, chopped, canned	12 samples, 5 brands	1.00	1140	275	14.4	1.3	23.6
514L	**Liver sausage**	24 samples	1.00	1283	310	12.9	4.0	26.9
515L	**Luncheon meat**, canned	18 samples	1.00	1295	313	12.6	5.0	26.9
516L	**Meat paste**	67 samples, beef, chicken, ham and tongue, liver and bacon	1.00	719	172	15.2	2.7	11.2
517L	**Pate**, liver	20 samples, assorted types	1.00	1307	316	13.1	0.9	28.9
518L	low fat	11 samples, assorted types; pork meat and liver based	1.00	794	190	18.0	2.6	12.0
519L	**Polony**	24 samples	1.00	1160	279	9.4	12.9	21.1
520L	**Pork pie**, *individual*	18 pies, average 55% pastry, 42% meat filling, 3% jelly	1.00	1552	373	9.8	22.7	27.0
521L	**Salami**	24 samples, 8 different countries of origin	1.00	2029	491	19.3	1.7	45.2
522L	**Sausage roll**, *flaky pastry*	Recipe	1.00	1974	475	7.4	29.5	36.4
523L	*short pastry*	Recipe	1.00	1901	457	8.3	34.1	31.9

No.	Food	Labelling information for Group 2 nutrients per 100g food				Additional nutrients and information per 100g food		
		Sugars (actual weight) g	Saturates g	Fibre (Englyst) g	Sodium g	Sodium mg	Starch (actual weight) g	Water g
	Meat products							
509L	**Faggots**	Tr	N	N	0.8	820	13.9	47.1
510L	**Frankfurters**	Tr	N	0.1	1.0	980	2.7	59.5
511L	**Grillsteaks**, *grilled*	0.5	11.0	Tr	0.7	650	Tr	50.1
512L	**Haggis**, *boiled*	Tr	7.6	N	0.8	770	17.5	46.2
513L	**Ham and pork**, chopped, canned	0.2	8.8	0.3	1.1	1090	1.1	58.5
514L	**Liver sausage**	0.8	7.9	0.5	0.9	860	3.2	51.8
515L	**Luncheon meat**, canned	Tr	9.8	0.3	1.1	1050	5.0	51.5
516L	**Meat paste**	Tr	N	0.1	0.7	740	2.7	67.1
517L	**Pate**, liver	0.3	8.4	Tr	0.8	790	0.6	50.6
518L	low fat	1.1	4.0	Tr	0.7	710	1.5	65.0
519L	**Polony**	Tr	N	N	0.9	870	12.9	52.0
520L	**Pork pie**, *individual*	0.5	10.2	0.9	0.7	720	22.2	36.8
521L	**Salami**	Tr	N	0.1	1.9	1850	1.7	28.0
522L	**Sausage roll**, *flaky pastry*	1.2	13.4	1.2	0.5	510	28.3	23.6
523L	*short pastry*	1.2	11.8	1.4	0.5	530	32.9	22.3

Labelling information for Group 1 nutrients per 100g food

No.	Food	Description and main data sources	Edible proportion	Energy kJ	Energy kcal	Protein (N × 6.25) g	Carbohydrate (actual wt.) g	Fat g
Meat products								
524L	**Sausages**, beef, *raw*	20 samples	1.00	1237	298	9.6	10.7	24.1
525L	*fried*	20 samples	1.00	1118	268	12.9	13.7	18.0
526L	*grilled*	20 samples	1.00	1097	263	13.0	13.9	17.3
527L	pork, *raw*	18 samples	1.00	1516	366	10.6	8.7	32.1
528L	*fried*	18 samples	1.00	1313	316	13.8	10.1	24.5
529L	*grilled*	18 samples	1.00	1315	317	13.3	10.5	24.6
530L	low fat, *raw*	7 samples, 5 brands; pork sausages	1.00	690	165	12.5	7.4	9.5
531L	*fried*	Samples as raw; fried 10-15 minutes	1.00	875	210	14.9	8.3	13.0
532L	*grilled*	Samples as raw; grilled 10-15 minutes	1.00	954	229	16.2	9.9	13.8
533L	**Saveloy**	60 samples	1.00	1083	261	9.9	9.2	20.5
534L	**Steak and kidney pie**, *individual*	10 pies, purchased cooked; pastry top and bottom	1.00	1335	320	9.1	23.3	21.2
535L	*pastry top only*	Recipe	1.00	1193	286	15.6	14.5	18.4
536L	**Stewed steak**, canned, *with gravy*	12 samples, 8 brands	1.00	729	175	14.8	0.9	12.5
537L	**Tongue**, canned	18 samples, lamb and ox	1.00	883	213	16.0	0	16.5
538L	**White pudding**	6 samples	1.00	1857	446	7.0	33.0	31.8

No.	Food	Labelling information for Group 2 nutrients per 100g food				Additional nutrients and information per 100g food		
		Sugars (actual weight) g	Saturates g	Fibre (Englyst) g	Sodium g	Sodium mg	Starch (actual weight) g	Water g
	Meat products							
524L	**Sausages**, beef, *raw*	1.7	10.0	0.5	0.8	810	9.0	50.3
525L	*fried*	2.3	7.2	0.7	1.1	1090	11.4	47.7
526L	*grilled*	2.3	6.7	0.7	1.1	1100	11.6	47.9
527L	pork, *raw*	1.3	12.2	0.5	0.8	760	7.4	45.4
528L	*fried*	1.7	9.4	0.7	1.1	1050	8.4	44.9
529L	*grilled*	1.7	9.5	0.7	1.0	1000	8.8	45.1
530L	low fat, *raw*	0.5	3.4	1.2	0.9	910	6.9	61.9
531L	*fried*	0.7	4.3	1.4	1.0	950	7.6	53.9
532L	*grilled*	0.9	5.0	1.5	1.2	1190	9.0	50.1
533L	**Saveloy**	Tr	N	N	0.9	890	9.2	56.7
534L	**Steak and kidney pie**, *individual*	2.1	8.4	0.9	0.5	510	21.2	42.6
535L	*pastry top only*	0.4	7.0	0.6	0.7	660	14.1	49.0
536L	**Stewed steak**, canned, *with gravy*	Tr	5.9	Tr	0.4	380	0.9	70.0
537L	**Tongue**, canned	0	6.4	0	1.1	1050	0	63.9
538L	**White pudding**	Tr	N	N	0.4	370	33.0	22.8

Labelling information for Group 1 nutrients per 100g food

No.	Food	Description and main data sources	Edible proportion	Energy kJ	Energy kcal	Protein (N × 6.25) g	Carbohydrate (actual wt.) g	Fat g
	Meat dishes							
539L	**Beef chow mein**	12 samples from different shops. Noodles with beef and vegetables in sauce	1.00	565	135	6.7	13.5	6.0
540L	**Beef curry**, *retail*	6 samples, 3 brands; cooked according to packet directions	1.00	576	137	13.5	6.0	6.6
541L	*with rice*	Calculated from sample proportions as 57% curry and 43% rice	1.00	576	137	8.9	15.6	4.3
542L	**Beef kheema**	Recipe	1.00	1711	414	18.3	0.3	37.7
543L	**Beef koftas**	Recipe	1.00	1472	354	23.3	3.2[a]	27.6
544L	**Beef steak pudding**	Recipe	1.00	936	224	11.1	17.2[a]	12.3
545L	**Beef stew**	Recipe	1.00	503	120	9.7	4.2[a]	7.2
546L	**Bolognese sauce**	Recipe	1.00	608	146	8.0	3.6[a]	11.1
547L	**Chicken curry**, *with bone*	Recipe	0.75	637	154	7.6	2.2[a]	12.7
548L	*without bone*	Recipe	1.00	853	206	10.2	3.0[a]	17.0
549L	*retail*	7 samples, 5 brands; Korma and Masala varieties cooked according to packet directions	1.00	623	149	12.1	5.2	8.9
550L	*with rice*	Calculated from sample proportions as 55% curry and 45% rice	1.00	603	144	7.9	15.6	5.5
551L	**Chilli con carne**	Recipe	1.00	638	153	11.1	7.9[a]	8.5
552L	**Curried meat**	Recipe	1.00	683	164	8.6	8.7[a]	10.5

[a] Including oligosaccharides

No.	Food	Labelling information for Group 2 nutrients per 100g food				Additional nutrients and information per 100g food		
		Sugars (actual weight) g	Saturates g	Fibre (Englyst) g	Sodium g	Sodium mg	Starch (actual weight) g	Water g
	Meat dishes							
539L	**Beef chow mein**	2.3	1.3	N	0.6	590	11.2	71.7
540L	**Beef curry**, *retail*	4.4	3.1	1.2	0.5	450	1.6	69.5
541L	*with rice*	2.6	1.9	0.7	0.3	260	13.0	68.9
542L	**Beef kheema**	0.3	13.0	0.1	0.2	150	Tr	42.7
543L	**Beef koftas**	1.4[a]	7.0	0.4	1.0	990	0.9	40.8
544L	**Beef steak pudding**	0.9[a]	6.1	0.8	0.3	330	15.9	57.5
545L	**Beef stew**	1.8[a]	3.3	0.6	0.3	330	2.2	77.3
546L	**Bolognese sauce**	3.2[a]	3.1	1.0	0.4	430	0.1	74.7
547L	**Chicken curry**, *with bone*	1.2[a]	1.7	0.7	0.5	460	0.4	49.5
548L	*without bone*	1.6[a]	2.2	0.9	0.6	620	0.5	66.0
549L	*retail*	4.3	4.0	1.3	0.5	450	0.9	68.7
550L	*with rice*	2.4	2.3	0.8	0.3	250	13.2	68.4
551L	**Chilli con carne**	2.9[a]	3.0	2.3	0.3	250	4.0	67.6
552L	**Curried meat**	6.2[a]	2.9	1.4	0.5	470	1.5	67.9

[a] Not including oligosaccharides

Labelling information for Group 1 nutrients per 100g food

No.	Food	Description and main data sources	Edible proportion	Energy kJ	Energy kcal	Protein (N × 6.25) g	Carbohydrate (actual wt.) g	Fat g
	Meat dishes							
553L	**Hot pot**	Recipe	1.00	486	116	9.4	9.4[a]	4.5
554L	**Irish stew**	Recipe	1.00	512	123	5.3	8.3[a]	7.6
555L	*weighed with bones*	Calculated from Irish stew	0.91	468	112	4.8	7.7[a]	6.9
556L	**Lamb kheema**	Recipe	1.00	1364	330	14.6	2.3[a]	29.1
557L	**Lasagne**, *frozen, cooked*	10 samples, 3 brands. Calculated from frozen using 5.3% weight loss	1.00	423	101	4.9	11.7	3.8
558L	**Moussaka**	Recipe	1.00	768	185	9.1	6.5[a]	13.6
559L	**Mutton biriani**	Recipe	1.00	1147	275	7.6	23.1[a]	16.9
560L	**Mutton curry**	Recipe	1.00	1554	375	14.9	3.8[a]	33.4
561L	**Pancake roll**	18 samples, 12 shops. Vegetable and beansprout filling	1.00	903	216	6.6	19.3	12.5
562L	**Shepherd's pie**	Recipe	1.00	495	118	8.0	7.6[a]	6.2

[a] Including oligosaccharides

No.	Food	Sugars (actual weight) g	Saturates g	Fibre (Englyst) g	Sodium g	Sodium mg	Starch (actual weight) g	Water g
		Labelling information for Group 2 nutrients per 100g food				Additional nutrients and information per 100g food		
	Meat dishes							
553L	**Hot pot**	2.7[a]	1.8	1.2	0.7	660	6.1	73.5
554L	**Irish stew**	1.4[a]	3.5	0.9	0.4	360	6.5	76.2
555L	*weighed with bones*	1.4[a]	3.2	0.8	0.3	330	5.9	69.3
556L	**Lamb kheema**	1.6[a]	16.7	0.5	0.7	650	0.2	51.2
557L	**Lasagne**, *frozen, cooked*	2.0	1.9	N	0.4	430	9.7	75.2
558L	**Moussaka**	2.5[a]	4.5	0.9	0.3	320	3.5	68.0
559L	**Mutton biriani**	3.2[a]	9.7	0.7	0.3	270	19.4	50.2
560L	**Mutton curry**	2.7[a]	19.5	0.8	0.8	830	0.3	44.0
561L	**Pancake roll**	3.0	3.7	N	0.6	610	16.3	58.3
562L	**Shepherd's pie**	1.0[a]	2.4	0.6	0.5	450	6.4	75.6

[a] Not including oligosaccharides

Labelling information for Group 1 nutrients per 100g food

No.	Food	Description and main data sources	Edible proportion	Energy kJ	Energy kcal	Protein (N × 6.25) g	Carbohydrate (actual wt.) g	Fat g
	White fish							
563L	**Cod**, *raw, fillets*	Samples from 3 different shops	0.89	322	76	17.4	0	0.7
564L	*baked, fillets*	Samples baked in the oven with added butter	1.00	408	96	21.4	0	1.2
565L	*-, fillets, weighed with bones and skin*	Samples baked in oven with butter added	0.85	348	82	18.3	0	1.0
566L	*poached, fillets*	Poached in milk with butter and salt added	1.00	396	94	20.9	0	1.1
567L	*-, fillets, weighed with bones and skin*	Calculated from poached fillets	0.87	346	82	18.2	0	1.0
568L	*frozen, raw, steaks*	12 packets, 3 brands	1.00	287	68	15.6	0	0.6
569L	*-, grilled, steaks*	12 samples; grilled with butter and salt added	1.00	402	95	20.8	0	1.3
570L	*in batter, fried in blended oil*	Cooked samples from fish and chip shops	1.00	832	199	19.6	6.9	10.3
571L	*-, fried in dripping*	Cooked samples from fish and chip shops	1.00	832	199	19.6	6.9	10.3
572L	dried, *salted, boiled*	Soaked 24 hours and boiled	0.83	586	138	32.5	0	0.9
573L	**Dogfish**, *in batter, fried in blended oil*	7 cooked samples from fish and chip shops	1.00	1177	282	21.4	6.9	18.8
574L	*in batter, fried in blended oil, weighed with waste*	Calculated from fried in blended oil	0.92	1086	261	19.7	6.5	17.3
575L	*-, fried in dripping*	7 cooked samples from fish and chip shops	1.00	1177	282	21.4	6.9	18.8
576L	*-, fried in dripping, weighed with waste*	Calculated from fried in dripping	0.92	1086	261	19.7	6.5	17.3

No.	Food	Labelling information for Group 2 nutrients per 100g food				Additional nutrients and information per 100g food		
		Sugars (actual weight) g	Saturates g	Fibre (Englyst) g	Sodium g	Sodium mg	Starch (actual weight) g	Water g
White fish								
563L	**Cod**, *raw, fillets*	0	0.1	0	0.1	77	0	82.1
564L	*baked, fillets*	0	0.5	0	0.3	340	0	76.6
565L	*-, fillets, weighed with bones and skin*	0	0.4	0	0.3	290	0	65.1
566L	*poached, fillets*	0	0.4	0	0.1	110	0	77.7
567L	*-, fillets, weighed with bones and skin*	0	0.4	0	0.1	96	0	67.6
568L	*frozen, raw, steaks*	0	0.1	0	0.1	68	0	83.9
569L	*-, grilled, steaks*	0	0.5	0	0.1	91	0	78.0
570L	*in batter, fried in blended oil*	0.2	0.9	0.3	0.1	100	6.7	60.9
571L	*-, fried in dripping*	0.2	4.7	0.3	0.1	100	6.7	60.9
572L	dried, *salted, boiled*	0	0.2	0	0.4	400	0	64.9
573L	**Dogfish**, *in batter, fried in blended oil*	0.1	1.6	0.3	0.3	290	6.8	54.2
574L	*in batter, fried in blended oil, weighed with waste*	0.1	1.5	0.3	0.3	270	6.4	49.9
575L	*-, fried in dripping*	0.1	10.4	0.3	0.3	290	6.8	54.2
576L	*-, fried in dripping, weighed with waste*	0.1	9.6	0.3	0.3	270	6.4	49.9

Labelling information for Group 1 nutrients per 100g food

No.	Food	Description and main data sources	Edible proportion	Energy kJ	Energy kcal	Protein (N × 6.25) g	Carbohydrate (actual wt.) g	Fat g
White fish								
577L	**Haddock**, *raw*	Fillets	N	308	73	16.8	0	0.6
578L	*steamed*	Middle cut	1.00	417	98	22.8	0	0.8
579L	*steamed, weighed with bones and skin*	Calculated from steamed	0.76	316	75	17.3	0	0.6
580L	*in crumbs, fried in blended oil*	Samples coated in crumbs and fried	1.00	727	174	21.4	3.3	8.3
581L	*-, fried in blended oil, weighed with bones*	Calculated from fried in blended oil	0.92	667	159	19.7	3.0	7.6
582L	*-, fried in dripping*	Samples coated in crumbs and fried	1.00	727	174	21.4	3.3	8.3
583L	*-, fried in dripping, weighed with bones*	Calculated from fried in dripping	0.92	667	159	19.7	3.0	7.6
584L	smoked, *steamed*	Flesh only	1.00	429	101	23.3	0	0.9
585L	*steamed, weighed with bones and skin*	Calculated from smoked, steamed	0.65	279	66	15.1	0	0.6
586L	**Halibut**, *raw*	Literature sources	N	390	92	17.7	0	2.4
587L	*steamed*	Middle cut	1.00	553	131	23.8	0	4.0
588L	*steamed, weighed with bones and skin*	Calculated from steamed	0.76	417	99	18.0	0	3.0

No.	Food	Labelling information for Group 2 nutrients per 100g food				Additional nutrients and information per 100g food		
		Sugars (actual weight) g	Saturates g	Fibre (Englyst) g	Sodium g	Sodium mg	Starch (actual weight) g	Water g
	White fish							
577L	**Haddock**, *raw*	0	0.1	0	0.1	120	0	81.3
578L	*steamed*	0	0.2	0	0.1	120	0	75.1
579L	*steamed, weighed with bones and skin*	0	0.1	0	0.1	92	0	57.1
580L	*in crumbs, fried in blended oil*	0.1	0.7	0.2	0.2	180	3.2	65.1
581L	*-, fried in blended oil, weighed with bones*	0.1	0.7	0.1	0.2	160	2.9	60.0
582L	*-, fried in dripping*	0.1	3.8	0.2	0.2	180	3.2	65.1
583L	*-, fried in dripping, weighed with bones*	0.1	3.5	0.1	0.2	160	2.9	60.0
584L	smoked, *steamed*	0	0.2	0	1.2	1220	0	71.6
585L	*steamed, weighed with bones and skin*	0	0.1	0	0.8	790	0	46.5
586L	**Halibut**, *raw*	0	0.3	0	0.1	84	0	78.1
587L	*steamed*	0	0.5	0	0.1	110	0	70.9
588L	*steamed, weighed with bones and skin*	0	0.4	0	0.1	84	0	53.8

Labelling information for Group 1 nutrients per 100g food

No.	Food	Description and main data sources	Edible proportion	Energy kJ	Energy kcal	Protein (N × 6.25) g	Carbohydrate (actual wt.) g	Fat g
	White fish							
589L	**Lemon sole**, *raw*	Literature sources	N	343	81	17.1	0	1.4
590L	*steamed*	Flesh only	1.00	384	91	20.6	0	0.9
591L	*steamed, weighed with bones and skin*	Calculated from steamed	0.71	270	64	14.6	0	0.6
592L	*in crumbs, fried*	Samples coated in crumbs and fried	1.00	898	215	16.1	8.4	13.0
593L	*-, fried, weighed with bones*	Calculated from fried	0.79	711	170	12.7	6.7	10.3
594L	**Plaice**, *raw*	8 fish, purchased whole	0.42	386	91	17.9	0	2.2
595L	*steamed*	Flesh only	1.00	392	93	18.9	0	1.9
596L	*steamed, weighed with bones and skin*	Calculated from steamed	0.54	210	50	10.2	0	1.0
597L	*in batter, fried in blended oil*	6 cooked samples from fish and chip shops	1.00	1157	278	15.8	13.1	18.0
598L	*-, fried in dripping*	6 cooked samples from fish and chip shops	1.00	1157	278	15.8	13.1	18.0
599L	*in crumbs, fried, fillets*	8 samples coated in egg and crumbs, and fried	1.00	944	226	18.0	7.7	13.7

No.	Food	Labelling information for Group 2 nutrients per 100g food				Additional nutrients and information per 100g food		
		Sugars (actual weight) g	Saturates g	Fibre (Englyst) g	Sodium g	Sodium mg	Starch (actual weight) g	Water g
White fish								
589L	**Lemon sole**, *raw*	0	0.2	0	0.1	95	0	81.2
590L	*steamed*	0	0.1	0	0.1	120	0	77.2
591L	*steamed, weighed with bones and skin*	0	0.1	0	0.1	82	0	54.9
592L	*in crumbs, fried*	0.2	1.3	0.4	0.1	140	8.2	60.4
593L	*-, fried, weighed with bones*	0.2	1.0	0.3	0.1	110	6.5	47.7
594L	**Plaice**, *raw*	0	0.3	0	0.1	120	0	79.5
595L	*steamed*	0	0.3	0	0.1	120	0	78.0
596L	*steamed, weighed with bones and skin*	0	0.2	0	0.1	65	0	42.1
597L	*in batter, fried in blended oil*	0.3	1.5	N	0.2	220	12.8	52.4
598L	*-, fried in dripping*	0.3	8.2	N	0.2	220	12.8	52.4
599L	*in crumbs, fried, fillets*	0.2	1.4	N	0.2	220	7.5	59.9

Labelling information for Group 1 nutrients per 100g food

No.	Food	Description and main data sources	Edible proportion	Energy kJ	Energy kcal	Protein (N × 6.25) g	Carbohydrate (actual wt.) g	Fat g
White fish								
600L	**Saithe**, *raw*	Literature sources	N	308	73	17.0	0	0.5
601L	*steamed*	Pieces from tail end	1.00	418	99	23.3	0	0.6
602L	*steamed, weighed with bones and skin*	Calculated from steamed	0.85	355	84	19.8	0	0.5
603L	**Skate**, *in batter, fried*	6 cooked samples from fish and chip shops	1.00	914	219	22.9	4.5	12.1
604L	*in batter, fried, weighed with waste*	Calculated from in batter, fried	0.82	747	179	18.8	3.6	9.9
605L	**Whiting**, *steamed*	Flesh only	1.00	389	92	20.9	0	0.9
606L	*steamed, weighed with bones*	Calculated from steamed	0.93	264	62	14.2	0	0.6
607L	*in crumbs, fried*	Samples coated in crumbs and fried	1.00	798	191	18.1	6.4	10.3
608L	*-, fried, weighed with bones*	Calculated from in crumbs, fried	0.90	716	171	16.3	5.6	9.3

No.	Food	Labelling information for Group 2 nutrients per 100g food				Additional nutrients and information per 100g food		
		Sugars (actual weight) g	Saturates g	Fibre (Englyst) g	Sodium g	Sodium mg	Starch (actual weight) g	Water g
	White fish							
600L	**Saithe**, *raw*	0	0.1	0	0.1	73	0	81.0
601L	*steamed*	0	0.1	0	0.1	97	0	74.8
602L	*steamed, weighed with bones and skin*	0	0.1	0	0.1	83	0	63.5
603L	**Skate**, *in batter, fried*	0.1	1.2	0.2	0.1	140	4.4	61.8
604L	*in batter, fried, weighed with waste*	0.1	1.0	0.2	0.1	110	3.5	50.7
605L	**Whiting**, *steamed*	0	0.1	0	0.1	130	0	76.9
606L	*steamed, weighed with bones*	0	0.1	0	0.1	86	0	52.2
607L	*in crumbs, fried*	0.2	1.0	0.3	0.2	200	6.2	63.0
608L	*-, fried, weighed with bones*	0.1	0.9	0.3	0.2	180	5.5	56.8

Labelling information for Group 1 nutrients per 100g food

No.	Food	Description and main data sources	Edible proportion	Energy		Protein (N × 6.25)	Carbohydrate (actual wt.)	Fat
				kJ	kcal	g	g	g
Fatty fish								
609L	**Anchovies**, canned in oil, *drained*	10 assorted brands	N	1165	280	25.2	0	19.9
610L	**Herring**, *raw*	12 fish, sampled in November; flesh only	0.55	970	234	16.8	0	18.5[a]
611L	*fried*	Flesh, skin and roes; covered in oatmeal	1.00	975	234	23.1	1.4	15.1
612L	*fried, weighed with bones*	Calculated from fried	0.88	858	206	20.3	1.2	13.3
613L	*grilled*	12 fish, flesh only	1.00	828	199	20.4	0	13.0
614L	*grilled, weighed with bones*	Calculated from grilled	0.68	562	135	13.9	0	8.8
615L	**Kipper**, *baked*	Flesh only	1.00	855	205	25.5	0	11.4
616L	*baked, weighed with bones*	Calculated from baked	0.54	464	111	13.8	0	6.2
617L	**Mackerel**, *raw*	Literature sources	N	926	223	19.0	0	16.3
618L	*fried*	Flesh only	1.00	784	188	21.5	0	11.3
619L	*fried, weighed with bones*	Calculated from fried	0.73	574	138	15.7	0	8.3
620L	smoked	10 samples, flesh and skin	0.98	1463	353	18.8	0	30.9
621L	**Pilchards**, canned in tomato sauce	6 cans, 4 brands; whole contents	1.00	530	126	18.8	0.6	5.4

[a] The values for fat content can vary throughout the year from about 5g per 100g in February – April to 20g per 100g in July – October

No.	Food	Labelling information for Group 2 nutrients per 100g food				Additional nutrients and information per 100g food		
		Sugars (actual weight) g	Saturates g	Fibre (Englyst) g	Sodium g	Sodium mg	Starch (actual weight) g	Water g
	Fatty fish							
609L	**Anchovies**, canned in oil, *drained*	0	N	0	3.9	3930	0	41.6
610L	**Herring**, *raw*	0	5.3	0	0.1	67	0	63.9[a]
611L	*fried*	Tr	4.3	N	0.1	100	1.4	58.7
612L	*fried, weighed with bones*	Tr	3.8	N	0.1	89	1.2	51.6
613L	*grilled*	0	3.7	0	0.2	170	0	65.5
614L	*grilled, weighed with bones*	0	2.5	0	0.1	120	0	44.5
615L	**Kipper**, *baked*	0	1.8	0	1.0	990	0	58.7
616L	*baked, weighed with bones*	0	1.0	0	0.5	540	0	31.6
617L	**Mackerel**, *raw*	0	3.3	0	0.1	130	0	64.0
618L	*fried*	0	2.3	0	0.2	150	0	65.6
619L	*fried, weighed with bones*	0	1.7	0	0.1	110	0	47.8
620L	smoked	0	6.3	0	0.8	750	0	47.1
621L	**Pilchards**, canned in tomato sauce	0.5	1.1	Tr	0.4	370	0.1	70.0

[a] The values for water content can vary throughout the year from about 75g per 100g in February – April to 60g per 100g in July – October

Labelling information for Group 1 nutrients per 100g food

No.	Food	Description and main data sources	Edible proportion	Energy kJ	Energy kcal	Protein (N × 6.25) g	Carbohydrate (actual wt.) g	Fat g
	Fatty fish							
622L	**Salmon**, *raw*	Atlantic salmon; literature sources	N	757	182	18.4	0	12.0
623L	*steamed*	Shoulder cut, flesh only	1.00	823	197	20.1	0	13.0
624L	*steamed, weighed with bones and skin*	Calculated from steamed	0.81	666	160	16.3	0	10.5
625L	canned	10 cans, red salmon; backbone and skin removed	0.98	649	155	20.3	0	8.2
626L	smoked	4 samples	1.00	598	142	25.4	0	4.5
627L	**Sardines**, canned in tomato sauce	10 cans, 4 brands; whole contents	1.00	740	178	17.8	0.5	11.6
628L	canned in oil, *drained*	10 cans, 6 brands	0.83	906	217	23.7	0	13.6
629L	**Trout**, brown, *steamed*	Flesh only	1.00	566	135	23.5	0	4.5
630L	*steamed, weighed with bones*	Calculated from steamed	0.66	375	89	15.5	0	3.0
631L	**Tuna**, canned in oil, *drained*	6 cans, 2 brands; skipjack tuna	0.79	790	189	26.9	0	9.0
632L	canned in brine, *drained*	10 cans, 9 brands	0.81	427	101	23.8	0	0.6
633L	**Whitebait**, *fried*	Whole fish; rolled in flour and fried	1.00	2171	525	19.5	4.8	47.5

No.	Food	Labelling information for Group 2 nutrients per 100g food				Additional nutrients and information per 100g food		
		Sugars (actual weight) g	Saturates g	Fibre (Englyst) g	Sodium g	Sodium mg	Starch (actual weight) g	Water g
Fatty fish								
622L	**Salmon**, *raw*	0	2.2	0	0.1	98	0	68.0
623L	*steamed*	0	2.4	0	0.1	110	0	65.4
624L	*steamed, weighed with bones and skin*	0	1.9	0	0.1	87	0	53.0
625L	canned	0	1.5	0	0.6	570	0	70.4
626L	smoked	0	0.8	0	1.9	1880	0	64.9
627L	**Sardines**, canned in tomato sauce	0.5	3.3	Tr	0.7	700	Tr	65.0
628L	canned in oil, *drained*	0	2.8	0	0.7	650	0	58.4
629L	**Trout**, brown, *steamed*	0	1.0	0	0.1	88[a]	0	70.6
630L	*steamed, weighed with bones*	0	0.7	0	0.1	58	0	46.5
631L	**Tuna**, canned in oil, *drained*	0	1.4	0	0.3	290	0	63.3
632L	canned in brine, *drained*	0	0.2	0	0.3	320	0	74.6
633L	**Whitebait**, *fried*	0.1	4.4	0.2	0.2	230	4.7	23.5

[a] Sea trout contains 210mg Na per 100g

Labelling information for Group 1 nutrients per 100g food

No.	Food	Description and main data sources	Edible proportion	Energy kJ	Energy kcal	Protein (N × 6.25) g	Carbohydrate (actual wt.) g	Fat g
Crustacea								
634L	**Crab**, *boiled*	Boiled in fresh water	1.00	534	127	20.1	0	5.2
635L	*boiled, weighed with shell*	Calculated from boiled	0.20	105	25	4.0	0	1.0
636L	canned	6 cans, 2 brands	1.00	341	81	18.1	0	0.9
637L	**Lobster**, *boiled*	Boiled in fresh water	1.00	502	119	22.1	0	3.4
638L	*boiled, weighed with shell*	Calculated from boiled	0.36	179	42	7.9	0	1.2
639L	**Prawns**, *boiled*	Samples cooked in sea or salt water	1.00	451	107	22.6	0	1.8
640L	*boiled, weighed with shell*	Calculated from boiled	0.38	172	41	8.6	0	0.7
641L	**Scampi**, *in breadcrumbs, frozen, fried*	5 packets	1.00	1306	312	12.2	26.3	17.6
642L	**Shrimps**, *frozen, shell removed*	10 assorted brands	1.00	310	73	16.5	0	0.8
643L	canned, *drained*	10 cans, 3 brands	0.65	398	94	20.8	0	1.2
Molluscs								
644L	**Cockles**, *boiled*	Samples cooked in sea or salt water	1.00	203	48	11.3	Tr	0.3
645L	**Mussels**, *boiled*	Boiled in fresh water	1.00	366	87	17.2	Tr	2.0
646L	*boiled, weighed with shell*	Calculated from boiled	0.30	111	26	5.2	Tr	0.6
647L	**Squid**, *frozen, raw*	5 assorted brands	0.59	278	66	13.1	0	1.5
648L	**Whelks**, *boiled, weighed with shell*	Samples cooked in sea or salt water	0.15	59	14	2.8	Tr	0.3
649L	**Winkles**, *boiled, weighed with shell*	Samples cooked in sea or salt water	0.19	60	14	2.9	Tr	0.3

No.	Food	Labelling information for Group 2 nutrients per 100g food				Additional nutrients and information per 100g food		
		Sugars (actual weight) g	Saturates g	Fibre (Englyst) g	Sodium g	Sodium mg	Starch (actual weight) g	Water g
	Crustacea							
634L	**Crab**, *boiled*	0	0.7	0	0.4	370	0	72.5
635L	*boiled, weighed with shell*	0	0.1	0	0.1	73	0	14.5
636L	canned	0	0.1	0	0.6	550	0	79.2
637L	**Lobster**, *boiled*	0	N	0	0.3	330	0	72.4
638L	*boiled, weighed with shell*	0	N	0	0.1	120	0	26.1
639L	**Prawns**, *boiled*	0	0.4	0	1.6	1590	0	70.0
640L	*boiled, weighed with shell*	0	0.2	0	0.6	610	0	26.6
641L	**Scampi**, *in breadcrumbs, frozen, fried*	Tr	1.7	N	0.4	380	26.3	39.4
642L	**Shrimps**, *frozen, shell removed*	0	0.1	0	0.4	375	0	81.2
643L	canned, *drained*	0	0.2	0	1.0	980	0	74.9
	Molluscs							
644L	**Cockles**, *boiled*	Tr	0.1	0	3.5	3520	Tr	78.9
645L	**Mussels**, *boiled*	Tr	0.4	0	0.2	210	Tr	79.0
646L	*boiled, weighed with shell*	Tr	0.1	0	0.1	63	Tr	23.7
647L	**Squid**, *frozen, raw*	0	N	0	0.2	185	0	84.2
648L	**Whelks**, *boiled, weighed with shell*	Tr	0.1	0	Tr	40	Tr	11.6
649L	**Winkles**, *boiled, weighed with shell*	Tr	Tr	0	0.2	220	Tr	15.1

Labelling information for Group 1 nutrients per 100g food

No.	Food	Description and main data sources	Edible proportion	Energy kJ	Energy kcal	Protein (N × 6.25) g	Carbohydrate (actual wt.) g	Fat g
	Fish products and dishes							
650L	**Fish cakes**, *fried*	14 packets, 4 brands, white fish	1.00	776	186	9.1	13.7	10.5
651L	**Fish fingers**, *fried in blended oil*	11 packets, 3 brands; coated in breadcrumbs	1.00	965	231	13.5	15.6	12.7
652L	*fried in lard*	Calculated from fried in blended oil	1.00	965	231	13.5	15.6	12.7
653L	*grilled*	Calculation from *fried in lard*	1.00	887	211	15.1	17.5	9.0
654L	**Fish paste**	30 samples, sardine, crab, lobster, salmon	1.00	703	168	15.3	3.4	10.4
655L	**Fish pie**	Recipe	1.00	436	103	8.0	11.1	3.0
656L	**Kedgeree**	Recipe	1.00	699	167	14.3	9.6	7.9
657L	**Roe**, cod, hard, *fried*	Parboiled, sliced and fried in crumbs	1.00	842	202	20.9	2.7	11.9
658L	herring, soft, *fried*	Rolled in flour and fried	1.00	1067	256	24.1	4.3	15.8
659L	**Taramasalata**	10 assorted samples	1.00	1834	445	3.2	3.7	46.4

No.	Food	Sugars (actual weight) g	Saturates g	Fibre (Englyst) g	Sodium g	Sodium mg	Starch (actual weight) g	Water g
		Labelling information for Group 2 nutrients per 100g food				**Additional nutrients and information per 100g food**		
	Fish products and dishes							
650L	**Fish cakes**, *fried*	Tr	1.0	N	0.5	500	13.7	63.3
651L	**Fish fingers**, *fried in blended oil*	Tr	2.8	0.6	0.4	350	15.6	55.6
652L	*fried in lard*	Tr	4.5	0.6	0.4	350	15.6	55.6
653L	*grilled*	Tr	2.8	0.7	0.4	380	17.5	56.2
654L	**Fish paste**	Tr	N	0.2	0.6	600	3.4	67.1
655L	**Fish pie**	1.3	1.2	0.7	0.3	250	9.8	75.7
656L	**Kedgeree**	0.1	2.3	Tr	0.9	870	9.5	65.6
657L	**Roe**, cod, hard, *fried*	Tr	1.2	0.1	0.1	130	2.7	62.0
658L	herring, soft, *fried*	Tr	1.6	N	0.1	87	4.3	52.3
659L	**Taramasalata**	Tr	3.2	N	0.7	650	3.7	35.9

Labelling information for Group 1 nutrients per 100g food

No.	Food	Description and main data sources	Edible proportion	Energy kJ	Energy kcal	Protein (N × 6.25) g	Carbohydrate (actual wt.) g	Fat g
	Early potatoes							
660L	**New potatoes**, *average, raw*	IFR; flesh only	0.89	293	69	1.8	14.8	0.3
661L	*boiled in unsalted water*	IFR. Samples as raw; boiled 20 minutes	1.00	314	74	1.5	16.3	0.3
662L	*in skins, boiled in unsalted water*	LGC; boiled 20 minutes	1.00	275	65	1.4	14.1	0.3
663L	canned, *re-heated, drained*	LGC; 10 samples, 4 brands	0.65	262	62	1.4	13.8	0.1
	Main crop potatoes							
664L	**Old potatoes**, *average, raw*	IFR; 4 varieties sampled over two years. Flesh only	0.80	310	73	2.1	15.7	0.2
665L	*baked, flesh and skin*	LGC. Samples as raw; baked 90 minutes 200C	1.00	565	133	3.9	28.9	0.2
666L	*-, flesh only*	IFR. Samples as raw; baked 90 minutes 200C	1.00	320	75	2.2	16.4	0.1
667L	*-, flesh only, weighed with skin*	Calcd. from *flesh only*	0.67	215	51	1.4	11.0	0.1
668L	*boiled in unsalted water*	IFR. Samples as raw; boiled 20 minutes	1.00	298	70	1.8	15.5	0.1
669L	*mashed with butter*	Calculation from boiled (100g), butter (5g), milk (7g)	1.00	431	103	1.8	14.2	4.3
670L	*mashed with margarine*	Calculation from boiled (100g), margarine (5g) and milk (7g)	1.00	431	103	1.8	14.2	4.3
671L	*roast in blended oil*	Calculation from *roast in corn oil*	1.00	617	147	2.9	23.6	4.5
672L	*roast in corn oil*	IFR. Samples as raw; roasted in shallow oil 90 minutes 200C	1.00	617	147	2.9	23.6	4.5
673L	*roast in lard*	Calculation from *roast in corn oil*	1.00	617	147	2.9	23.6	4.5

No.	Food	Labelling information for Group 2 nutrients per 100g food				Additional nutrients and information per 100g food		
		Sugars (actual weight) g	Saturates g	Fibre (Englyst) g	Sodium g	Sodium mg	Starch (actual weight) g	Water g
	Early potatoes							
660L	**New potatoes**, *average, raw*	1.3	0.1	1.0	Tr	11	13.5	81.7
661L	*boiled in unsalted water*	1.1	0.1	1.1	Tr	9	15.2	80.5
662L	*in skins, boiled in unsalted water*	1.0	0.1	1.5	Tr	10	13.1	81.1
663L	canned, *re-heated, drained*	0.7	Tr	0.8	0.3	250	13.1	81.3
	Main crop potatoes							
664L	**Old potatoes**, *average, raw*	0.6	Tr	1.3	Tr	7	15.1	79.0
665L	*baked, flesh and skin*	1.2	Tr	2.7	Tr	12	27.7	62.6
666L	*-, flesh only*	0.7	Tr	1.4	Tr	7	15.7	78.9
667L	*-, flesh only, weighed with skin*	0.5	Tr	0.9	Tr	5	10.5	52.9
668L	*boiled in unsalted water*	0.7	Tr	1.2	Tr	7	14.8	80.3
669L	*mashed with butter*	1.0	2.8	1.1	Tr	43	13.2	77.6
670L	*mashed with margarine*	1.0	1.4	1.1	Tr	49	13.2	77.6
671L	*roast in blended oil*	0.6	0.4	1.8	Tr	9	23.0	64.7
672L	*roast in corn oil*	0.6	0.6	1.8	Tr	9	23.0	64.7
673L	*roast in lard*	0.6	1.8	1.8	Tr	9	23.0	64.7

Labelling information for Group 1 nutrients per 100g food

No.	Food	Description and main data sources	Edible proportion	Energy kJ	Energy kcal	Protein (N × 6.25) g	Carbohydrate (actual wt.) g	Fat g
	Chipped old potatoes							
674L	**Chips**, homemade, *fried in blended oil*	Calculation from *fried in corn oil*	1.00	780	186	3.9	27.4	6.7[a]
675L	*fried in corn oil*	IFR. Samples as raw potatoes; deep fried 6 minutes 190C	1.00	780	186	3.9	27.4	6.7[a]
676L	*fried in dripping*	Calculation from *fried in corn oil*	1.00	780	186	3.9	27.4	6.7[a]
677L	retail, *fried in blended oil*	Calculation from *fried in vegetable oil*	1.00	988	236	3.2	27.9	12.4
678L	*fried in dripping*	Calculation from *fried in vegetable oil*	1.00	988	236	3.2	27.9	12.4
679L	*fried in vegetable oil*	5 samples from fish and chip shops	1.00	988	236	3.2	27.9	12.4
680L	French fries, retail	5 samples from burger outlets. Manufacturers' data	1.00	1158	277	3.4	31.0	15.5
681L	straight cut, *frozen, fried in blended oil*	Calculation from *fried in corn oil*	1.00	1127	269	4.1	32.8	13.5
682L	*frozen, fried in corn oil*	LGC; 10 samples, 10 brands. Deep fried 3-5 minutes	1.00	1127	269	4.1	32.8	13.5
683L	*-, fried in dripping*	Calculation from *fried in corn oil*	1.00	1127	269	4.1	32.8	13.5
684L	fine cut, *frozen, fried in blended oil*	Calculation from *fried in corn oil*	1.00	1502	360	4.5	37.5	21.3
685L	*frozen, fried in corn oil*	LGC; 10 samples, 4 brands. Deep fried 1-4 minutes	1.00	1502	360	4.5	37.5	21.3
686L	*-, fried in dripping*	Calculation from *fried in corn oil*	1.00	1502	360	4.5	37.5	21.3
687L	**Oven chips**, *frozen, baked*	LGC; 10 samples, 7 brands. Oven baked 15-20 minutes	1.00	674	160	3.3	27.2	4.2

[a] The fat content of homemade chips will be variable and dependent on a number of factors related to their preparation

No.	Food	Sugars (actual weight) g	Saturates g	Fibre (Englyst) g	Sodium g	Sodium mg	Starch (actual weight) g	Water g
		Labelling information for Group 2 nutrients per 100g food				Additional nutrients and information per 100g food		
	Chipped old potatoes							
674L	**Chips**, homemade, *fried in blended oil*	0.6	0.6	2.2	Tr	12	26.8	56.5
675L	*fried in corn oil*	0.6	0.9	2.2	Tr	12	26.8	56.5
676L	*fried in dripping*	0.6	3.7	2.2	Tr	12	26.8	56.5
677L	retail, *fried in blended oil*	1.7	1.1	2.2	Tr	35	26.2	52.3
678L	*fried in dripping*	1.7	6.8	2.2	Tr	35	26.2	52.3
679L	*fried in vegetable oil*	1.7	3.6	2.2	Tr	35	26.2	52.3
680L	French fries, retail	1.3	5.8	2.1	0.3	310	29.7	43.8
681L	straight cut, *frozen, fried in blended oil*	0.7	1.2	2.4	Tr	29	32.1	40.3
682L	*frozen, fried in corn oil*	0.7	2.5	2.4	Tr	29	32.1	40.3
683L	*-, fried in dripping*	0.7	7.5	2.4	Tr	30	32.1	40.3
684L	fine cut, *frozen, fried in blended oil*	0.6	1.8	2.4	0.1	97	36.9	26.0
685L	*frozen, fried in corn oil*	0.6	4.0	2.7	0.1	97	36.9	26.0
686L	*-, fried in dripping*	0.6	11.8	2.7	0.1	98	36.9	26.0
687L	**Oven chips**, *frozen, baked*	0.7	1.8	2.0	0.1	53	26.5	58.5

Labelling information for Group 1 nutrients per 100g food

No.	Food	Description and main data sources	Edible proportion	Energy kJ	Energy kcal	Protein (N × 6.25) g	Carbohydrate (actual wt.) g	Fat g
	Potato products							
688L	**Instant potato powder**, *made up with water*	Calcd. from ingredients; made up as packet directions	1.00	238	56	1.5	12.3	0.1
689L	*made up with whole milk*	Calcd. from ingredients; made up as packet directions	1.00	313	74	2.3	13.5	1.2
690L	**Potato croquettes**, *fried in blended oil*	LGC; 10 samples, 5 brands. Shallow fried 5-7 minutes	1.00	884	212	3.7	19.8	13.1
691L	**Potato waffles**, *frozen, cooked*	IFR. 10 samples (Birds Eye); grilled, shallow and deep fried in corn oil, oven baked	1.00	829	197	3.2	27.7	8.2
	Beans and lentils							
692L	**Aduki beans**, *dried, raw*	LGC; 6 samples, whole beans	1.00	1132	267	19.9	45.6[a]	0.5
693L	*dried, boiled in unsalted water*	LGC analysis and calculation from dried	1.00	512	121	9.3	20.4[a]	0.2
694L	**Baked beans**, canned in tomato sauce, *re-heated*	LGC; 10 cans, 7 brands	1.00	350	83	5.2	14.1	0.6
695L	reduced sugar, reduced salt	LGC; 5 cans, 2 own brands	1.00	308	73	5.3	11.5	0.6
696L	**Beansprouts**, mung, *raw*	IFR; as purchased	1.00	132	31	2.9	3.8	0.5
697L	*stir-fried in blended oil*	LGC. 6 samples; stir-fried 2 minutes. And calcd. from raw	1.00	299	72	1.9	2.4	6.1
698L	**Black gram**, urad gram, *dried, raw*	Whole beans. Literature sources	1.00	1169	275	24.9	40.8[a]	1.4
699L	*dried, boiled in unsalted water*	As raw; soaked and boiled	1.00	379	89	7.8	13.6[a]	0.4

[a] Including oligosaccharides

No.	Food	Labelling information for Group 2 nutrients per 100g food				Additional nutrients and information per 100g food		
		Sugars (actual weight) g	Saturates g	Fibre (Englyst) g	Sodium g	Sodium mg	Starch (actual weight) g	Water g
	Potato products							
688L	**Instant potato powder**, *made up with water*	0.8	Tr	1.0	0.2	200	11.5	83.3
689L	*made up with whole milk*	2.0	0.7	1.0	0.2	210	11.5	80.0
690L	**Potato croquettes**, *fried in blended oil*	0.6	1.7	1.3	0.4	420	19.2	58.2
691L	**Potato waffles**, *frozen, cooked*	0.6	1.0	2.3	0.4	430	27.1	52.7
	Beans and lentils							
692L	**Aduki beans**, *dried, raw*	1.0[a]	N	11.1	Tr	5	40.6	12.7
693L	*dried, boiled in unsalted water*	0.4[a]	N	5.5	Tr	2	18.9	59.4
694L	**Baked beans**, canned in tomato sauce, *re-heated*	5.6	0.1	3.7	0.5	530	8.5	71.5
695L	reduced sugar, reduced salt	2.7	0.1	3.8	0.3	330	8.8	73.6
696L	**Beansprouts**, mung, *raw*	2.2	0.1	1.5	Tr	5	1.6	90.4
697L	*stir-fried in blended oil*	1.4	0.5	0.9	Tr	3	1.0	88.4
698L	**Black gram**, urad gram, *dried, raw*	1.2[a]	0.2	N	Tr	40	37.6	11.5
699L	*dried, boiled in unsalted water*	0.3[a]	0.1	N	Tr	13	13.0	71.3

[a] Not including oligosaccharides

No.	Food	Description and main data sources	Edible proportion	Energy kJ	Energy kcal	Protein (N × 6.25) g	Carbohydrate (actual wt.) g	Fat g
Beans and lentils								
700L	**Blackeye beans**, *dried, raw*	Whole beans. Analysis and literature sources	1.00	1299	306	23.5	49.4[a]	1.6
701L	*dried, boiled in unsalted water*	As raw; soaked and boiled	1.00	482	114	8.8	18.0[a]	0.7
702L	**Broad beans**, *frozen, boiled in unsalted water*	LGC; 10 samples, 7 brands. Boiled 3-10 minutes	1.00	338	80	7.9	10.7[a]	0.6
703L	**Butter beans**, canned, *re-heated, drained*	LGC; 10 cans, 5 brands	0.57	319	75	5.9	11.8[a]	0.5
704L	**Chick peas**, whole, *dried, raw*	Analytical and literature sources. Kabuli variety	1.00	1332	315	21.4	45.2[a]	5.4
705L	*dried, boiled in unsalted water*	As raw. Soaked and boiled	1.00	504	119	8.4	16.7[a]	2.1
706L	canned, *re-heated, drained*	LGC. Whole peas; 10 samples, 5 brands	0.60	480	114	7.2	14.7[a]	2.9
707L	**Green beans/French beans**, *raw*	IFR; pods and beans, ends trimmed	0.83	104	25	1.9	3.1	0.5
708L	*frozen, boiled in unsalted water*	LGC; 10 samples, 8 brands. Boiled 3-8 minutes	1.00	111	26	1.8	4.5	0.1
709L	**Hummus**	LGC. Chick pea spread; 10 samples, retail and homemade	1.00	779	187	7.6	10.8[a]	12.6
710L	**Lentils**, green and brown, whole, *dried, raw*	LGC; 10 samples, 6 brands. Continental type	1.00	1240	292	24.4	44.4[a]	1.9
711L	*dried, boiled in salted water*	LGC; as raw. Boiled 10 minutes, simmered 25 minutes	1.00	439	104	8.8	15.5[a]	0.7
712L	red, split, *dried, raw*	LGC; as purchased	1.00	1325	312	23.8	51.3[a]	1.3
713L	*dried, boiled in unsalted water*	LGC. As purchased; boiled 20 minutes	1.00	416	98	7.6	16.0[a]	0.4

[a] Including oligosaccharides

No.	Food	Labelling information for Group 2 nutrients per 100g food				Additional nutrients and information per 100g food		
		Sugars (actual weight) g	Saturates g	Fibre (Englyst) g	Sodium g	Sodium mg	Starch (actual weight) g	Water g
Beans and lentils								
700L	**Blackeye beans**, *dried, raw*	2.8[a]	0.5	8.2	Tr	16	43.2	10.7
701L	*dried, boiled in unsalted water*	1.0[a]	0.2	3.5	Tr	5	16.4	66.2
702L	**Broad beans**, *frozen, boiled in unsalted water*	1.2[a]	0.1	6.5	Tr	8	9.1	73.8
703L	**Butter beans**, canned, *re-heated, drained*	1.0[a]	0.1	4.6	0.4	420	9.9	74.0
704L	**Chick peas**, whole, *dried, raw*	2.5[a]	0.5	10.7	Tr	39	39.8	10.0
705L	*dried, boiled in unsalted water*	1.0[a]	0.2	4.3	Tr	5	15.1	65.8
706L	canned, *re-heated, drained*	0.4[a]	0.3	4.1	0.2	220	13.7	67.5
707L	**Green beans/French beans**, *raw*	2.3	0.1	2.2	Tr	Tr	0.8	90.7
708L	*frozen, boiled in unsalted water*	2.1	Tr	4.1	Tr	8	2.4	90.0
709L	**Hummus**	1.8[a]	N	2.4	0.7	670	8.5	61.4
710L	**Lentils**, green and brown, whole, *dried, raw*	1.1[a]	0.2	8.9	Tr	12	40.5	10.8
711L	*dried, boiled in salted water*	0.4[a]	0.1	3.8	Tr	3	14.5	66.7
712L	red, split, *dried, raw*	2.3[a]	0.2	4.9	Tr	36	46.2	11.1
713L	*dried, boiled in unsalted water*	0.8[a]	Tr	1.9	Tr	12	14.7	72.1

[a] Not including oligosaccharides

Labelling information for Group 1 nutrients per 100g food

No.	Food	Description and main data sources	Edible proportion	Energy		Protein (N × 6.25)	Carbohydrate (actual wt.)	Fat
				kJ	kcal	g	g	g
Beans and lentils								
714L	**Mung beans**, whole, *dried, raw*	Literature sources	1.00	1164	274	23.8	42.3[a]	1.1
715L	*dried, boiled in unsalted water*	As raw, soaked and boiled	1.00	380	90	7.6	13.9[a]	0.4
716L	**Red kidney beans**, *dried, raw*	Whole beans. Analytical and literature sources	1.00	1111	262	22.1	40.2[a]	1.4
717L	*dried, boiled in unsalted water*	As raw, soaked and boiled	1.00	415	98	8.4	14.9[a]	0.5
718L	canned, *re-heated, drained*	LGC; 10 cans, 6 brands	0.64	413	97	6.9	16.1[a]	0.6
719L	**Runner beans**, *raw*	IFR; ends and sides trimmed	0.86	96	23	1.6	3.2	0.4
720L	*boiled in unsalted water*	IFR. Sliced and boiled 20 minutes	1.00	78	19	1.2	2.3	0.5
721L	**Soya beans**, *dried, raw*	Whole beans. Analysis and literature sources	1.00	1550	370	35.9	14.8[a]	18.6
722L	*dried, boiled in unsalted water*	As raw	1.00	590	141	14.0	4.8[a]	7.3
723L	**Tofu**, soya bean, *steamed*	LGC. Soya bean curd; 7 assorted samples	1.00	303	73	8.1	0.6[a]	4.2
724L	*steamed, fried*	Calcd. from *steamed* and ref. Haytowitz and Matthews (1986)	1.00	1087	261	23.5	1.9[a]	17.7

[a] Including oligosaccharides

No.	Food	Labelling information for Group 2 nutrients per 100g food				Additional nutrients and information per 100g food		
		Sugars (actual weight) g	Saturates g	Fibre (Englyst) g	Sodium g	Sodium mg	Starch (actual weight) g	Water g
	Beans and lentils							
714L	**Mung beans**, whole, *dried, raw*	1.5[a]	0.3	10.0	Tr	12	37.2	11.0
715L	*dried, boiled in unsalted water*	0.5[a]	0.1	3.0	Tr	2	12.8	69.3
716L	**Red kidney beans**, *dried, raw*	2.4[a]	0.2	15.7	Tr	18	34.5	11.2
717L	*dried, boiled in unsalted water*	0.9[a]	0.1	6.7	Tr	2	13.2	66.0
718L	canned, *re-heated, drained*	3.3[a]	0.1	6.2	0.4	390	11.6	67.5
719L	**Runner beans**, *raw*	2.8	0.1	2.0	Tr	Tr	0.4	91.2
720L	*boiled in unsalted water*	2.0	0.1	1.9	Tr	1	0.3	92.8
721L	**Soya beans**, *dried, raw*	5.3[a]	2.3	15.7	Tr	5	4.4	8.5
722L	*dried, boiled in unsalted water*	2.1[a]	0.9	6.1	Tr	1	1.7	64.3
723L	**Tofu**, soya bean, *steamed*	0.2[a]	0.5	N	Tr	4	0.3	85.0
724L	*steamed, fried*	0.8[a]	N	N	Tr	12	0.8	51.0

[a] Not including oligosaccharides

Labelling information for Group 1 nutrients per 100g food

No.	Food	Description and main data sources	Edible proportion	Energy kJ	Energy kcal	Protein (N × 6.25) g	Carbohydrate (actual wt.) g	Fat g
	Peas							
725L	**Mange-tout peas**, *raw*	LGC. Whole pods, ends trimmed; 10 samples	0.92	138	33	3.6	4.1	0.2
726L	*boiled in salted water*	LGC. As raw; boiled 3 minutes. And calcd. from raw	1.00	114	27	3.2	3.3	0.1
727L	*stir-fried in blended oil*	LGC. As raw; stir-fried 5 minutes. And calcd. from raw	1.00	302	72	3.8	3.5	4.8
728L	**Mushy peas**, canned, *re-heated*	LGC; 10 samples, 3 brands	1.00	337	80	5.8	12.5[a]	0.7
729L	**Peas**, *raw*	IFR; whole peas, no pods	0.37	350	83	6.9	10.4[a]	1.5
730L	*boiled in unsalted water*	IFR. As raw; boiled 20 minutes	1.00	326	77	6.7	9.0[a]	1.6
731L	*frozen, boiled in salted water*	Based on *frozen, boiled in unsalted water*	1.00	287	68	5.9	9.0[a]	0.9
732L	*-, boiled in unsalted water*	LGC; 10 samples, 8 brands. Boiled 2-5 minutes	1.00	287	68	5.9	9.0[a]	0.9
733L	canned, *re-heated, drained*	LGC; 10 samples, 9 brands	0.67	334	79	5.3	12.4[a]	0.9
734L	**Petit pois**, *frozen, boiled in salted water*	LGC; 10 samples, 4 brands. Boiled 2-5 minutes	1.00	207	49	5.0	5.2[a]	0.9
735L	*frozen, boiled in unsalted water*	Based on *boiled in salted water*	1.00	207	49	5.0	5.2[a]	0.9
736L	**Processed peas**, canned, *re-heated, drained*	LGC; 10 samples, 7 brands	0.65	415	98	6.9	16.0[a]	0.7

[a] Including oligosaccharides

No.	Food	Labelling information for Group 2 nutrients per 100g food				Additional nutrients and information per 100g food		
		Sugars (actual weight) g	Saturates g	Fibre (Englyst) g	Sodium g	Sodium mg	Starch (actual weight) g	Water g
Peas								
725L	**Mange-tout peas**, *raw*	3.4	Tr	2.3	Tr	2	0.7	88.7
726L	*boiled in salted water*	2.8	Tr	2.2	Tr	42	0.5	89.2
727L	*stir-fried in blended oil*	3.3	0.4	2.4	Tr	2	0.2	83.6
728L	**Mushy peas**, canned, *re-heated*	1.5[a]	0.1	1.8	0.3	340	9.7	76.5
729L	**Peas**, *raw*	2.2[a]	0.3	4.7	Tr	1	6.4	74.6
730L	*boiled in unsalted water*	1.1[a]	0.3	4.5	Tr	Tr	6.9	75.6
731L	*frozen, boiled in salted water*	2.6[a]	0.2	5.1	0.1	94	4.3	78.3
732L	*-, boiled in unsalted water*	2.6[a]	0.2	5.1	Tr	2	4.3	78.3
733L	canned, *re-heated, drained*	3.7[a]	0.2	5.1	0.3	250	5.7	77.9
734L	**Petit pois**, *frozen, boiled in salted water*	2.9[a]	0.2	4.5	0.1	69	Tr	81.1
735L	*frozen, boiled in unsalted water*	2.9[a]	0.2	4.5	Tr	2	Tr	81.1
736L	**Processed peas**, canned, *re-heated, drained*	1.4[a]	0.1	4.8	0.4	380	13.4	69.6

[a] Not including oligosaccharides

Labelling information for Group 1 nutrients per 100g food

No.	Food	Description and main data sources	Edible proportion	Energy kJ	Energy kcal	Protein (N × 6.25) g	Carbohydrate (actual wt.) g	Fat g
	Vegetables, general							
737L	**Asparagus**, *raw*	IFR; tough base of stems removed	0.75	106	25	2.9	2.0	0.6
738L	*boiled in salted water*	IFR. Soft tips only; boiled 15 minutes	0.48	111	26	3.4	1.4	0.8
739L	**Aubergine**, *raw*	IFR; ends trimmed	0.96[a]	68	16	0.9	2.2	0.4
740L	*fried in corn oil*	IFR. Sliced; shallow fried 10 minutes	1.00	1248	303	1.2	2.8	31.9
741L	**Beetroot**, *raw*	IFR; top and root trimmed, peeled	0.80	155	37	1.7	7.2	0.1
742L	*boiled in salted water*	IFR. As raw; boiled 45 minutes	0.80	196	46	2.3	9.0	0.1
743L	pickled, *drained*	LGC; 10 samples, 5 brands. Whole and sliced	0.65	120[b]	28[b]	1.2	5.4	0.2
744L	**Broccoli**, green, *raw*	IFR; tough stems removed	0.61	139	33	4.4	1.8[c]	0.9
745L	*boiled in unsalted water*	IFR. As raw, cut into florets; boiled 15 minutes	1.00	99	24	3.1	1.0[c]	0.8
746L	**Brussels sprouts**, *raw*	IFR; base trimmed, outer leaves removed	0.69	179	43	3.5	4.0[c]	1.4
747L	*boiled in unsalted water*	IFR. As raw; boiled 15 minutes	1.00	157	37	2.9	3.5[c]	1.3
748L	*frozen, boiled in unsalted water*	LGC. 10 samples, 8 brands; boiled 5-10 minutes	1.00	159	38	3.5	3.0[c]	1.3
749L	**Cabbage**, *raw, average*	Average of January King, Savoy, summer and white	0.77	117	28	1.8	4.2	0.4
750L	*boiled in unsalted water, average*	As raw	1.00	68	16	1.0	2.1	0.4
751L	January King, *raw*	IFR; outer leaves and stem removed	0.66	112	26	1.8	3.9	0.4
752L	*boiled in salted water*	IFR. As raw; shredded and boiled 19 minutes	1.00	77	18	0.8	2.4	0.6
753L	white, *raw*	IFR; outer leaves and stem removed	0.91	116	27	1.4	5.0	0.2

[a] If peeled = 0.77

[b] Acetic acid from vinegar will contribute to the energy value

[c] Including oligosaccharides

No.	Food	Labelling information for Group 2 nutrients per 100g food				Additional nutrients and information per 100g food		
		Sugars (actual weight) g	Saturates g	Fibre (Englyst) g	Sodium g	Sodium mg	Starch (actual weight) g	Water g
Vegetables, general								
737L	**Asparagus**, *raw*	1.9	0.1	1.7	Tr	1	0.1	91.4
738L	*boiled in salted water*	1.4	0.1	1.4	0.1	60	Tr	91.5
739L	**Aubergine**, *raw*	2.0	0.1	2.0	Tr	2	0.2	92.9
740L	*fried in corn oil*	2.6	4.1	2.3	Tr	2	0.2	59.5
741L	**Beetroot**, *raw*	6.7	Tr	1.9	0.1	66	0.5	87.1
742L	*boiled in salted water*	8.4	Tr	1.9	0.1	110	0.6	82.4
743L	pickled, *drained*	5.4	Tr	1.7	0.1	120	Tr	88.6
744L	**Broccoli**, green, *raw*	1.5[a]	0.2	2.6	Tr	8	0.1	88.2
745L	*boiled in unsalted water*	0.9[a]	0.2	2.3	Tr	13	Tr	91.1
746L	**Brussels sprouts**, *raw*	3.1[a]	0.3	4.1	Tr	6	0.7	84.3
747L	*boiled in unsalted water*	3.0[a]	0.3	3.1	Tr	2	0.3	86.9
748L	*frozen, boiled in unsalted water*	2.4[a]	0.3	4.3	Tr	8	0.4	86.8
749L	**Cabbage**, *raw, average*	4.1	0.1	2.4	Tr	5	0.1	90.1
750L	*boiled in unsalted water, average*	2.0	0.1	1.8	Tr	8	0.1	93.1
751L	January King, *raw*	3.8	0.1	2.3	Tr	3	0.1	89.7
752L	*boiled in salted water*	2.2	0.1	2.1	0.1	100	0.2	92.5
753L	white, *raw*	4.9	Tr	2.1	Tr	7	0.1	90.7

[a] Not including oligosaccharides

Labelling information for Group 1 nutrients per 100g food

No.	Food	Description and main data sources	Edible proportion	Energy kJ	Energy kcal	Protein (N × 6.25) g	Carbohydrate (actual wt.) g	Fat g
	Vegetables, general							
754L	**Carrots**, old, *raw*	IFR; ends trimmed, peeled	0.70	152	36	0.6	7.7[a]	0.3
755L	*boiled in unsalted water*	IFR. As raw; sliced and boiled 12.5 minutes	1.00	108	26	0.6	4.9[a]	0.4
756L	young, *raw*	IFR; ends trimmed, scrubbed	0.87	131	31	0.7	5.9[a]	0.5
757L	*boiled in unsalted water*	IFR. As raw; sliced and boiled 15 minutes	1.00	102	24	0.6	4.5[a]	0.4
758L	canned, *re-heated, drained*	LGC; 10 cans, 5 brands	0.61	93	22	0.6	4.2[a]	0.3
759L	**Cauliflower**, *raw*	IFR; florets only	0.45	146	35	3.6	3.0[a]	0.9
760L	*boiled in unsalted water*	IFR. As raw; boiled 13 minutes	1.00	118	28	2.9	2.1[a]	0.9
761L	**Celery**, *raw*	IFR; stem only	0.91	31	7	0.5	0.9	0.2
762L	*boiled in salted water*	IFR. Stem only; boiled 20 minutes	1.00	33	8	0.5	0.8	0.3
763L	**Chicory**, *raw*	IFR. Stem and inner leaves; pale variety	0.80	48[b]	11[b]	0.6	2.8	0.6
764L	**Courgette**, *raw*	IFR; ends trimmed	0.88	76	18	1.8	1.8	0.4
765L	*boiled in unsalted water*	Analysis and calculation from raw	1.00	83	20	2.0	2.0	0.4
766L	*fried in corn oil*	IFR. As raw; sliced and shallow fried 5 minutes	1.00	266	64	2.6	2.6	4.8
767L	**Cucumber**, *raw*	IFR; ends trimmed, not peeled	0.97[c]	41	10	0.7	1.5	0.1
768L	**Curly kale**, *raw*	IFR; main ribs and stalks removed	0.85	141	34	3.4	1.4	1.6
769L	*boiled in salted water*	IFR. As raw; shredded and boiled 7 minutes	1.00	99	24	2.4	1.0	1.1
770L	**Fennel**, Florence, *raw*	IFR; inner leaves and bulb only	0.80	53	13	0.9	1.8	0.2
771L	*boiled in salted water*	IFR. As raw; boiled 14 minutes	1.00	48	11	0.9	1.5	0.2

[a] Including oligosaccharides

[b] Contains inulin; 32 per cent total carbohydrate taken to be available for energy purposes

[c] If peeled = 0.77

No.	Food	Labelling information for Group 2 nutrients per 100g food				Additional nutrients and information per 100g food		
		Sugars (actual weight) g	Saturates g	Fibre (Englyst) g	Sodium g	Sodium mg	Starch (actual weight) g	Water g
	Vegetables, general							
754L	**Carrots**, old, *raw*	7.2[a]	0.1	2.4	Tr	25	0.3	89.8
755L	*boiled in unsalted water*	4.5[a]	0.1	2.5	0.1	50	0.2	90.5
756L	young, *raw*	5.5[a]	0.1	2.4	Tr	40	0.2	88.8
757L	*boiled in unsalted water*	4.1[a]	0.1	2.3	Tr	23	0.2	90.7
758L	canned, *re-heated, drained*	3.6[a]	0.1	1.9	0.4	370	0.4	91.9
759L	**Cauliflower**, *raw*	2.5[a]	0.2	1.8	Tr	9	0.4	88.4
760L	*boiled in unsalted water*	1.8[a]	0.2	1.6	Tr	4	0.2	90.6
761L	**Celery**, *raw*	0.9	Tr	1.1	0.1	60	Tr	95.1
762L	*boiled in salted water*	0.8	0.1	1.2	0.2	160	Tr	95.2
763L	**Chicory**, *raw*	0.7	0.2	0.9	Tr	1	0.2	94.3
764L	**Courgette**, *raw*	1.7	0.1	0.9	Tr	1	0.1	93.7
765L	*boiled in unsalted water*	1.9	0.1	1.2	Tr	1	0.1	93.0
766L	*fried in corn oil*	2.5	0.6	1.2	Tr	1	0.1	86.8
767L	**Cucumber**, *raw*	1.4[b]	Tr	0.6	Tr	3	0.1	96.4
768L	**Curly kale**, *raw*	1.3	0.2	3.1	Tr	43	0.1	88.4
769L	*boiled in salted water*	0.9	0.2	2.8	0.1	100	0.1	90.9
770L	**Fennel**, Florence, *raw*	1.7	Tr	2.4	Tr	11	0.1	94.2
771L	*boiled in salted water*	1.4	Tr	2.3	0.1	96	0.1	94.4

[a] Not including oligosaccharides

[b] Peeled cucumbers contain approximately 2.0g total sugars per 100g

Labelling information for Group 1 nutrients per 100g food

No.	Food	Description and main data sources	Edible proportion	Energy kJ	Energy kcal	Protein (N × 6.25) g	Carbohydrate (actual wt.) g	Fat g
Vegetables, general								
772L	**Garlic**, *raw*	IFR; peeled cloves	0.79	412	97	7.9	15.0	0.6
773L	**Gherkins**, pickled, *drained*	LGC; 10 samples, 5 brands	0.67	62[a]	15[a]	0.9	2.5	0.1
774L	**Gourd**, karela, *raw*	LGC; 5 samples. Ends trimmed	0.93	47	11	1.6	0.7	0.2
775L	**Leeks**, *raw*	IFR; trimmed and outer leaves removed	0.57[b]	95	23	1.6	2.9[c]	0.5
776L	*boiled in unsalted water*	IFR. As raw; chopped and boiled 22 minutes	1.00	92	22	1.3	2.6[c]	0.7
777L	**Lettuce**, *average, raw*	Average of 4 varieties	0.74	61	15	0.8	1.7	0.5
778L	butterhead, *raw*	IFR; outer leaves removed	0.76	55	13	0.9	1.0	0.6
779L	Iceberg, *raw*	IFR; outer leaves removed	0.83	54	13	0.7	1.8	0.3
780L	**Marrow**, *raw*	IFR; flesh only, seeds removed	0.54	53	13	0.5	2.2	0.2
781L	*boiled in unsalted water*	IFR. As raw; cut and boiled 19 minutes	1.00	40	9	0.4	1.5	0.2
782L	**Mixed vegetables**, *frozen, boiled in salted water*	LGC; 10 samples. Assorted varieties. Simmered 3-7 minutes	1.00	180	43	3.3	6.2	0.5
783L	**Mushrooms**, common, *raw*	IFR; stalks trimmed where necessary	0.97[d]	95	23	4.0	0.5	0.5
784L	*boiled in salted water*	LGC. 10 samples, button and sliced; boiled 5-10 minutes. And calcd. from raw	1.00	88	21	4.0	0.5	0.3
785L	*fried in blended oil*	Calculation from *fried in corn oil*	1.00	705	171	5.9	0.3	16.2
786L	*fried in butter*	Calculation from *fried in corn oil*	1.00	705	171	5.9	0.3	16.2
787L	*fried in corn oil*	IFR. As raw; sliced and fried 8 minutes	1.00	705	171	5.9	0.3	16.2

[a] Acetic acid from vinegar will contribute to the energy value

[b] Bulb only = 0.36

[c] Including oligosaccharides

[d] If peeled = 0.75

No.	Food	Labelling information for Group 2 nutrients per 100g food				Additional nutrients and information per 100g food		
		Sugars (actual weight) g	Saturates g	Fibre (Englyst) g	Sodium g	Sodium mg	Starch (actual weight) g	Water g
	Vegetables, general							
772L	**Garlic**, *raw*	1.6	0.1	4.1	Tr	4	13.4	64.3
773L	**Gherkins**, pickled, *drained*	2.3	Tr	1.2	0.7	690	0.2	92.8
774L	**Gourd**, karela, *raw*	Tr	N	2.6	Tr	1	0.7	93.3
775L	**Leeks**, *raw*	2.2[a]	0.1	2.2	Tr	2	0.3	90.8
776L	*boiled in unsalted water*	2.0[a]	0.1	1.7	Tr	6	0.2	92.2
777L	**Lettuce**, *average, raw*	1.7	0.1	0.9	Tr	3	Tr	95.1
778L	butterhead, *raw*	1.0	0.1	1.2	Tr	5	Tr	94.4
779L	Iceberg, *raw*	1.8	Tr	0.6	Tr	2	Tr	95.6
780L	**Marrow**, *raw*	2.1	Tr	0.5	Tr	1	0.1	95.6
781L	*boiled in unsalted water*	1.3	Tr	0.6	Tr	1	0.2	95.9
782L	**Mixed vegetables**, *frozen, boiled in salted water*	3.5	N	N	0.1	96	2.7	85.8
783L	**Mushrooms**, common, *raw*	0.3	0.1	1.1	Tr	5	0.2	92.6
784L	*boiled in salted water*	0.3	0.1	1.1	0.1	71	0.2	92.7
785L	*fried in blended oil*	0.1	1.4	1.5	Tr	4	0.2	74.8
786L	*fried in butter*	0.1	10.7	1.5	0.2	150	0.2	74.8
787L	*fried in corn oil*	0.1	2.1	1.5	Tr	4	0.2	74.8

[a] Not including oligosaccharides

Labelling information for Group 1 nutrients per 100g food

No.	Food	Description and main data sources	Edible proportion	Energy kJ	Energy kcal	Protein (N × 6.25) g	Carbohydrate (actual wt.) g	Fat g
	Vegetables, general							
788L	**Mustard and cress**, *raw*	IFR; leaves and cut stems	1.00[a]	56	13	1.6	0.4	0.6
789L	**Okra**, *raw*	IFR and literature sources. Ends trimmed	0.74	129	31	2.5	2.9	1.0
790L	*boiled in unsalted water*	Calcd. from raw	1.00	123	29	2.5	2.8	0.9
791L	*stir-fried in corn oil*	IFR. As raw; sliced and fried 5 minutes	1.00	1110	269	4.3	4.2	26.1
792L	**Onions**, *raw*	IFR; flesh only	0.91	159	37	1.3	7.6[b]	0.2
793L	*boiled in unsalted water*	Calcd. from raw	1.00	75	18	0.6	3.6[b]	0.1
794L	*fried in blended oil*	Calculation from *fried in corn oil*	1.00	686	165	2.3	13.7[b]	11.2[c]
795L	*fried in corn oil*	IFR. As raw: sliced into rings and fried 15 minutes	1.00	686	165	2.3	13.7[b]	11.2[c]
796L	*fried in lard*	Calculation from *fried in corn oil*	1.00	686	165	2.3	13.7[b]	11.2[c]
797L	pickled, *drained*	LGC; 10 samples, 7 brands	0.58	101[d]	24[d]	0.9	4.6[b]	0.2
798L	*cocktail/silverskin, drained*	LGC; 10 samples, 8 brands	0.59	63[d]	15[d]	0.6	2.9[b]	0.1
799L	**Parsnip**, *raw*	LGC; ends trimmed and peeled	0.72	269	64	1.8	11.6[b]	1.1
800L	*boiled in unsalted water*	LGC. As raw; sliced and boiled 12 minutes	1.00	276	65	1.6	12.0[b]	1.2[e]
801L	**Peppers**, capsicum, chilli, green, *raw*	Refs. Cashel *et al.* (1989), Gopalan *et al.* (1980)	0.90	83	20	2.9	0.7	0.6
802L	capsicum, green, *raw*	IFR; stalk and seeds removed	0.84	69	16	0.8	2.6[b]	0.3
803L	*boiled in salted water*	IFR. As raw; sliced and boiled 15 minutes	1.00	80	19	1.0	2.6[b]	0.5
804L	capsicum, red, *raw*	IFR; stalk and seeds removed	0.83	142	34	1.1	6.4[b]	0.4
805L	*boiled in salted water*	Calculation from raw	1.00	153	36	1.2	6.9[b]	0.4

[a] If purchased on soil block = 0.27

[b] Including oligosaccharides

[c] The fat content of fried onions can vary considerably

[d] Acetic acid from vinegar will contribute to the energy value

[e] Roast parsnips contain 6.5g fat per 100g

No.	Food	Labelling information for Group 2 nutrients per 100g food				Additional nutrients and information per 100g food		
		Sugars (actual weight) g	Saturates g	Fibre (Englyst) g	Sodium g	Sodium mg	Starch (actual weight) g	Water g
	Vegetables, general							
788L	**Mustard and cress**, *raw*	0.4	Tr	1.1	Tr	19	Tr	95.3
789L	**Okra**, *raw*	2.4	0.3	4.0	Tr	8	0.5	86.6
790L	*boiled in unsalted water*	2.3	0.3	3.6	Tr	5	0.5	87.9
791L	*stir-fried in corn oil*	3.5	3.3	6.3	Tr	13	0.7	54.5
792L	**Onions**, *raw*	5.5[a]	Tr	1.4	Tr	3	Tr	89.0
793L	*boiled in unsalted water*	2.6[a]	Tr	0.7	Tr	2	Tr	92.6
794L	*fried in blended oil*	9.8[a]	1.0	3.1	Tr	4	0.1	65.7
795L	*fried in corn oil*	9.8[a]	1.4	3.1	Tr	4	0.1	65.7
796L	*fried in lard*	9.8[a]	4.6	3.1	Tr	4	0.1	65.7
797L	pickled, *drained*	3.4[a]	Tr	1.2	0.5	450	Tr	90.6
798L	*cocktail/silverskin, drained*	2.2[a]	Tr	N	0.6	620	Tr	91.8
799L	**Parsnip**, *raw*	5.4[a]	0.2	4.6	Tr	10	5.6	79.3
800L	*boiled in unsalted water*	5.6[a]	0.2	4.7	Tr	4	5.8	78.7
801L	**Peppers**, capsicum, chilli, green, *raw*	0.7	N	N	Tr	7	Tr	85.7
802L	capsicum, green, *raw*	2.4[a]	0.1	1.6	Tr	4	0.1	93.3
803L	*boiled in salted water*	2.3[a]	0.1	1.8	0.1	70	0.2	92.6
804L	capsicum, red, *raw*	6.1[a]	0.1	1.6	Tr	4	0.1	90.4
805L	*boiled in salted water*	6.6[a]	0.1	1.7	0.1	70	0.1	89.5

[a] Not including oligosaccharides

Labelling information for Group 1 nutrients per 100g food

No.	Food	Description and main data sources	Edible proportion	Energy kJ	Energy kcal	Protein (N × 6.25) g	Carbohydrate (actual wt.) g	Fat g
	Vegetables, general							
806L	**Plantain**, *raw*	Literature sources. Green flesh	0.65	489	115	1.1	27.0	0.3
807L	*boiled in unsalted water*	10 samples. Flesh only; boiled 30 minutes. And literature sources	1.00	468	110	0.8	26.3	0.2
808L	ripe, *fried in vegetable oil*	8 samples	1.00	1112	264	1.5	43.9	9.2
809L	**Pumpkin**, *raw*	IFR; flesh only, peeled thickly, seeds removed	0.67	58	14	0.8	2.2	0.2
810L	*boiled in salted water*	IFR. As raw; boiled 15 minutes	1.00	55	13	0.6	2.0	0.3
811L	**Quorn**, myco-protein	Manufacturer's data (Marlow Foods)	1.00	362	86	11.9	1.8[a]	3.5
812L	**Radish**, red, *raw*	IFR; ends trimmed, flesh and skin	0.81	52	12	0.7	1.9	0.2
813L	**Spinach**, *raw*	IFR; ribs and stems removed	0.81	104	25	2.8	1.6	0.8
814L	*boiled in unsalted water*	IFR. As raw; shredded	1.00	82	20	2.2	0.9	0.8
815L	*frozen, boiled in unsalted water*	LGC; 10 samples, 8 brands. Boiled 2-10 minutes	1.00	89	21	3.1	0.4	0.8
816L	**Spring greens**, *raw*	IFR; main ribs and stems removed	0.84	141	33	3.0	3.1	1.0
817L	*boiled in unsalted water*	IFR. As raw; boiled 12 minutes	1.00	85	20	1.9	1.6	0.7
818L	**Spring onions**, *bulbs and tops, raw*	IFR; peeled bulb and leaves	0.69	104	25	2.0	3.0	0.5
819L	**Swede**, *raw*	IFR; flesh only, peeled thinly	0.73	108	26	0.7	5.0	0.3
820L	*boiled in unsalted water*	IFR. As raw; diced and boiled 22 minutes	1.00	48	11	0.3	2.3	0.1
821L	**Sweet potato**, *raw*	IFR; flesh only, yellow variety	0.84	366	86	1.2	19.7	0.3
822L	*boiled in salted water*	IFR. As raw; boiled 27 minutes	1.00	355	84	1.1	19.1	0.3

[a] Including oligosaccharides

No.	Food	Labelling information for Group 2 nutrients per 100g food				Additional nutrients and information per 100g food		
		Sugars (actual weight) g	Saturates g	Fibre (Englyst) g	Sodium g	Sodium mg	Starch (actual weight) g	Water g
	Vegetables, general							
806L	**Plantain**, *raw*	5.5	0.1	1.3	Tr	4	21.5	67.5
807L	*boiled in unsalted water*	5.4	0.1	1.2	Tr	4	20.9	68.5
808L	ripe, *fried in vegetable oil*	11.2	1.0	2.3	Tr	3	32.7	34.7
809L	**Pumpkin**, *raw*	1.7	0.1	1.0	Tr	Tr	0.3	95.0
810L	*boiled in salted water*	1.7	0.1	1.1	0.1	76	0.1	94.9
811L	**Quorn**, myco-protein	1.1[a]	0.6	4.8	0.2	240	Tr	75.0
812L	**Radish**, red, *raw*	1.9	0.1	0.9	Tr	11	Tr	95.4
813L	**Spinach**, *raw*	1.5	0.1	2.1	0.1	140	0.1	89.7
814L	*boiled in unsalted water*	0.9	0.1	2.1	0.1	120	Tr	91.8
815L	*frozen, boiled in unsalted water*	0.2	0.1	2.1	Tr	16	0.2	91.6
816L	**Spring greens**, *raw*	2.7	0.1	3.4	Tr	20	0.4	86.2
817L	*boiled in unsalted water*	1.4	0.1	2.6	Tr	10	0.2	92.2
818L	**Spring onions**, *bulbs and tops, raw*	2.8	0.1	1.5	Tr	7	0.2	92.2
819L	**Swede**, *raw*	4.9	Tr	1.9	Tr	15	0.1	91.2
820L	*boiled in unsalted water*	2.2	Tr	0.7	Tr	14	0.1	95.8
821L	**Sweet potato**, *raw*	5.5	0.1	2.4	Tr	40	14.2	73.7
822L	*boiled in salted water*	11.0	0.1	2.3	Tr	32	8.1	74.7

[a] Not including oligosaccharides

Labelling information for Group 1 nutrients per 100g food

No.	Food	Description and main data sources	Edible proportion	Energy kJ	Energy kcal	Protein (N × 6.25) g	Carbohydrate (actual wt.) g	Fat g
	Vegetables, general							
823L	**Sweetcorn**, baby, canned, *drained*	Ref. Wu Leung *et al.* (1972)	0.53	96	23	2.9	1.9	0.4
824L	kernels, canned, *re-heated, drained*	LGC; 10 samples, 5 brands	0.82	515	122	2.9	24.8[a]	1.2
825L	on-the-cob, *whole, boiled in unsalted water*	IFR; boiled 19 minutes	0.59	276	65	2.5	10.7[a]	1.4
826L	**Tomato purée**	LGC; 10 samples, 8 brands	1.00	302	71	4.4	12.9	0.2
827L	**Tomatoes**, *raw*	IFR; flesh, skin and seeds	1.00	74	18	0.7	3.0	0.3
828L	*fried in blended oil*	Calculation from *fried in corn oil*	1.00	385	93	0.8	5.1	7.7
829L	*fried in corn oil*	IFR. As raw; sliced and fried 10 minutes	1.00	385	93	0.8	5.1	7.7
830L	*fried in lard*	Calculation from *fried in corn oil*	1.00	385	93	0.8	5.1	7.7
831L	*grilled*	Calcd. from raw using water loss of 13%	1.00	214	51	2.0	8.6	0.9
832L	canned, *whole contents*	LGC; 10 samples, 10 brands. Tomatoes and juice	1.00[b]	70	17	1.0	2.9	0.1
833L	**Turnip**, *raw*	IFR; flesh only, peeled thinly	0.75	108	26	0.9	4.8	0.3
834L	*boiled in unsalted water*	IFR. As raw; diced and boiled 19 minutes	1.00	52	12	0.6	2.0	0.2
835L	**Watercress**, *raw*	IFR; large stalks removed	0.62	95	23	3.0	0.4	1.0
836L	**Yam**, *raw*	IFR; flesh only	0.81	475	112	1.6	25.7	0.3
837L	*boiled in unsalted water*	IFR. As raw; boiled 25 minutes	1.00	552	130	1.7	30.1	0.3

[a] Including oligosaccharides

[b] Drained = 0.60

No.	Food	Sugars (actual weight) g	Saturates g	Fibre (Englyst) g	Sodium g	Sodium mg	Starch (actual weight) g	Water g
		Labelling information for Group 2 nutrients per 100g food				**Additional nutrients and information per 100g food**		
	Vegetables, general							
823L	**Sweetcorn**, baby, canned, *drained*	1.4	N	1.5	1.1	1140	0.5	92.5
824L	kernels, canned, *re-heated, drained*	9.3[a]	0.2	1.4	0.3	270	15.1	72.3
825L	on-the-cob, *whole, boiled in unsalted water*	1.4[a]	0.2	1.3	Tr	1	9.1	41.2
826L	**Tomato purée**	12.6	Tr	2.8	0.2	240[b]	0.3	71.9
827L	**Tomatoes**, *raw*	3.0	0.1	1.0	Tr	9	Tr	93.1
828L	*fried in blended oil*	5.0	0.7	1.3	Tr	10	0.1	84.4
829L	*fried in corn oil*	5.0	1.0	1.3	Tr	10	0.1	84.4
830L	*fried in lard*	5.0	4.2	1.3	Tr	10	0.1	84.4
831L	*grilled*	8.6	0.3	2.9	Tr	26	Tr	80.1
832L	canned, *whole contents*	2.7	Tr	0.7	Tr	39	0.2	94.0
833L	**Turnip**, *raw*	4.6	Tr	2.4	Tr	15	0.2	91.2
834L	*boiled in unsalted water*	1.9	Tr	1.9	Tr	28	0.1	93.1
835L	**Watercress**, *raw*	0.4	0.3	1.5	Tr	49	Tr	92.5
836L	**Yam**, *raw*	0.7	0.1	1.3	Tr	2	25.0	67.2
837L	*boiled in unsalted water*	0.7	0.1	1.4	Tr	17	29.4	64.4

[a] Not including oligosaccharides

[b] The sodium content of unsalted tomato purée is approximately 20mg per 100g

Labelling information for Group 1 nutrients per 100g food

No.	Food	Description and main data sources	Edible proportion	Energy kJ	Energy kcal	Protein (N × 6.25) g	Carbohydrate (actual wt.) g	Fat g
838L	**Chilli powder**[a]	Ref. Marsh *et al.* (1977)	1.00	N	N	12.3	N	16.8
839L	**Cinnamon**, *ground*	Ref. Marsh *et al.* (1977)	1.00	N	N	3.9	N	3.2
840L	**Curry powder**[b]	2 samples	1.00	984	235	9.5	24.9	10.8
841L	**Garam masala**	Ref. Wharton *et al.* (1983)	1.00	1592	379	15.6	45.2	15.1
842L	**Mint**, *fresh*	Literature sources	1.00	181	43	3.8	5.3	0.7
843L	**Mustard powder**	2 brands	1.00	1888	453	28.9	19.7	28.7
844L	**Nutmeg**, *ground*	Ref. Marsh *et al.* (1977)	1.00	N	N	6.9	N	36.3
845L	**Paprika**	Ref. Marsh *et al.* (1977)	1.00	1326	316	14.8	34.9	13.0
846L	**Parsley**, *fresh*	IFR; tough stalks removed	0.80	143	34	2.9	2.7	1.3
847L	**Pepper**, black	Ref. Marsh *et al.* (1977)	1.00	N	N	12.8	N	3.3
848L	white	Ref. Marsh *et al.* (1977)	1.00	N	N	12.2	N	2.1
849L	**Rosemary**, dried	Ref. Marsh *et al.* (1977)	1.00	1435	342	4.9	46.4	15.2
850L	**Sage**, dried, *ground*	Ref. Marsh *et al.* (1977)	1.00	1376	328	10.6	42.7	12.7
851L	**Thyme**, dried, *ground*	Ref. Marsh *et al.* (1977)	1.00	1199	284	9.1	45.3	7.4

[a] Mix of chilli pepper 83%, cumin 9%, oregano 4%, salt 2.5% and garlic powder 1.5%

[b] Composition will vary according to variety

No.	Food	Labelling information for Group 2 nutrients per 100g food				Additional nutrients and information per 100g food		
		Sugars (actual weight) g	Saturates g	Fibre (Englyst) g	Sodium g	Sodium mg	Starch (actual weight) g	Water g
838L	**Chilli powder**	N	N	N	1.0	1010	N	7.8
839L	**Cinnamon**, *ground*	N	0.7	N	Tr	26	N	9.5
840L	**Curry powder**	N	N	23.0	0.5	450	N	8.5
841L	**Garam masala**	N	N	N	0.1	97	N	10.1
842L	**Mint**, *fresh*	N	N	N	Tr	15	N	86.4
843L	**Mustard powder**	N	1.5	N	Tr	5	N	8.0
844L	**Nutmeg**, *ground*	N	25.9	N	Tr	16	N	6.2
845L	**Paprika**	N	1.9	N	Tr	34	N	9.5
846L	**Parsley**, *fresh*	2.3	N	5.0	Tr	33	0.4	83.1
847L	**Pepper**, black	N	N	N	Tr	44	Tr	10.5
848L	white	N	N	N	Tr	5	Tr	11.4
849L	**Rosemary**, dried	N	N	N	0.1	50	N	9.3
850L	**Sage**, dried, *ground*	N	7.0	N	Tr	11	N	8.0
851L	**Thyme**, dried, *ground*	N	2.7	N	0.1	55	N	7.8

Labelling information for Group 1 nutrients per 100g food

No.	Food	Description and main data sources	Edible proportion	Energy kJ	Energy kcal	Protein (N × 6.25) g	Carbohydrate (actual wt.) g	Fat g
852L	**Apples**, cooking, *raw, peeled*	Bramley variety; flesh only	1.00	160	38	0.3	8.9	0.1
853L	*raw, peeled, weighed with skin and core*	Calculated from No. 852	0.73	116	27	0.3	6.3	0.1
854L	*stewed with sugar*	Samples as raw. 1000g fruit, 100g water, 120g sugar	1.00	327	77	0.3	18.7	0.1
855L	*stewed without sugar*	Samples as raw. 1000g fruit, 100g water and calculation from No. 854	1.00	146	35	0.3	8.1	0.1
856L	eating, *average, raw*	15 varieties; flesh and skin	1.00	208	49	0.4	11.6	0.1
857L	*average, raw, weighed with core*	Calculated from No. 856	0.89	186	44	0.4	10.3	0.1
858L	*-, raw, peeled*	Literature sources and calculation from No. 856; flesh only	1.00	198	47	0.4	11.0	0.1
859L	*-, raw, peeled, weighed with skin and core*	Calculated from No. 858	0.76	152	36	0.3	8.4	0.1
860L	**Apricots**, *raw*	18 samples; flesh and skin	1.00	136	32	0.9	6.9	0.1
861L	*raw, weighed with stones*	Calculated from No. 860	0.92	124	29	0.8	6.3	0.1
862L	*ready-to-eat*	10 samples, no stones; semi-dried	1.00	701	165	3.9	36.0	0.6
863L	canned in syrup	10 samples, 9 brands	1.00	283	67	0.4	16.0	0.1
864L	canned in juice	10 samples, 5 brands	1.00	155	37	0.5	8.4	0.1
865L	**Avocado**, *average*	Average of Fuerte and Hass varieties	1.00	786	191	1.9	1.9[a]	19.5[b]
866L	*average, weighed with skin and stone*	Calculated from No. 865	0.71	555	135	1.3	1.3[a]	13.8

[a] Including mannoheptulose

[b] Fat can range from 10 to 40g per 100g

		Labelling information for Group 2 nutrients per 100g food				Additional nutrients and information per 100g food		
No.	Food	Sugars (actual weight) g	Saturates g	Fibre (Englyst) g	Sodium g	Sodium mg	Starch (actual weight) g	Water g
852L	**Apples**, cooking, *raw, peeled*	8.9	Tr	1.6	Tr	2	Tr	87.7
853L	*raw, peeled, weighed with skin and core*	6.3	Tr	1.1	Tr	1	Tr	63.1
854L	*stewed with sugar*	18.7	Tr	1.2	Tr	4	Tr	77.7
855L	*stewed without sugar*	8.1	Tr	1.5	Tr	4	Tr	87.5
856L	eating, *average, raw*	11.6[a]	Tr	1.8	Tr	3	Tr	84.5
857L	*average, raw, weighed with core*	10.3	Tr	1.6	Tr	3	Tr	75.2
858L	*-, raw, peeled*	11.0	Tr	1.6	Tr	3	Tr	85.4
859L	*-, raw, peeled, weighed with skin and core*	8.4	Tr	1.2	Tr	2	Tr	64.9
860L	**Apricots**, *raw*	6.9	Tr	1.7	Tr	2	0	87.2
861L	*raw, weighed with stones*	6.3	Tr	1.6	Tr	2	0	80.2
862L	*ready-to-eat*	36.0	N	6.3	Tr	14	0	29.7
863L	canned in syrup	16.0	Tr	0.9	Tr	10	0	80.0
864L	canned in juice	8.4	Tr	0.9	Tr	5	0	87.5
865L	**Avocado**, *average*	0.5[b]	4.1	3.4	Tr	6	Tr	72.5[c]
866L	*average, weighed with skin and stone*	0.4[b]	2.9	2.4	Tr	4	Tr	51.5

[a] Levels ranged from 9.5 to 12.9g total sugars per 100g

[b] Not including mannoheptulose

[c] Water can range from 50 to 80g per 100g

Labelling information for Group 1 nutrients per 100g food

No.	Food	Description and main data sources	Edible proportion	Energy kJ	Energy kcal	Protein (N × 6.25) g	Carbohydrate (actual wt.) g	Fat g
867L	**Bananas**	10 samples; flesh only	1.00	414	98	1.2	22.5	0.3
868L	*weighed with skin*	Calculated from No. 867	0.66	274	65	0.8	14.9	0.2
869L	**Blackberries**, *raw*	Cultivated and wild berries; whole fruit	1.00	109	26	0.9	5.1	0.2
870L	*stewed with sugar*	Calculated from 700g fruit, 210g water, 84g sugar	1.00	249	59	0.7	13.5	0.2
871L	*stewed without sugar*	Calculated from 700g fruit, 210g water	1.00	94	22	0.8	4.3	0.2
872L	**Blackcurrants**, *raw*	Whole fruit, stalks removed	0.98	129	30	0.9	6.7	Tr
873L	*stewed with sugar*	Calculated from 700g fruit, 210g water, 84g sugar	1.00	262	62	0.8	14.6	Tr
874L	canned in juice	4 samples, 2 brands	1.00	143	34	0.8	7.6	Tr
875L	canned in syrup	3 samples of the same brand (Hartley's)	1.00	323	76	0.7	18.3	Tr
876L	**Cherries**, *raw*	10 samples of black and red cherries; flesh and skin	1.00	213	50	0.9	11.4	0.1
877L	*raw, weighed with stones*	Calculated from No. 876	0.83	179	42	0.8	9.5	0.1
878L	canned in syrup	10 samples, red and black	1.00	321	76	0.6	18.3	Tr
879L	glacé	10 samples, 8 brands; red and multicoloured	1.00	1113	262	0.4	65.1	Tr
880L	**Cherry pie filling**	10 samples, 7 brands	1.00	362	85	0.4	20.9	Tr
881L	**Clementines**	10 samples; flesh only	1.00	164	39	0.9	8.5	0.1
882L	*weighed with peel and pips*	Calculated from No. 881	0.75	124	29	0.7	6.4	0.1
883L	**Currants**	10 samples, 9 brands	1.00	1205	284	2.3	67.7	0.4

No.	Food	Labelling information for Group 2 nutrients per 100g food: Sugars (actual weight) g	Saturates g	Fibre (Englyst) g	Sodium g	Additional nutrients and information per 100g food: Sodium mg	Starch (actual weight) g	Water g
867L	**Bananas**	20.4[a]	0.1	1.1	Tr	1	2.1[a]	75.1
868L	*weighed with skin*	13.5	0.1	0.7	Tr	1	1.4	49.6
869L	**Blackberries**, *raw*	5.1	Tr	3.1	Tr	2	0	85.0
870L	*stewed with sugar*	13.5	Tr	2.4	Tr	1	0	78.9
871L	*stewed without sugar*	4.3	Tr	2.6	Tr	1	0	87.2
872L	**Blackcurrants**, *raw*	6.7	Tr	3.6	Tr	3	0	77.4
873L	*stewed with sugar*	14.6	Tr	2.8	Tr	2	0	72.9
874L	canned in juice	7.6	N	3.1	Tr	Tr	0	84.0
875L	canned in syrup	18.3	N	2.6	Tr	Tr	0	75.0
876L	**Cherries**, *raw*	11.4	Tr	0.9	Tr	1	0	82.8
877L	*raw, weighed with stones*	9.5	Tr	0.7	Tr	1	0	68.7
878L	canned in syrup	18.3	Tr	0.6	Tr	8	0	77.8
879L	glacé	65.1	Tr	0.9	Tr	27	0	23.6
880L	**Cherry pie filling**	17.4	Tr	0.4	Tr	30	3.5	75.8
881L	**Clementines**	8.5	Tr	1.2	Tr	4	0	87.5
882L	*weighed with peel and pips*	6.4	Tr	0.9	Tr	3	0	65.6
883L	**Currants**	67.7	N	1.9	Tr	14	0	15.7

[a] These are proportions for yellow ripe bananas. The starch content falls and the sugar content rises on ripening

Labelling information for Group 1 nutrients per 100g food

No.	Food	Description and main data sources	Edible proportion	Energy kJ	Energy kcal	Protein (N × 6.25) g	Carbohydrate (actual wt.) g	Fat g
884L	**Damsons**, *raw, weighed with stones*	Calculated from raw damsons, *weighed without stones*	0.90	155	36	0.4	8.7	Tr
885L	*stewed with sugar*	Calculated from 1050g fruit, 210g water, 126g sugar	1.00	328	77	0.4	18.9	Tr
886L	**Dates**, *raw, weighed with stones*	Calculated from whole raw dates	0.86	483	114	1.3	26.9	0.1
887L	*dried, weighed with stones*	Calculated from whole dried dates	0.84	1026	241	2.8	57.1	0.2
888L	**Dried mixed fruit**[a]	Calculated from recipe proportions	1.00	1208	284	2.3	67.9	0.4
889L	**Figs**, *dried*	Analysis and literature sources; whole fruit	1.00	1018	240	3.6	52.8	1.6
890L	*ready-to-eat*	6 samples; semi-dried	1.00	934	220	3.3	48.4	1.5
891L	**Fruit cocktail**, canned in juice	10 samples, 6 brands	1.00	129	30	0.4	7.2	Tr
892L	canned in syrup[b]	Analysis and calculation from recipe proportions	1.00	255	60	0.4	14.6	Tr
893L	**Fruit pie filling**	10 samples, 7 brands. Assorted flavours	1.00	337	79	0.4	19.4	Tr
894L	**Fruit salad**, *homemade*	Calculated from equal proportions of bananas, oranges, apples, pears and grapes	1.00	247	58	0.7	13.6	0.1
895L	**Gooseberries**, cooking, *raw*	Tops and tails removed	0.91	83	20	1.1	2.9	0.4
896L	*stewed with sugar*	1000g fruit, 150g water, 120g sugar	1.00	234	55	0.7	12.4	0.3
897L	*stewed without sugar*	500g fruit, 100g water and calculation from No. 896	1.00	67	16	0.9	2.4	0.3
898L	dessert, canned in syrup	4 samples, 2 brands	1.00	325	77	0.4	18.3	0.2

[a] Calculated as sultanas 49%, currants 24%, raisins 18% and peel 9%

[b] Calculated as pears 42%, peaches 41%, pineapple 8%, grapes 5% and cherries 4%

No.	Food	Labelling information for Group 2 nutrients per 100g food				Additional nutrients and information per 100g food		
		Sugars (actual weight) g	Saturates g	Fibre (Englyst) g	Sodium g	Sodium mg	Starch (actual weight) g	Water g
884L	**Damsons**, *raw, weighed with stones*	8.7	Tr	1.6	Tr	2	0	69.7
885L	*stewed with sugar*	18.9	Tr	1.5	Tr	1	0	70.6
886L	**Dates**, *raw, weighed with stones*	26.9	Tr	1.5	Tr	6	0	52.2
887L	*dried, weighed with stones*	57.1	0.1	3.4	Tr	8	0	12.3
888L	**Dried mixed fruit**	67.9	N	2.2	Tr	48	0	15.5
889L	**Figs**, *dried*	52.8	N	7.5	0.1	62	0	16.8
890L	*ready-to-eat*	48.4	N	6.9	0.1	57	0	23.6
891L	**Fruit cocktail**, canned in juice	7.2	Tr	1.0	Tr	3	0	86.9
892L	canned in syrup	14.6	Tr	1.0	Tr	3	0	81.8
893L	**Fruit pie filling**	14.4	N	1.0	Tr	43	5.0	79.5
894L	**Fruit salad**, *homemade*	13.1	Tr	1.5	Tr	2	0.5	82.3
895L	**Gooseberries**, cooking, *raw*	2.9	N	2.4	Tr	2	0	90.1
896L	*stewed with sugar*	12.4	N	1.9	Tr	7	0	82.1
897L	*stewed without sugar*	2.4	N	2.0	Tr	2	0	90.6
898L	dessert, canned in syrup	18.3	Tr	1.7	Tr	2	0	78.9

899L to 915L

Labelling information for Group 1 nutrients per 100g food

No.	Food	Description and main data sources	Edible proportion	Energy kJ	Energy kcal	Protein (N × 6.25) g	Carbohydrate (actual wt.) g	Fat g
899L	**Grapefruit**, *raw*	10 samples; flesh only	1.00	131	31	0.8	6.7	0.1
900L	*raw, weighed with peel and pips*	Calculated from No.899	0.68	90	21	0.6	4.5	0.1
901L	canned in juice	10 samples, 8 brands	1.00	134	32	0.6	7.3	Tr
902L	canned in syrup	10 samples	1.00	270	64	0.5	15.4	Tr
903L	**Grapes**, *average*[a]	10 samples, white, black and seedless	1.00	274	65	0.4	15.5	0.1
904L	*weighed with pips*	Calculated from No. 903	0.95	260	61	0.4	14.7	0.1
905L	**Guava**, *raw*	Literature sources	1.00	117	28	0.8	5.0	0.5
906L	*raw, weighed with skin and pips*	Calculated from No. 905	0.90	110	26	0.8	4.6	0.5
907L	canned in syrup	10 samples	1.00	270	64	0.4	15.5	Tr
908L	**Kiwi fruit**	Analysis and literature sources, flesh and seeds	1.00	214	51	1.1	10.4	0.5
909L	*weighed with skin*	Calculated from No. 908	0.86	183	43	0.9	9.0	0.4
910L	**Lemons**, *whole, without pips*	Analysis and literature sources; includes peel but no pips	0.99	83	20	1.0	3.2	0.3
911L	**Lychees**, *raw*	Analysis and literature sources; flesh only	1.00	262	62	0.9	14.3	0.1
912L	*raw, weighed with skin and stone*	Calculated from No. 911	0.62	164	39	0.6	8.8	0.1
913L	canned in syrup	Analysis and literature sources	1.00	308	72	0.4	17.7	Tr
914L	**Mandarin oranges**, canned in juice	10 samples, 4 brands	1.00	141	33	0.7	7.6	Tr
915L	canned in syrup	10 samples, 10 brands	1.00	233	55	0.5	13.2	Tr

[a] Few significant differences reported between varieties

No.	Food	Labelling information for Group 2 nutrients per 100g food				Additional nutrients and information per 100g food		
		Sugars (actual weight) g	Saturates g	Fibre (Englyst) g	Sodium g	Sodium mg	Starch (actual weight) g	Water g
899L	**Grapefruit**, *raw*	6.7	Tr	1.3	Tr	3	0	89.0
900L	*raw, weighed with peel and pips*	4.5	Tr	0.9	Tr	2	0	60.5
901L	canned in juice	7.3	Tr	0.4	Tr	10	0	88.6
902L	canned in syrup	15.4	Tr	0.6	Tr	10	0	81.8
903L	**Grapes**, *average*	15.5	Tr	0.7	Tr	2	0	81.8
904L	*weighed with pips*	14.7	Tr	0.7	Tr	2	0	77.7
905L	**Guava**, *raw*	4.9	N	3.7	Tr	5	0.1	84.7
906L	*raw, weighed with skin and pips*	4.5	N	3.3	Tr	5	0.1	76.2
907L	canned in syrup	15.5	Tr	3.0	Tr	7	Tr	77.6
908L	**Kiwi fruit**	10.1	N	1.9	Tr	4	0.3	84.0
909L	*weighed with skin*	8.7	N	1.6	Tr	3	0.3	72.2
910L	**Lemons**, *whole, without pips*	3.2	0.1	N	Tr	5	0	86.3
911L	**Lychees**, *raw*	14.3	Tr	0.7	Tr	1	0	81.1
912L	*raw, weighed with skin and stone*	8.8	Tr	0.4	Tr	1	0	50.3
913L	canned in syrup	17.7	Tr	0.5	Tr	2	0	79.3
914L	**Mandarin oranges**, canned in juice	7.6	Tr	0.3	Tr	6	0	89.6
915L	canned in syrup	13.2	Tr	0.2	Tr	6	0	84.8

Labelling information for Group 1 nutrients per 100g food

No.	Food	Description and main data sources	Edible proportion	Energy kJ	Energy kcal	Protein (N × 6.25) g	Carbohydrate (actual wt.) g	Fat g
916L	**Mangoes**, ripe, *raw*	Literature sources; flesh only	1.00	251	59	0.7	13.6	0.2
917L	*raw, weighed with skin and stone*	Calculated from No. 916	0.68	169	40	0.4	9.3	0.1
918L	canned in syrup	10 samples	1.00	347	82	0.3	20.1	Tr
919L	**Melon**, Canteloupe-type	10 samples, Canteloupe, Charantais and Rock; flesh only	1.00	84	20	0.6	4.1	0.1
920L	*weighed with skin*	Calculated from No. 919; no pips	0.66	58	14	0.4	2.8	0.1
921L	Galia	11 samples; flesh only	1.00	106	25	0.5	5.5	0.1
922L	*weighed with skin*	Calculated from No. 921; no pips	0.68	73	17	0.3	3.8	0.1
923L	Honeydew	10 samples; flesh only	1.00	126	30	0.6	6.6	0.1
924L	*weighed with skin*	Calculated from No. 923; no pips	0.65	84	20	0.4	4.3	0.1
925L	**watermelon**	Literature sources; flesh only	1.00	134	32	0.4	6.8	0.3
926L	**Mixed peel**	10 samples, 9 brands	1.00	1014	239	0.3	57.4	0.9
927L	**Nectarines**	10 samples; flesh and skin	1.00	174	41	1.4	8.6	0.1
928L	*weighed with stones*	Calculated from No. 927	0.89	157	37	1.3	7.7	0.1

No.	Food	Labelling information for Group 2 nutrients per 100g food				Additional nutrients and information per 100g food		
		Sugars (actual weight) g	Saturates g	Fibre (Englyst) g	Sodium g	Sodium mg	Starch (actual weight) g	Water g
916L	**Mangoes**, ripe, *raw*	13.3	0.1	2.6	Tr	2	0.3	82.4
917L	*raw, weighed with skin and stone*	9.1	Tr	1.8	Tr	1	0.2	56.0
918L	canned in syrup	20.0	Tr	0.7	Tr	3	0.1	74.8
919L	**Melon**, Canteloupe-type	4.1	Tr	1.0	Tr	8	0	92.1
920L	*weighed with skin*	2.8	Tr	0.7	Tr	5	0	60.8
921L	Galia	5.5	Tr	0.4	Tr	31	0	91.7
922L	*weighed with skin*	3.8	Tr	0.3	Tr	21	0	63.4
923L	Honeydew	6.6	Tr	0.6	Tr	32	0	92.2
924L	*weighed with skin*	4.3	Tr	0.4	Tr	21	0	59.9
925L	**watermelon**	6.8	0.1	0.1	Tr	2	0	92.3
926L	**Mixed peel**	57.4	N	4.8	0.3	280	0	20.9
927L	**Nectarines**	8.6	Tr	1.2	Tr	1	0	88.9
928L	*weighed with stones*	7.7	Tr	1.1	Tr	1	0	79.1

Labelling information for Group 1 nutrients per 100g food

No.	Food	Description and main data sources	Edible proportion	Energy kJ	Energy kcal	Protein (N × 6.25) g	Carbohydrate (actual wt.) g	Fat g
929L	**Olives**, *in brine*	Bottled, drained; flesh and skin, green	1.00	422	103	0.9	Tr	11.0
930L	*in brine, weighed with stones*	Calculated from No. 929	0.80	338	82	0.7	Tr	8.8
931L	**Oranges**	Assorted varieties; flesh only	1.00	164	39	1.1	8.3	0.1
932L	*weighed with peel and pips*[a]	Calculated from No. 931	0.70	116	27	0.8	5.8	0.1
933L	**Passion fruit**	Analysis and literature sources; flesh and pips	1.00	159	38	2.8	5.7	0.4
934L	*weighed with skin*	Calculated from No. 933	0.61	94	22	1.7	3.4	0.2
935L	**Paw-paw**, *raw*	Literature sources; flesh only	1.00	158	37	0.5	8.6	0.1
936L	*raw, weighed with skin and pips*	Calculated from No. 935	0.75	119	28	0.4	6.4	0.1
937L	canned in juice	10 samples	1.00	291	68	0.2	16.9	Tr
938L	**Peaches**, *raw*	10 samples; flesh and skin	1.00	143	34	1.0	7.2	0.1
939L	*raw, weighed with stone*	Calculated from No. 938	0.90	130	31	0.9	6.5	0.1
940L	canned in juice	10 samples, 7 brands; halves and slices	1.00	172	40	0.6	9.5	Tr
941L	canned in syrup	10 samples, 9 brands; halves and slices	1.00	241	57	0.5	13.7	Tr

[a] Levels ranged from 0.60 to 0.74

No.	Food	Sugars (actual weight) g	Saturates g	Fibre (Englyst) g	Sodium g	Sodium mg	Starch (actual weight) g	Water g
		Labelling information for Group 2 nutrients per 100g food				**Additional nutrients and information per 100g food**		
929L	**Olives**, *in brine*	Tr	1.7	2.9	2.3	2250	0	76.5
930L	*in brine, weighed with stones*	Tr	1.4	2.3	1.8	1800	0	61.2
931L	**Oranges**	8.3	Tr	1.7	Tr	5	0	86.1
932L	*weighed with peel and pips*	5.8	Tr	1.2	Tr	3	0	60.3
933L	**Passion fruit**	5.7	0.1	3.3	Tr	19	0	74.9
934L	*weighed with skin*	3.4	Tr	2.0	Tr	12	0	45.7
935L	**Paw-paw**, *raw*	8.6	Tr	2.2	Tr	5	0	88.5
936L	*raw, weighed with skin and pips*	6.4	Tr	1.7	Tr	4	0	66.4
937L	canned in juice	16.9	Tr	0.7	Tr	8	0	80.4
938L	**Peaches**, *raw*	7.2	Tr	1.5	Tr	1	0	88.9
939L	*raw, weighed with stone*	6.5	Tr	1.3	Tr	1	0	80.0
940L	canned in juice	9.5	Tr	0.8	Tr	12	0	86.7
941L	canned in syrup	13.7	Tr	0.9	Tr	4	0	81.1

Labelling information for Group 1 nutrients per 100g food

No.	Food	Description and main data sources	Edible proportion	Energy kJ	Energy kcal	Protein (N × 6.25) g	Carbohydrate (actual wt.) g	Fat g
942L	**Pears**, *average, raw*	Average of Comice, Conference and Williams varieties; flesh and skin	1.00	180	43	0.3	10.1	0.1
943L	*average, raw, weighed with core*	Calculated from No. 942	0.91	165	39	0.3	9.2	0.1
944L	*-, raw, peeled*	Literature sources and calculation from No. 942; flesh only	1.00	187	44	0.3	10.5	0.1
945L	canned in juice	10 samples, 7 brands	1.00	151	36	0.3	8.6	Tr
946L	canned in syrup	10 samples, 8 brands	1.00	224	53	0.3	12.9	Tr
947L	**Pineapple**, *raw*	10 samples; flesh only	1.00	179	42	0.4	9.7	0.2
948L	canned in juice	10 samples, 10 brands; cubes and slices	1.00	209	49	0.3	12.0	Tr
949L	canned in syrup	10 samples, 10 brands; cubes and slices	1.00	286	67	0.5	16.3	Tr
950L	**Plums**, *average, raw*	Assorted varieties; flesh and skin	1.00	162	38	0.6	8.7	0.1
951L	*average, raw, weighed with stones*	Calculated from No. 950	0.94	150	35	0.5	8.1	0.1
952L	*-, stewed with sugar, weighed with stones*	Calculated from Plums stewed with sugar	0.95	330	78	0.5	18.7	0.1
953L	*-, stewed without sugar, weighed with stones*	Calculated from Plums stewed without sugar	0.95	126	30	0.4	6.8	0.1
954L	canned in syrup	10 samples, 7 brands; Red, Golden and Victoria	1.00	267	63	0.3	15.4	Tr
955L	**Prunes**, canned in juice	10 samples; stones removed	0.93	354	83	0.8	19.6	0.2
956L	canned in syrup	11 samples, 6 brands; stones removed	0.92	403	95	0.6	22.7	0.2
957L	ready-to-eat	4 samples; semi-dried	1.00	634	149	2.5	33.9	0.4

No.	Food	Sugars (actual weight) g	Saturates g	Fibre (Englyst) g	Sodium g	Sodium mg	Starch (actual weight) g	Water g
		Labelling information for Group 2 nutrients per 100g food				**Additional nutrients and information per 100g food**		
942L	**Pears**, *average, raw*	10.1	Tr	2.2	Tr	3	0	83.8
943L	*average, raw, weighed with core*	9.2	Tr	2.0	Tr	3	0	76.3
944L	*-, raw, peeled*	10.5	Tr	1.7	Tr	3	0	83.8
945L	canned in juice	8.6	Tr	1.4	Tr	3	0	86.8
946L	canned in syrup	12.9	Tr	1.1	Tr	3	0	82.6
947L	**Pineapple**, *raw*	9.7	Tr	1.2	Tr	2	0	86.5
948L	canned in juice	12.0	Tr	0.5	Tr	1	0	86.8
949L	canned in syrup	16.3	Tr	0.7	Tr	2	0	82.2
950L	**Plums**, *average, raw*	8.7	Tr	1.6	Tr	2	0	83.9
951L	*average, raw, weighed with stones*	8.1	Tr	1.5	Tr	2	0	78.9
952L	*-, stewed with sugar, weighed with stones*	18.7	Tr	1.2	Tr	2	0	70.5
953L	*-, stewed without sugar, weighed with stones*	6.8	Tr	1.2	Tr	2	0	81.0
954L	canned in syrup	15.4	Tr	0.8	Tr	6	0	81.4
955L	**Prunes**, canned in juice	19.6	Tr	2.4	Tr	18	0	74.1
956L	canned in syrup	22.7	Tr	2.8	Tr	18	0	69.9
957L	ready-to-eat	33.9	N	5.7	Tr	11	0	31.1

Labelling information for Group 1 nutrients per 100g food

No.	Food	Description and main data sources	Edible proportion	Energy kJ	Energy kcal	Protein ($N \times 6.25$) g	Carbohydrate (actual wt.) g	Fat g
958L	**Raisins**	10 samples, 8 brands. Large stoned variety	1.00	1229	289	2.1	69.3	0.4
959L	**Raspberries**, *raw*	9 samples; whole fruit	1.00	111	26	1.4	4.5	0.3
960L	canned in syrup	Mixed sample	1.00	378	89	0.6	21.4	0.1
961L	**Rhubarb**, *raw*	Stems only	0.87	34	8	0.9	0.9	0.1
962L	*stewed with sugar*	1000g fruit, 100g water, 120g sugar	1.00	208	49	0.9	11.1	0.1
963L	*stewed without sugar*	500g fruit, 50g water and calculation from No. 962	1.00	31	7	0.9	0.7	0.1
964L	canned in syrup	10 samples, 6 brands	1.00	136	32	0.5	7.5	Tr
965L	**Satsumas**	10 samples; flesh only	1.00	158	37	0.9	8.2	0.1
966L	*weighed with peel*	Calculated from No. 965	0.71	113	26	0.6	5.8	0.1
967L	**Strawberries**, *raw*	9 samples; flesh and pips	0.95	118	28	0.8	5.9	0.1
968L	canned in syrup	10 samples	1.00	289	68	0.4	16.6	Tr
969L	**Sultanas**	10 samples, 9 brands; whole fruit	1.00	1241	292	2.7	69.4	0.4
970L	**Tangerines**	Flesh only	1.00	153	36	0.9	7.9	0.1
971L	*weighed with peel and pips*	Calculated from No. 970	0.73	111	26	0.6	5.7	0.1

No.	Food	Labelling information for Group 2 nutrients per 100g food				Additional nutrients and information per 100g food		
		Sugars (actual weight) g	Saturates g	Fibre (Englyst) g	Sodium g	Sodium mg	Starch (actual weight) g	Water g
958L	**Raisins**	69.3	N	2.0	0.1	60	0	13.2
959L	**Raspberries**, *raw*	4.5	0.1	2.5	Tr	3	0	87.0
960L	canned in syrup	21.4	Tr	1.5	Tr	4	0	74.0
961L	**Rhubarb**, *raw*	0.9	Tr	1.4	Tr	3	0	94.2
962L	*stewed with sugar*	11.1	Tr	1.2	Tr	1	0	84.6
963L	*stewed without sugar*	0.7	Tr	1.3	Tr	1	0	94.1
964L	canned in syrup	7.5	Tr	0.8	Tr	4	0	90.6
965L	**Satsumas**	8.2	Tr	1.3	Tr	4	0	87.4
966L	*weighed with peel*	5.8	Tr	0.9	Tr	3	0	62.1
967L	**Strawberries**, *raw*	5.9	Tr	1.1	Tr	6	0	89.5
968L	canned in syrup	16.6	Tr	0.7	Tr	9	0	81.7
969L	**Sultanas**	69.4	N	2.0	Tr	19	0	15.2
970L	**Tangerines**	7.9	Tr	1.3	Tr	2	0	86.7
971L	*weighed with peel and pips*	5.7	Tr	0.9	Tr	1	0	63.3

Labelling information for Group 1 nutrients per 100g food

No.	Food	Description and main data sources	Edible proportion	Energy kJ	Energy kcal	Protein (N × 6.25) g	Carbohydrate (actual wt.) g	Fat g
972L	**Almonds**	10 blanched samples, flaked and ground	1.00	2607	630	25.4	6.5	55.8
973L	*weighed with shells*	Calculated from No. 972	0.37	961	232	9.4	2.3	20.6
974L	**Brazil nuts**	10 samples, kernel only	1.00	2850	691	16.3	2.9	68.2
975L	*weighed with shells*	Calculated from No. 974	0.46	1311	318	7.5	1.3	31.4
976L	**Cashew nuts**, *roasted and salted*	10 samples, kernels only	1.00	2589	624	24.2	17.3	50.9
977L	**Chestnuts**	Analysis and literature sources; kernel only	1.00	710	168	2.3	33.6	2.7
978L	**Coconut**, *creamed block*	7 samples, 2 brands; block of dried kernel	1.00	2780	674	7.1	6.7	68.8
979L	*desiccated*	Analytical and literature sources	1.00	2510	609	6.6	6.1	62.0
980L	**Hazelnuts**	10 samples, kernel only	1.00	2727	660	16.6	5.6	63.5
981L	*weighed with shells*	Calculated from No. 980	0.38	1035	251	6.3	2.1	24.1
982L	**Macadamia nuts**, salted	8 samples	1.00	3106	754	9.3	4.5	77.6
983L	**Marzipan**, *homemade*	Recipe	1.00	1976	473	12.4	47.7	25.8
984L	*retail*	10 samples, white and yellow	1.00	1740	414	6.4	64.6	14.4
985L	**Mixed nuts**[a]	Calculated from recipe proportions	1.00	2580	623	26.7	7.3	54.1

[a] Calculated as peanuts 67%, almonds 17%, cashews 8% and hazelnuts 7%

No.	Food	Labelling information for Group 2 nutrients per 100g food				Additional nutrients and information per 100g food		
		Sugars (actual weight) g	Saturates g	Fibre (Englyst) g	Sodium g	Sodium mg	Starch (actual weight) g	Water g
972L	**Almonds**	4.0	4.7	7.4	Tr	14	2.5	4.2
973L	*weighed with shells*	1.4	1.7	2.7	Tr	5	0.9	1.5
974L	**Brazil nuts**	2.3	16.4	4.3	Tr	3	0.6	2.8
975L	*weighed with shells*	1.0	7.5	2.0	Tr	1	0.3	1.3
976L	**Cashew nuts**, *roasted and salted*	5.3	10.1	3.2	0.3	290	12.0	2.4
977L	**Chestnuts**	6.7	0.5	4.1	Tr	11	26.9	51.7
978L	**Coconut**, *creamed block*	6.7	59.3	N	Tr	30	0	2.5
979L	*desiccated*	6.1	53.4	13.7	Tr	28	0	2.3
980L	**Hazelnuts**	3.8	4.7	6.5	Tr	6	1.8	4.6
981L	*weighed with shells*	1.4	1.8	2.5	Tr	2	0.7	1.7
982L	**Macadamia nuts**, salted	3.8	11.2	5.3	0.3	280	0.7	1.3
983L	**Marzipan**, *homemade*	46.6	2.3	3.3	Tr	16	1.1	10.2
984L	*retail*	64.6	1.2	1.9	Tr	20	Tr	7.9
985L	**Mixed nuts**	3.8	8.4	6.0	0.3	300	3.5	2.5

Nuts and seeds *continued*

Labelling information for Group 1 nutrients per 100g food

No.	Food	Description and main data sources	Edible proportion	Energy		Protein (N × 6.25)	Carbohydrate (actual wt.)	Fat
				kJ	kcal	g	g	g
986L	**Peanut butter**, smooth	10 samples, 3 brands	1.00	2638	637	26.1	12.2	53.7
987L	**Peanuts**, *plain*	10 samples, kernel only	1.00	2406	580	29.6	11.6	46.1
988L	*plain, weighed with shells*	Calculated from No. 987	0.69	1659	400	20.4	8.0	31.8
989L	*dry roasted*	10 samples, 5 brands	1.00	2504	604	29.4	9.5	49.8
990L	*roasted and salted*	20 samples	1.00	2554	617	28.3	6.6	53.0
991L	**Pecan nuts**	9 samples, kernel only	1.00	2873	697	10.9	5.5	70.1
992L	**Pine nuts**	20 samples, pine kernels	1.00	2883	699	16.5	3.8	68.6
993L	**Pistachio nuts**, *weighed with shells*	Calculated from Pistachio nuts without shells	0.55	1399	338	11.6	4.3	30.5
994L	**Sesame seeds**	10 samples, with and without hulls	1.00	2527	612	21.5	0.9	58.0
995L	**Sunflower seeds**	Analysis and literature sources	1.00	2472	596	23.4	18.6[a]	47.5
996L	**Tahini paste**	Ref. McCarthy and Matthews (1984) and calculation from No. 994	1.00	2565	621	21.8	0.9	58.9
997L	**Walnuts**	10 samples, kernel only	1.00	2881	698	17.3	3.1	68.5
998L	*weighed with shells*	Calculated from No. 997	0.43	1237	300	7.4	1.4	29.4

[a] Including oligosaccharides

No.	Food	Labelling information for Group 2 nutrients per 100g food				Additional nutrients and information per 100g food		
		Sugars (actual weight) g	Saturates g	Fibre (Englyst) g	Sodium g	Sodium mg	Starch (actual weight) g	Water g
986L	**Peanut butter**, smooth	6.4	11.7	5.4	0.4	350	5.8	1.1
987L	**Peanuts**, *plain*	5.9	8.2	6.2	Tr	2	5.7	6.3
988L	*plain, weighed with shells*	4.1	5.7	4.3	Tr	1	3.9	4.3
989L	*dry roasted*	3.6	8.9	6.4	0.8	790	5.9	1.8
990L	*roasted and salted*	3.6	9.5	6.0	0.4	400	3.0	1.9
991L	**Pecan nuts**	4.1	5.7	4.7	Tr	1	1.4	3.7
992L	**Pine nuts**	3.7	4.6	1.9	Tr	1	0.1	2.7
993L	**Pistachio nuts**, *weighed with shells*	3.0	4.1	3.3	0.3	290	1.3	1.1
994L	**Sesame seeds**	0.4	8.3	7.9	Tr	20	0.5	4.6
995L	**Sunflower seeds**	1.6[a]	4.5	6.0	Tr	3	16.3	4.4
996L	**Tahini paste**	0.4	8.4	8.0	Tr	20	0.5	3.1
997L	**Walnuts**	2.5	5.6	3.5	Tr	7	0.6	2.8
998L	*weighed with shells*	1.1	2.4	1.5	Tr	3	0.3	1.2

[a] Not including oligosaccharides

Labelling information for Group 1 nutrients per 100g food

No.	Food	Description and main data sources	Edible proportion	Energy kJ	Energy kcal	Protein (N × 6.25) g	Carbohydrate (actual wt.) g	Fat g
	Sugars, syrups and preserves							
999L	**Chocolate nut spread**	8 samples, 5 brands	1.00	2306	552	6.2	57.6	33.0
1000L	**Glucose liquid**, BP	1 sample	1.00	1372	323	Tr	80.7	0
1001L	**Honey**	2 samples	1.00	1304	307	0.4	76.3	0
1002L	**Honeycomb**	2 samples, honey and comb together	1.00	1275	300	0.6	74.4	4.6[a]
1003L	**Jaggery**	5 assorted samples	1.00	1576	371	0.5	92.2	0
1004L	**Jam**, *fruit with edible seeds*	10 samples, 5 flavours	1.00	1161	273	0.6	67.7	0
1005L	*stone fruit*	8 samples, 4 flavours	1.00	1161	273	0.4	67.9	0
1006L	reduced sugar	9 samples, 5 brands; assorted flavours	1.00	549	129	0.5	31.6	0.1
1007L	**Lemon curd**, *starch base*	10 jars, 4 brands	1.00	1217	288	0.6	59.9	5.1
1008L	**Marmalade**	4 brands	1.00	1159	273	0.1	68.1	0
1009L	**Mincemeat**	10 samples of the same brand	1.00	1225	290	0.6	62.1	4.3
1010L	**Sugar**, demerara	5 samples	1.00	1700	400	0.5	99.5	0
1011L	white	Granulated and loaf sugar	1.00	1700	400	Tr	100.0	0
1012L	**Syrup**, golden	3 samples of the same brand	1.00	1321	311	0.3	77.4	0
1013L	**Treacle**, black	3 samples	1.00	1129	266	1.2	65.2	0

[a] Waxy material, probably not available as fat; disregarded in calculating energy values

No.	Food	Labelling information for Group 2 nutrients per 100g food				Additional nutrients and information per 100g food		
		Sugars (actual weight) g	Saturates g	Fibre (Englyst) g	Sodium g	Sodium mg	Starch (actual weight) g	Water g
Sugars, syrups and preserves								
999L	**Chocolate nut spread**	56.9	10.1	0.8	0.1	50	0.7	Tr
1000L	**Glucose liquid**, BP	40.2	0	0	0.2	150	40.5[a]	20.4
1001L	**Honey**	76.3	0	0	Tr	11	0	23.0
1002L	**Honeycomb**	74.4	0	0	Tr	7	0	20.2
1003L	**Jaggery**	85.0	0	0	0.1	79	7.2	3.4
1004L	**Jam**, *fruit with edible seeds*	67.7	0	N	Tr	16	0	29.8
1005L	*stone fruit*	67.9	0	N	Tr	12	0	29.6
1006L	reduced sugar	31.6	Tr	N	Tr	17	0	65.3
1007L	**Lemon curd**, *starch base*	39.6	N	0.2	0.1	65	20.3	30.1
1008L	**Marmalade**	68.1	0	0.6	Tr	18	0	28.0
1009L	**Mincemeat**	62.1	2.4	1.3	0.1	140	Tr	27.5
1010L	**Sugar**, demerara	99.5	0	0	Tr	6	0	Tr
1011L	white	100.0	0	0	Tr	Tr	0	Tr
1012L	**Syrup**, golden	77.4	0	0	0.3	270	0	20.0
1013L	**Treacle**, black	65.2	0	0	0.1	96	0	28.5

[a] Including oligosaccharides

Labelling information for Group 1 nutrients per 100g food

No.	Food	Description and main data sources	Edible proportion	Energy kJ	Energy kcal	Protein (N × 6.25) g	Carbohydrate (actual wt.) g	Fat g
Chocolate confectionery								
1014L	**Bounty bar**	8 samples; Mars	1.00	1989	476	4.8	55.4	26.1
1015L	**Chocolate**, milk	10 samples of the same brand	1.00	2223	532	8.4	56.4	30.3
1016L	plain	10 samples of the same brand	1.00	2206	528	4.7	61.5	29.2
1017L	white	14 samples; buttons and bars	1.00	2223	532	8.0	55.5	30.9
1018L	**Chocolates**, fancy and filled	8 samples of different brands, mixed, milk and plain	1.00	1947	464	4.1	69.5	18.8
1019L	**Creme eggs**	10 samples; Cadbury's	1.00	1635	390	4.1	55.5	16.8
1020L	**Kit Kat**	12 samples; Rowntree Mackintosh	1.00	2094	501	8.2	57.1	26.6
1021L	**Mars bar**	8 samples: Mars	1.00	1872	446	5.3	63.7	18.9
1022L	**Milky Way**	10 samples; Mars	1.00	1691	403	4.4	60.7	15.8
1023L	**Smartie-type sweets**	10 samples; Smarties and M and M's	1.00	1928	459	5.4	69.9	17.5
1024L	**Twix**	10 samples; Mars	1.00	2018	482	5.6	59.8	24.5
Non chocolate confectionery								
1025L	**Boiled sweets**	6 samples	1.00	1418	334	Tr	83.4	Tr
1026L	**Fruit gums**	8 samples of the same brand	1.00	757	178	1.0	43.5	0
1027L	**Liquorice allsorts**	6 samples	1.00	1355	319	3.9	71.0	2.2
1028L	**Pastilles**	6 samples of different brands	1.00	1107	260	5.3	59.8	0
1029L	**Peppermints**	Several samples of 6 different brands	1.00	1699	400	0.5	97.9	0.7
1030L	**Popcorn**, candied	Recipe	1.00	2020	481	2.1	73.2	20.0
1031L	plain	Recipe	1.00	2444	588	6.2	44.4	42.8
1032L	**Toffees**, *mixed*	8 samples of different brands	1.00	1828	435	2.1	68.0	17.2
1033L	**Turkish delight**, *without nuts*	7 assorted samples	1.00	1265	298	0.6	73.8	0

No.	Food	Labelling information for Group 2 nutrients per 100g food				Additional nutrients and information per 100g food		
		Sugars (actual weight) g	Saturates g	Fibre (Englyst) g	Sodium g	Sodium mg	Starch (actual weight) g	Water g
Chocolate confectionery								
1014L	**Bounty bar**	51.2	21.2	N	0.2	180	4.2	7.6
1015L	**Chocolate**, milk	53.8	17.8	Tr	0.1	120	2.6	2.2
1016L	plain	56.7	16.9	N	Tr	11	4.8	0.6
1017L	white	55.5	18.2	0	0.1	110	Tr	0.6
1018L	**Chocolates**, fancy and filled	62.7	N	N	0.1	60	6.8	5.7
1019L	**Creme eggs**	55.5	N	Tr	0.1	55	Tr	5.3
1020L	**Kit Kat**	44.6	13.8	N	0.1	110	12.5	1.3
1021L	**Mars bar**	63.1	10.0	Tr	0.2	150	0.6	6.9
1022L	**Milky Way**	60.0	8.3	Tr	0.1	100	0.7	6.6
1023L	**Smartie-type sweets**	67.1	10.3	Tr	0.1	58	2.8	1.5
1024L	**Twix**	45.7	12.0	N	0.2	190	14.1	3.5
Non chocolate confectionery								
1025L	**Boiled sweets**	83.0	0	0	Tr	25	0.4	N
1026L	**Fruit gums**	41.5	0	0	0.1	64	2.0	12.0
1027L	**Liquorice allsorts**	64.7	0.6	N	0.1	75	6.3	6.6
1028L	**Pastilles**	59.8	0	0	0.1	77	0	10.2
1029L	**Peppermints**	97.9	N	0	Tr	9	0	0.2
1030L	**Popcorn**, candied	59.1	2.0	N	0.1	56	14.1	2.6
1031L	plain	1.1	4.3	N	Tr	4	43.3	0.9
1032L	**Toffees**, *mixed*	67.1	13.7	0	0.3	320	0.9	4.8
1033L	**Turkish delight**, *without nuts*	65.3	0	0	Tr	31	8.5	16.1

Labelling information for Group 1 nutrients per 100g food

No.	Food	Description and main data sources	Edible proportion	Energy kJ	Energy kcal	Protein (N × 6.25) g	Carbohydrate (actual wt.) g	Fat g
	Savoury snacks							
1034L	**Bombay Mix**	20 samples; savoury mix of gram flour, assorted peas, lentils, nuts and seeds	1.00	2083	500	18.8	32.1	32.9
1035L	**Corn snacks**	20 samples, assorted types e.g. Wotsits, Monster Munch, Nik-Naks	1.00	2143	514	7.0	49.6	31.9
1036L	**Peanuts and raisins**[a]	Calculated from recipe proportions	1.00	1889	452	17.5	37.0	26.0
1037L	**Potato crisps**	20 samples, mixed plain and flavoured	1.00	2250	540	5.6	44.9	37.6
1038L	low fat	20 samples, mixed plain and flavoured	1.00	1882	449	6.6	57.3	21.5
1039L	**Potato hoops**	18 samples, assorted flavours; Hula Hoop type	1.00	2153	516	3.9	53.1	32.0
1040L	**Tortilla chips**	20 samples, 6 brands, maize chips	1.00	1895	453	7.6	54.7	22.6
1041L	**Trail Mix**	10 samples; mix of nuts and dried fruit	1.00	1840	441	9.1	37.1	28.5
1042L	**Twiglets**	20 samples, savoury wholewheat sticks	1.00	1603	381	12.4	56.4	11.7

[a] Calculated as peanuts 56% and raisins 44%

No.	Food	Labelling information for Group 2 nutrients per 100g food: Sugars (actual weight) g	Saturates g	Fibre (Englyst) g	Sodium g	Additional nutrients and information per 100g food: Sodium mg	Starch (actual weight) g	Water g
	Savoury snacks							
1034L	**Bombay Mix**	2.3	4.0	6.2	0.8	770	29.8	3.5
1035L	**Corn snacks**	4.4	11.8	1.0	1.1	1130	45.2	3.3
1036L	**Peanuts and raisins**	33.8	4.6	4.4	Tr	27	3.2	9.3
1037L	**Potato crisps**	0.7	9.2	4.9	1.1	1070	44.2	1.9
1038L	low fat	0.9	6.2	6.3	1.1	1070	56.4	1.1
1039L	**Potato hoops**	0.4	N	2.6	1.1	1070	52.7	2.8
1040L	**Tortilla chips**	1.2	4.0	4.9	0.9	850	53.5	0.9
1041L	**Trail Mix**	37.0	N	4.3	Tr	27	0.1	8.9
1042L	**Twiglets**	1.0	4.9	10.3	1.3	1330	55.4	3.2

Labelling information for Group 1 nutrients per 100g food

No.	Food	Description and main data sources	Edible proportion	Energy kJ	Energy kcal	Protein (N × 6.25) g	Carbohydrate (actual wt.) g	Fat g
	Powdered drinks and essences							
1043L	**Bournvita powder**	6 samples	1.00	1444	340	7.7	74.0	1.5
1044L	*made up with whole milk*	Calculated from 8g powder to 200ml milk	1.00	319	76	3.3	7.2	3.8
1045L	*made up with semi-skimmed milk*	Calculated from 8g powder to 200ml milk	1.00	243	58	3.4	7.4	1.6
1046L	**Build-up powder**	Manufacturer's data (Nestlé)	1.00	1487	350	24.0	61.5[a]	0.9
1047L	*made up with whole milk*	Made up according to packet directions	1.00	415	99	5.5	11.1	3.6
1048L	*made up with semi-skimmed milk*	Made up according to packet directions	1.00	343	81	5.6	11.3	1.5
1049L	*made up with skimmed milk*	Made up according to packet directions	1.00	295	69	5.6	11.3	0.2
1050L	**Cocoa powder**	10 samples, 2 brands	1.00	1374	330	23.1	10.5	21.7
1051L	*made up with whole milk*	Calculated from 4g powder, 4g sugar and 200ml milk	1.00	324	77	3.4	6.5	4.2
1052L	*made up with semi-skimmed milk*	Calculated from 4g powder, 4g sugar and 200ml milk	1.00	245	58	3.6	6.7	1.9
1053L	**Coffee**, *infusion, 5 minutes*	60g ground coffee from mixed sample; boiled in percolator with 900ml water and strained	1.00	141	33	8.0	0.3	Tr
1054L	instant	10 jars, 2 brands	1.00	522	123	20.4	10.3	0
1055L	**Coffee and chicory essence**	7 bottles of the same brand	1.00	953	224	2.1	53.5	0.2
1056L	**Coffeemate**	Analysis and manufacturer's data (Nestlé)	1.00	2240	537	2.6	53.2[a]	34.9

[a] Including oligosaccharides from the glucose syrup/maltodextrins in the product

No.	Food	Labelling information for Group 2 nutrients per 100g food				Additional nutrients and information per 100g food		
		Sugars (actual weight) g	Saturates g	Fibre (Englyst) g	Sodium g	Sodium mg	Starch (actual weight) g	Water g
	Powdered drinks and essences							
1043L	**Bournvita powder**	49.5	N	N	0.2	190	24.5	1.5
1044L	*made up with whole milk*	6.3	N	Tr	0.1	59	0.9	84.6
1045L	*made up with semi-skimmed milk*	6.5	N	Tr	0.1	59	0.9	86.5
1046L	**Build-up powder**	52.1[a]	0.6	Tr	0.4	380	Tr	3.0
1047L	*made up with whole milk*	10.0	2.2	Tr	0.1	92	Tr	78.1
1048L	*made up with semi-skimmed milk*	10.2	0.9	Tr	0.1	92	Tr	79.8
1049L	*made up with skimmed milk*	10.2	0.1	Tr	0.1	92	Tr	81.0
1050L	**Cocoa powder**	Tr	12.8	12.1	1.0	950	10.5	3.4
1051L	*made up with whole milk*	6.3	2.6	0.2	0.1	70	0.2	84.6
1052L	*made up with semi-skimmed milk*	6.5	1.2	0.2	0.1	70	0.2	86.5
1053L	**Coffee**, *infusion, 5 minutes*	0.3	Tr	0	Tr	Tr	0	N
1054L	instant	6.2	Tr	0	Tr	41	4.1	3.4
1055L	**Coffee and chicory essence**	51.5	Tr	0	0.1	65	2.0	36.9
1056L	**Coffeemate**	9.6[a]	32.1	0	0.2	200	Tr	3.0

[a] Not including oligosaccharides from the glucose syrup/maltodextrins in the product

Labelling information for Group 1 nutrients per 100g food

No.	Food	Description and main data sources	Edible proportion	Energy kJ	Energy kcal	Protein (N × 6.25) g	Carbohydrate (actual wt.) g	Fat g
	Powdered drinks and essences							
1057L	**Complan powder**, savoury	Chicken flavour, manufacturer's data (Farley's)	1.00	1825	434	21.6	50.9[a]	16.0
1058L	savoury, *made up with water*	Made up according to packet directions	1.00	403	96	4.8	11.3	3.5
1059L	sweet	3 flavours, manufacturer's data (Farley's)	1.00	1815	431	19.6	56.7[a]	14.0
1060L	sweet, *made up with water*	Made up according to packet directions	1.00	405	96	4.4	12.7	3.1
1061L	sweet, *made up with whole milk*	Made up according to packet directions	1.00	567	135	6.8	13.3	6.1
1062L	sweet, *made up with semi-skimmed milk*	Made up according to packet directions	1.00	504	120	6.8	13.5	4.3
1063L	sweet, *made up with skimmed milk*	Made up according to packet directions	1.00	460	109	6.8	13.5	3.1
1064L	**Drinking chocolate powder**	10 tins, 3 brands	1.00	1584	374	6.5	73.6	6.0
1065L	*made up with whole milk*	Calculated from 18g powder to 200ml milk	1.00	381	91	3.4	10.1	4.1
1066L	*made up with semi-skimmed milk*	Calculated from 18g powder to 200ml milk	1.00	305	72	3.5	10.3	1.9
1067L	**Horlicks LowFat Instant powder**	Manufacturer's data (SmithKline Beechams)	1.00	1598	377	17.4	69.4	3.3
1068L	*made up with water*	Calculated from 32g powder to 200ml water	1.00	223	53	2.4	9.6	0.5
1069L	**Horlicks powder**	Manufacturer's data (SmithKline Beechams)	1.00	1603	378	12.4	73.2	4.0
1070L	*made up with whole milk*	Calculated from 25g powder to 200ml milk	1.00	418	100	4.1	12.0	3.9
1071L	*made up with semi-skimmed milk*	Calculated from 25g powder to 200ml milk	1.00	351	83	4.3	12.2	1.9

[a] Including oligosaccharides from the glucose syrup/maltodextrins in the product

No.	Food	Labelling information for Group 2 nutrients per 100g food				Additional nutrients and information per 100g food		
		Sugars (actual weight) g	Saturates g	Fibre (Englyst) g	Sodium g	Sodium mg	Starch (actual weight) g	Water g
	Powdered drinks and essences							
1057L	**Complan powder**, savoury	13.1[a]	7.5	0	1.8	1800	8.0	3.8
1058L	savoury, *made up with water*	2.9	1.7	0	0.4	400	1.8	78.7
1059L	sweet	44.7[a]	5.9	Tr	0.3	290	Tr	3.5
1060L	sweet, *made up with water*	10.0	1.3	Tr	0.1	65	Tr	78.3
1061L	sweet, *made up with whole milk*	13.3	3.2	Tr	0.1	110	Tr	69.3
1062L	sweet, *made up with semi-skimmed milk*	13.5	2.1	Tr	0.1	110	Tr	70.8
1063L	sweet, *made up with skimmed milk*	13.5	1.3	Tr	0.1	110	Tr	71.9
1064L	**Drinking chocolate powder**	70.3	3.5	N	0.3	250	3.3	2.1
1065L	*made up with whole milk*	9.8	2.5	Tr	0.1	70	0.3	80.9
1066L	*made up with semi-skimmed milk*	10.0	1.2	Tr	0.1	70	0.3	82.8
1067L	**Horlicks LowFat Instant powder**	N	N	N	0.6	590	N	N
1068L	*made up with water*	N	N	Tr	0.1	81	N	86.2
1069L	**Horlicks powder**	50.5	N	N	0.5	460	22.7	2.5
1070L	*made up with whole milk*	9.5	N	Tr	0.1	98	2.5	78.6
1071L	*made up with semi-skimmed milk*	9.7	N	Tr	0.1	98	2.5	80.4

[a] Not including oligosaccharides from the glucose syrup/maltodextrins in the product

Labelling information for Group 1 nutrients per 100g food

No.	Food	Description and main data sources	Edible proportion	Energy kJ	Energy kcal	Protein (N × 6.25) g	Carbohydrate (actual wt.) g	Fat g
	Powdered drinks and essences							
1072L	**Milk shake**, *purchased*	21 samples, thick take-away type	1.00	384	91	2.9	12.7	3.2
1073L	**Milk shake powder**	6 samples (Nesquik), 3 flavours	1.00	1672	394	1.3	93.6	1.6
1074L	*made up with whole milk*	Calculated from 15g powder to 200ml milk	1.00	370	88	3.0	10.7	3.7
1075L	*made up with semi-skimmed milk*	Calculated from 15g powder to 200ml milk	1.00	297	70	3.1	10.9	1.6
1076L	**Ovaltine powder**	Manufacturer's data (Wander)	1.00	1535	362	8.8	75.6	2.7
1077L	*made up with whole milk*	Calculated from 25g powder to 200ml milk	1.00	414	99	3.8	12.3	3.8
1078L	*made up with semi-skimmed milk*	Calculated from 25g powder to 200ml milk	1.00	340	81	3.9	12.4	1.7
1079L	**Tea**, Indian, *infusion*	10g leaves from mixed sample; infused with 1000ml boiling water 2-10 minutes and strained	1.00	Tr	Tr	Tr	Tr	Tr

No.	Food	Labelling information for Group 2 nutrients per 100g food				Additional nutrients and information per 100g food		
		Sugars (actual weight) g	Saturates g	Fibre (Englyst) g	Sodium g	Sodium mg	Starch (actual weight) g	Water g
	Powdered drinks and essences							
1072L	**Milk shake**, *purchased*	12.7	2.0	Tr	0.1	55	Tr	80.0
1073L	**Milk shake powder**	93.6	N	Tr	Tr	20	Tr	0.5
1074L	*made up with whole milk*	10.7	N	Tr	0.1	52	Tr	81.9
1075L	*made up with semi-skimmed milk*	10.9	N	Tr	0.1	52	Tr	83.7
1076L	**Ovaltine powder**	N	N	N	0.2	160	N	2.0
1077L	*made up with whole milk*	N	N	Tr	0.1	66	N	78.5
1078L	*made up with semi-skimmed milk*	N	N	Tr	0.1	66	N	80.3
1079L	**Tea**, Indian, *infusion*	Tr	Tr	0	Tr	Tr	0	N

Labelling information for Group 1 nutrients per 100g food

No.	Food	Description and main data sources	Edible proportion	Energy kJ	Energy kcal	Protein (N × 6.25) g	Carbohydrate (actual wt.) g	Fat g
	Carbonated drinks							
1080L	**Coca-cola**	8 cans and 5 bottles	1.00	179	42	Tr	10.5	0
1081L	**Lemonade**, *bottled*	7 bottles of the same brand	1.00	95	22	Tr	5.6	0
1082L	**Lucozade**	Mixed sample and manufacturer's data (SmithKline Beechams)	1.00	292	69	Tr	17.2[a]	0
	Squash and cordials							
1083L	**Lime juice cordial**, *undiluted*	6 bottles of the same brand	1.00	503	118	0.1	29.5	0
1084L	**Orange drink**, *undiluted*	Mixed sample; orange squash	1.00	479	113	Tr	28.2	0
1085L	**Ribena**, *undiluted*	Mixed sample and manufacturer's data (SmithKline Beechams); blackcurrant juice drink	1.00	1000	235	0.1	58.7[a]	0
1086L	**Rosehip syrup**, *undiluted*	9 bottles, 4 brands	1.00	1003	236	Tr	59.0	0
	Juices							
1087L	**Apple juice**, *unsweetened*	10 samples; bottles and cartons	1.00	174	41	0.1	9.9	0.1
1088L	**Grape juice**, *unsweetened*	10 samples, 6 brands; red and white juice	1.00	208	49	0.3	11.7	0.1
1089L	**Grapefruit juice**, *unsweetened*	50 samples; fresh, canned, bottled and frozen	1.00	150	35	0.4	8.2	0.1
1090L	**Lemon juice**	Analysis and literature sources; juice from fresh lemon	1.00	32	8	0.3	1.6	Tr
1091L	**Orange juice**, *unsweetened*	60 samples; fresh, canned, bottled and frozen	1.00	160	38	0.5	8.7	0.1
1092L	**Pineapple juice**, *unsweetened*	18 samples; fresh juice	1.00	184	43	0.3	10.3	0.1
1093L	**Tomato juice**	10 samples, 9 brands	1.00	65	15	0.8	3.0	Tr

[a] Including oligosaccharides

No.	Food	Sugars (actual weight) g	Saturates g	Fibre (Englyst) g	Sodium g	Sodium mg	Starch (actual weight) g	Water g
		Labelling information for Group 2 nutrients per 100g food				**Additional nutrients and information per 100g food**		
	Carbonated drinks							
1080L	**Coca-cola**	10.5	0	0	Tr	8	Tr	89.8
1081L	**Lemonade**, *bottled*	5.6	0	0	Tr	7	0	94.6
1082L	**Lucozade**	8.6[a]	0	0	Tr	28	Tr	81.7
	Squash and cordials							
1083L	**Lime juice cordial**, *undiluted*	29.5	0	0	Tr	8	Tr	70.5
1084L	**Orange drink**, *undiluted*	28.2	0	0	Tr	21	0	71.2
1085L	**Ribena**, *undiluted*	57.1[a]	0	0	Tr	26	Tr	40.3
1086L	**Rosehip syrup**, *undiluted*	58.9	0	0	0.3	280	0.1	32.5
	Juices							
1087L	**Apple juice**, *unsweetened*	9.9	Tr	Tr	Tr	2	0	88.0
1088L	**Grape juice**, *unsweetened*	11.7	Tr	0	Tr	7	0	85.4
1089L	**Grapefruit juice**, *unsweetened*	8.2	Tr	Tr	Tr	7	0	89.4
1090L	**Lemon juice**	1.6	Tr	0.1	Tr	1	0	91.4
1091L	**Orange juice**, *unsweetened*	8.7	Tr	0.1	Tr	10	0	89.2
1092L	**Pineapple juice**, *unsweetened*	10.3	Tr	Tr	Tr	8	0	87.8
1093L	**Tomato juice**	3.0	Tr	0.6	0.2	230	Tr	93.8

[a] Not including oligosaccharides

Labelling information for Group 1 nutrients per 100ml food

No.	Food	Description and main data sources	Solids	Energy		Protein (N × 6.25)	Carbohydrate (actual wt.)	Fat
				kJ	kcal	g	g	g
Beers								
1094L	**Beer**, bitter, *canned*	6 samples	3.3	132	32	0.3	2.2	Tr
1095L	*draught*	5 samples from different brewers	3.3	132	32	0.3	2.2	Tr
1096L	*keg*	6 samples from different brewers	3.6	130	31	0.3	2.2	Tr
1097L	mild, *draught*	5 samples from different brewers	2.5	104	25	0.2	1.5	Tr
1098L	**Brown ale**, *bottled*	6 samples from different brewers	4.2	118	28	0.3	2.9	Tr
1099L	**Lager**, *bottled*	6 samples	2.4	120	29	0.2	1.4	Tr
1100L	**Pale ale**, *bottled*	6 samples from different brewers	3.3	133	32	0.3	1.9	Tr
1101L	**Stout**, *bottled*	4 samples from different brewers	5.8	157	38	0.3	4.0	Tr
1102L	extra	6 samples of the same brand	3.6	164	39	0.3	2.0	Tr
1103L	**Strong ale**	6 samples from different brewers, barley wine type	8.0	302	72	0.7	5.8	Tr
Ciders								
1104L	**Cider**, dry	3 samples of different brands	3.7	153	37	Tr	2.5	0
1105L	sweet	3 samples of different brands	5.1	177	42	Tr	4.1	0
1106L	vintage	3 samples of the same brand	8.9	424	102	Tr	7.0	0
Wines[a]								
1107L	**Red wine**	3 samples, Beaujolais, Burgundy, claret	–	–	–	–	–	–
1108L	**Rosé wine**, medium	5 samples from different vintners	–	–	–	–	–	–
1109L	**White wine**, dry	5 samples from different vintners	–	–	–	–	–	–
1110L	medium	1 sample, Graves	–	–	–	–	–	–
1111L	sparkling	1 sample, Champagne	–	–	–	–	–	–
1112L	sweet	1 sample, Sauternes	–	–	–	–	–	–

[a] The EC Wine Regulations currently prohibit labelling showing nutritional or ingredient information other than alcohol content on a % by volume basis

No.	Food	Labelling information for Group 2 nutrients per 100ml food				Additional nutrients and information per 100ml food		
		Sugars (actual weight) g	Saturates g	Fibre (Englyst) g	Sodium g	Alcohol % vol.	Sodium mg	Starch (actual weight) g
Beers								
1094L	**Beer**, bitter, *canned*	2.2	Tr	0	Tr	3.9	9	0
1095L	*draught*	2.2	Tr	0	Tr	3.9	12	0
1096L	*keg*	2.2	Tr	0	Tr	3.8	8	0
1097L	mild, *draught*	1.5	Tr	0	Tr	3.3	11	0
1098L	**Brown ale**, *bottled*	2.9	Tr	0	Tr	2.8	16	0
1099L	**Lager**, *bottled*	1.4	Tr	0	Tr	4.1	4	0
1100L	**Pale ale**, *bottled*	1.9	Tr	0	Tr	4.2	10	0
1101L	**Stout**, *bottled*	4.0	Tr	0	Tr	3.7	23	0
1102L	extra	2.0	Tr	0	Tr	5.4	4	0
1103L	**Strong ale**	5.8	Tr	0	Tr	8.4	15	0
Ciders								
1104L	**Cider**, dry	2.5	0	0	Tr	4.8	7	0
1105L	sweet	4.1	0	0	Tr	4.7	7	0
1106L	vintage	7.0	0	0	Tr	13.3	2	0
Wines[a]								
1107L	**Red wine**	–	–	–	–	12.0	–	–
1108L	**Rosé wine**, medium	–	–	–	–	11.0	–	–
1109L	**White wine**, dry	–	–	–	–	11.5	–	–
1110L	medium	–	–	–	–	11.1	–	–
1111L	sparkling	–	–	–	–	12.5	–	–
1112L	sweet	–	–	–	–	12.9	–	–

[a] The EC Wine Regulations currently prohibit labelling showing nutritional or ingredient information other than alcohol content on a % by volume basis

Labelling information for Group 1 nutrients per 100ml food

No.	Food	Description and main data sources	Solids	Energy		Protein ($N \times 6.25$)	Carbohydrate (actual wt.)	Fat
				kJ	kcal	g	g	g
Fortified wines[a]								
1113L	**Port**	2 samples	–	–	–	–	–	–
1114L	**Sherry**, dry	1 sample	–	–	–	–	–	–
1115L	medium	5 samples from different importers	–	–	–	–	–	–
1116L	sweet	1 sample	–	–	–	–	–	–
Vermouths[a]								
1117L	**Vermouth**, dry	5 samples of different brands	–	–	–	–	–	–
1118L	sweet	5 samples of different brands	–	–	–	–	–	–
Liqueurs								
1119L	**Advocaat**	4 samples of different brands	39.6	1143	273	4.7	27.0	6.3
1120L	**Cherry brandy**	6 samples of different brands	33.3	1078	257	Tr	31.0	0
1121L	**Curacao**	4 samples of different brands	27.8	1309	313	Tr	27.0	0
Spirits								
1122L	**40% volume**	Mean of brandy, gin, rum, whisky	Tr	919	222	Tr	Tr	0

[a] The EC Wine Regulations currently prohibit labelling showing nutritional or ingredient information other than alcohol content on a % by volume basis

No.	Food	Labelling information for Group 2 nutrients per 100ml food				Additional nutrients and information per 100ml food		
		Sugars (actual weight) g	Saturates g	Fibre (Englyst) g	Sodium g	Alcohol % vol.	Sodium mg	Starch (actual weight) g
	Fortified wines[a]							
1113L	**Port**	–	–	–	–	20.1	–	–
1114L	**Sherry**, dry	–	–	–	–	19.9	–	–
1115L	medium	–	–	–	–	18.7	–	–
1116L	sweet	–	–	–	–	19.7	–	–
	Vermouths[a]							
1117L	**Vermouth**, dry	–	–	–	–	17.6	–	–
1118L	sweet	–	–	–	–	16.5	–	–
	Liqueurs							
1119L	**Advocaat**	27.0	0	0	N	16.2	N	0
1120L	**Cherry brandy**	31.0	0	0	N	24.1	N	0
1121L	**Curacao**	27.0	0	0	N	37.1	N	0
	Spirits							
1122L	**40% volume**	Tr	0	0	Tr	40.1	Tr	0

[a] The EC Wine Regulations currently prohibit labelling showing nutritional or ingredient information other than alcohol content on a % by volume basis

Labelling information for Group 1 nutrients per 100g food

No.	Food	Description and main data sources	Edible proportion	Energy kJ	Energy kcal	Protein (N × 6.25) g	Carbohydrate (actual wt.) g	Fat g
Homemade soups								
1123L	**Lentil soup**	Recipe	1.00	414	99	4.4	11.7[a]	3.8
Canned soups								
1124L	**Cream of chicken soup**, canned, *ready to serve*	10 cans, 3 brands	1.00	241	58	1.7	4.2	3.8
1125L	**condensed**, canned	7 cans of the same brand	1.00	404	97	2.6	5.5	7.2
1126L	*ready to serve*	Diluted with an equal volume of water	1.00	203	49	1.3	2.8	3.6
1127L	**Cream of mushroom soup**, canned, *ready to serve*	10 cans, 3 brands	1.00	221	53	1.1	3.6	3.8
1128L	**Cream of tomato soup**, canned, *ready to serve*	10 cans, 3 brands	1.00	229	55	0.8	5.5	3.3
1129L	**condensed**, canned	7 cans, 2 brands	1.00	519	124	1.7	14.0	6.8
1130L	*ready to serve*	Diluted with an equal volume of water	1.00	258	62	0.9	6.9	3.4
1131L	**Low calorie soup**, canned	7 cans, 3 brands; tomato, vegetable and minestrone varieties	1.00	87	21	0.9	3.8	0.2
1132L	**Oxtail soup**, canned, *ready to serve*	10 cans, 3 brands	1.00	184	44	2.4	4.7	1.7
1133L	**Vegetable soup**, canned, *ready to serve*	10 cans, 4 brands	1.00	157	37	1.5	6.2	0.7

[a] Including oligosaccharides

No.	Food	Labelling information for Group 2 nutrients per 100g food				Additional nutrients and information per 100g food		
		Sugars (actual weight) g	Saturates g	Fibre (Englyst) g	Sodium g	Sodium mg	Starch (actual weight) g	Water g
	Homemade soups							
1123L	**Lentil soup**	2.2[a]	1.3	1.1	Tr	45	8.9	77.7
	Canned soups							
1124L	**Cream of chicken soup**, canned, *ready to serve*	1.1	N	N	0.5	460	3.1	87.9
1125L	**condensed**, canned	1.3	N	N	0.7	710	4.2	82.2
1126L	*ready to serve*	0.7	N	N	0.4	350	2.1	91.1
1127L	**Cream of mushroom soup**, canned, *ready to serve*	0.8	N	N	0.5	470	2.8	89.2
1128L	**Cream of tomato soup**, canned, *ready to serve*	2.5	N	N	0.5	460	3.0	84.2
1129L	**condensed**, canned	10.9	N	N	0.8	830	3.1	70.6
1130L	*ready to serve*	5.4	N	N	0.4	410	1.5	85.3
1131L	**Low calorie soup**, canned	2.0	Tr	N	0.4	370	1.8	93.3
1132L	**Oxtail soup**, canned, *ready to serve*	0.9	N	N	0.4	440	3.8	88.5
1133L	**Vegetable soup**, canned, *ready to serve*	2.4	N	1.5	0.5	500	3.8	86.4

[a] Not including oligosaccharides

Labelling information for Group 1 nutrients per 100g food

No.	Food	Description and main data sources	Edible proportion	Energy kJ	Energy kcal	Protein (N × 6.25) g	Carbohydrate (actual wt.) g	Fat g
	Packet soups							
1134L	**Chicken noodle soup**, dried	10 packets, 5 brands	1.00	1368	323	13.8	55.8	5.0
1135L	dried, *ready to serve*	Calculated from 35g soup powder to 570ml water	1.00	84	20	0.8	3.5	0.3
1136L	**Instant soup powder**, dried	10 packets, 3 brands; assorted flavours	1.00	1640	390	6.5	59.5[a]	14.0
1137L	dried, *made up with water*	Calculated from 37g powder to 190ml water	1.00	269	64	1.1	9.7[a]	2.3
1138L	**Minestrone soup**, dried	10 packets, 3 brands	1.00	1247	296	10.1	44.1	8.8
1139L	dried, *ready to serve*	Calculated from 45g soup powder to 570ml water	1.00	99	24	0.8	3.5	0.7
1140L	**Oxtail soup**, dried	10 packets, 5 brands	1.00	1480	351	17.6	46.6	10.5
1141L	dried, *ready to serve*	Calculated from 45g soup powder to 570ml water	1.00	115	27	1.4	3.6	0.8
1142L	**Tomato soup**, dried	10 packets, 4 brands	1.00	1356	321	6.6	61.0	5.6
1143L	dried, *ready to serve*	Calculated from 58g soup powder to 570ml water	1.00	132	31	0.6	6.1	0.5

[a] Including maltodextrins

No.	Food	Sugars (actual weight) g	Saturates g	Fibre (Englyst) g	Sodium g	Sodium mg	Starch (actual weight) g	Water g
		Labelling information for Group 2 nutrients per 100g food				**Additional nutrients and information per 100g food**		
	Packet soups							
1134L	**Chicken noodle soup**, dried	9.7	N	4.3	6.1	6120	46.1	4.8
1135L	dried, *ready to serve*	0.7	Tr	0.2	0.4	370	2.8	94.2
1136L	**Instant soup powder**, dried	11.3[a]	N	N	3.4	3440	31.0	4.1
1137L	dried, *made up with water*	1.8[a]	N	N	0.6	560	5.1	84.4
1138L	**Minestrone soup**, dried	14.5	N	N	5.6	5600	29.6	3.9
1139L	dried, *ready to serve*	1.2	N	N	0.4	430	2.3	92.6
1140L	**Oxtail soup**, dried	8.6	N	N	5.3	5250	38.0	3.0
1141L	dried, *ready to serve*	0.7	N	N	0.4	400	2.9	92.5
1142L	**Tomato soup**, dried	34.7	N	N	4.0	4040	26.3	2.8
1143L	dried, *ready to serve*	3.6	N	N	0.4	390	2.5	90.6

[a] Not including maltodextrins

Labelling information for Group 1 nutrients per 100g food

No.	Food	Description and main data sources	Edible proportion	Energy kJ	Energy kcal	Protein (N × 6.25) g	Carbohydrate (actual wt.) g	Fat g
	Dairy sauces							
1144L	**Bread sauce**, *made with whole milk*	Recipe	1.00	462	110	4.3	11.8	5.1
1145L	*made with semi-skimmed milk*	Recipe	1.00	392	93	4.4	11.9	3.1
1146L	**Cheese sauce**, *made with whole milk*	Recipe	1.00	816	196	7.9	8.3	14.6
1147L	*made with semi-skimmed milk*	Recipe	1.00	745	179	8.0	8.4	12.6
1148L	**Cheese sauce packet mix**, *made up with whole milk*	Recipe	1.00	460	110	5.3	8.5	6.1
1149L	*made up with semi-skimmed milk*	Recipe	1.00	380	91	5.4	8.7	3.8
1150L	**Onion sauce**, *made with whole milk*	Recipe	1.00	419	101	2.8	7.7	6.5
1151L	*made with semi-skimmed milk*	Recipe	1.00	367	88	2.9	7.8	5.0
1152L	**White sauce**, savoury, *made with whole milk*	Recipe	1.00	623	150	4.1	10.1	10.3
1153L	*made with semi-skimmed milk*	Recipe	1.00	535	128	4.3	10.2	7.8
1154L	sweet, *made with whole milk*	Recipe	1.00	714	171	3.8	17.5	9.5
1155L	*made with semi-skimmed milk*	Recipe	1.00	634	151	3.9	17.7	7.2

No.	Food	Labelling information for Group 2 nutrients per 100g food				Additional nutrients and information per 100g food		
		Sugars (actual weight) g	Saturates g	Fibre (Englyst) g	Sodium g	Sodium mg	Starch (actual weight) g	Water g
	Dairy sauces							
1144L	**Bread sauce**, *made with whole milk*	4.5	2.6	0.3	0.5	480	7.3	76.3
1145L	*made with semi-skimmed milk*	4.6	1.4	0.3	0.5	480	7.3	78.1
1146L	**Cheese sauce**, *made with whole milk*	4.1	7.5	0.2	0.5	450	4.2	66.9
1147L	*made with semi-skimmed milk*	4.2	6.3	0.2	0.5	450	4.2	68.7
1148L	**Cheese sauce packet mix**, *made up with whole milk*	5.0	N	N	0.5	460	3.5	77.2
1149L	*made up with semi-skimmed milk*	5.2	N	N	0.5	460	3.5	79.2
1150L	**Onion sauce**, *made with whole milk*	4.5	2.8	0.4	0.4	430	3.2	80.4
1151L	*made with semi-skimmed milk*	4.6	1.8	0.4	0.4	435	3.2	81.7
1152L	**White sauce**, savoury, *made with whole milk*	5.0	4.4	0.2	0.4	400	5.1	73.7
1153L	*made with semi-skimmed milk*	5.1	2.9	0.2	0.4	400	5.1	75.8
1154L	sweet, *made with whole milk*	12.8	4.1	0.2	0.1	110	4.7	68.3
1155L	*made with semi-skimmed milk*	13.0	2.7	0.2	0.1	110	4.7	70.2

Labelling information for Group 1 nutrients per 100g food

No.	Food	Description and main data sources	Edible proportion	Energy kJ	Energy kcal	Protein (N × 6.25) g	Carbohydrate (actual wt.) g	Fat g
Salad sauces, dressings and pickles								
1156L	**Apple chutney**	Recipe	1.00	902	212	1.0	51.6[a]	0.2
1157L	**French dressing**	Recipe	1.00	2676	651	0.4	0.1	72.1
1158L	**Mango chutney**, oily	10 assorted samples	1.00	1252	298	0.4	49.5	10.9
1159L	**Mayonnaise**, retail	6 samples, 5 brands	1.00	2843	691	1.1	1.6	75.6
1160L	**Pickle**, sweet	10 jars, 3 brands, including Branston, Pan Yan	1.00	599	141	0.6	34.0	0.3
1161L	**Salad cream**	3 samples, different brands	1.00	1445	349	1.4	16.1	31.0
1162L	reduced calorie	Analysis and manufacturer's data	1.00	810	196	1.0	9.2	17.2
1163L	**Tomato chutney**	Recipe	1.00	725	171	1.2	40.6[a]	0.4
Non salad sauces								
1164L	**Barbecue sauce**	Ref. Marsh (1980)	1.00	305	72	1.8	12.2	1.8
1165L	**Brown sauce**, *bottled*	6 bottles of different brands	1.00	442	104	1.1	24.9	0
1166L	**Cook-in-sauces**, canned	9 samples, 3 brands; assorted flavours	1.00	183	43	1.1	7.9	0.8
1167L	**Curry sauce**, canned	10 samples, 4 brands; assorted flavours	1.00	326	78	1.5	6.8	5.0
1168L	**Horseradish sauce**	8 samples, 5 brands; creamed and plain samples	1.00	642	154	2.5	17.0	8.4
1169L	**Mint sauce**	8 samples, 4 brands	1.00	382	90	1.6	20.9	Tr
1170L	**Pasta sauce**, tomato based	9 samples, 4 brands; assorted types	1.00	205	49	2.0	6.8	1.5
1171L	**Soy sauce**	Ref. Marsh (1980); dark, thick variety	1.00	289	68	8.7	8.3	0
1172L	**Tomato ketchup**	6 bottles of different brands	1.00	433	102	2.1	23.4	Tr
1173L	**Tomato sauce**	Recipe	1.00	380	91	2.3	8.1[a]	5.5

[a] Including oligosaccharides

No.	Food	Labelling information for Group 2 nutrients per 100g food				Additional nutrients and information per 100g food		
		Sugars (actual weight) g	Saturates g	Fibre (Englyst) g	Sodium g	Sodium mg	Starch (actual weight) g	Water g
	Salad sauces, dressings and pickles							
1156L	**Apple chutney**	50.6[a]	Tr	1.2	0.2	180	0.2	43.5
1157L	**French dressing**	0.1	10.0	0	0.9	930	0	22.8
1158L	**Mango chutney**, oily	49.1	N	0.9	1.1	1090	0.4	34.8
1159L	**Mayonnaise**, retail	1.2	11.1	0	0.5	450	0.4	18.8
1160L	**Pickle**, sweet	32.4	Tr	1.2	1.7	1700	1.6	58.9
1161L	**Salad cream**	16.1	3.9	N	1.0	1040	Tr	47.2
1162L	reduced calorie	9.0	2.5	N	N	N	0.2	N
1163L	**Tomato chutney**	39.9[a]	0.1	1.4	0.1	130	0.1	54.0
	Non salad sauces							
1164L	**Barbecue sauce**	N	0.3	N	0.8	810	N	80.9
1165L	**Brown sauce**, *bottled*	23.0	Tr	0.7	1.0	980	1.9	64.0
1166L	**Cook-in-sauces**, canned	4.9	0.1	N	0.9	940	3.0	87.4
1167L	**Curry sauce**, canned	3.7	N	N	1.0	980	3.1	81.4
1168L	**Horseradish sauce**	14.3	1.1	2.5	0.9	910	2.7	64.0
1169L	**Mint sauce**	20.9	Tr	N	0.7	700	0	68.7
1170L	**Pasta sauce**, tomato based	5.7	0.2	N	0.4	410	1.1	83.9
1171L	**Soy sauce**	N	0	0	5.7	5720	N	67.6
1172L	**Tomato ketchup**	22.4	Tr	0.9	1.1	1120	1.0	64.8
1173L	**Tomato sauce**	3.9[a]	1.8	1.4	0.3	340	3.9	80.3

[a] Not including oligosaccharides

Labelling information for Group 1 nutrients per 100g food

No.	Food	Description and main data sources	Edible proportion	Energy		Protein (N × 6.25)	Carbohydrate (actual wt.)	Fat
				kJ	kcal	g	g	g
Miscellaneous foods								
1174L	**Baking powder**	6 samples of the same brand	1.00	682	160	5.7	34.4	Tr
1175L	**Bovril**	9 jars	1.00	735	173	39.1	2.6	0.7
1176L	**Gelatin**	Literature sources	1.00	1615	380	95.0	0	0
1177L	**Gravy instant granules**	7 samples, 3 brands	1.00	1906	458	4.4	37.0	32.5
1178L	*made up with water*	Calculated from 23.5g granules and 300ml water	1.00	140	34	0.3	2.7	2.4
1179L	**Marmite**	7 jars	1.00	757	178	41.4	1.6	0.7
1180L	**Mustard**, smooth	10 samples, 7 types; English and French	1.00	584	140	7.1	9.4	8.2
1181L	wholegrain	9 samples, 5 brands	1.00	588	141	8.2	4.2	10.2
1182L	**Oxo cubes**	10 samples	1.00	979	231	39.3	10.9	3.4
1183L	**Salt**, block	2 samples	1.00	0	0	0	0	0
1184L	table	2 samples	1.00	0	0	0	0	0
1185L	**Vinegar**[a]	4 samples	1.00	87	21	0.4	0.6	0
1186L	**Water**	Included for recipe calculation	1.00	0	0	0	0	0
1187L	**Yeast**, bakers, *compressed*	Literature sources	1.00	246	58	12.6	1.0	0.4
1188L	dried	Literature sources	1.00	781	184	39.5	3.2	1.5

[a] Contains 4.8ml acetic acid per 100ml

		Labelling information for Group 2 nutrients per 100g food				Additional nutrients and information per 100g food		
No.	Food	Sugars (actual weight) g	Saturates g	Fibre (Englyst) g	Sodium g	Sodium mg	Starch (actual weight) g	Water g
	Miscellaneous foods							
1174L	**Baking powder**	Tr	0	0	11.8	11800[a]	34.4	6.3
1175L	**Bovril**	0	N	0	4.8	4800	2.6	38.7
1176L	**Gelatin**	0	0	0	N	N	0	13.0
1177L	**Gravy instant granules**	1.3	N	Tr	6.3	6330	35.7	4.0
1178L	*made up with water*	0.1	N	Tr	0.5	460	2.6	93.0
1179L	**Marmite**	0	N	0	4.5	4500	1.6	25.4
1180L	**Mustard**, smooth	7.7	0.5	N	3.0	2950	1.7	63.7
1181L	wholegrain	3.9	0.6	4.9	1.6	1620	0.3	65.0
1182L	**Oxo cubes**	0	N	0	10.3	10300	10.9	9.1
1183L	**Salt**, block	0	0	0	38.7	38700	0	0.2
1184L	table	0	0	0	38.9	38850	0	Tr
1185L	**Vinegar**	0.6	0	0	Tr	20	0	N
1186L	**Water**	0	0	0	N	N	0	100.0
1187L	**Yeast**, bakers, *compressed*	Tr	N	N	Tr	16	1.0	70.0
1188L	dried	Tr	N	N	0.1	50	3.2	5.0

[a] The sodium content will depend on the brand

The

Appendices

ALTERNATIVE AND TAXONOMIC NAMES

- Foods are listed below in the same order as in the main tables.
- The alternative names listed in the left-hand column below are those that were most frequently encountered during data collection and are included to help in identifying foods. It is important to recognise that in some cases such names may be used for more than one food and that all such usages may not appear in this list.
- To see if a name is listed, the food index should be consulted first. If the term is included as an alternative name, a cross reference entry indicates the food name to which it refers. This allows all alternatives to be listed together.
- Taxonomic names listed in the right-hand column refer as specifically as possible to the data used. Where two or more taxonomic names are listed, the data are representative of a mixture of these varieties.
- The abbreviation 'var' is used to indicate the specific variety or unspecified variety(ies); 'sp' and 'spp' are used to indicate that one or more than one species of the specified Genus is included.

	Alternative names	Food names	Taxonomic names
Cereals			
		Oats	*Avena sativa*
		Rye	*Secale cereale*
		Sago	*Metroxylon* spp
		Tapioca	*Manihot esculenta*
		Wheat	*Triticum aestivum*
		Rice	*Oryza sativa*
		Pasta wheat	*Triticum durum*
Meat			
		Beef	*Bos taurus*
		Lamb	*Ovis aries*
		Pork	*Sus scrofa*
		Veal	*Bos taurus*
Poultry			
		Chicken	*Gallus domesticus*

	Alternative names	Food names	Taxonomic names
		Duck	*Anas platyrhynchos*
		Goose	*Anser anser*
		Grouse	*Lagopus scroticus*
		Partridge	*Perdix perdix*
		Pheasant	*Phasianus colchicus*
		Pigeon	*Columba* spp
		Turkey	*Meleagris gallopavo*
	Game		
		Hare	*Lepus europaeus*
		Rabbit	*Lepus cuniculus*
		Venison	*Cervus* spp
Fish			
	White fish		
		Cod	*Gadus morhua*
	Rock eel Rock salmon	**Dogfish**	Probably *Squalus acanthias*
		Haddock	*Melanogrammus aeglefinus*
		Halibut	*Hippoglossus hippoglossus*
		Lemon sole	*Microstomus kitt*
		Plaice	*Pleuronectes platessa*
	Coalfish Coley	**Saithe**	*Pollachius virens*
		Skate **Whiting**	*Raja* spp *Merlangius merlangus*
	Fatty fish		
		Anchovies	*Engraulis encrasicholus*
		Herring	*Clupea harengus*

Alternative names	Food names	Taxonomic names
	Kipper	*Clupea harengus*
	Mackerel	*Scomber scombrus*
	Pilchards	*Sardinops sagex ocellata*
	Salmon, Atlantic red	*Salmo salar* *Oncorhynchus nerka*
	Sardines	*Sardina pilchardus*
	Trout, brown	*Salmo trutta*
	Tuna	*Euthynnus* sp *Katsuwonus pelamis*
	Whitebait	Young of *Clupea harengus* and *Sprattus sprattus*
Crustacea		
	Crab	*Cancer pagurus*
	Lobster	*Homarus vulgaris*
	Prawns	*Paleamon serratus*
	Scampi	*Nephrops norvegicus*
	Shrimps	*Crangon crangon* *Pandalus montagui* *Pandalus borealis*
Molluscs		
	Cockles	*Cardium edule*
	Mussels	*Mytilus edulis*
	Squid	*Loligo vulgaris*
	Whelks	*Buccinum undatum*
	Winkles	*Littorina littorea*

Vegetables

Alternative names	Food names	Taxonomic names
Potatoes		
Aloo Batata	**Potatoes**	*Solanum tuberosum*

Alternative names	Food names	Taxonomic names
Beans and lentils		
Adzuki beans	**Aduki beans**	*Vigna angularis*
	Baked beans	*Phaseolus vulgaris* (navy beans)
	Beansprouts, mung	*Phaseolus aureus*
Alad Urad	**Black gram**, urad gram	*Vigna mungo*
Blackeye peas Cowpeas Chori Lobia	**Blackeye beans**	*Vigna unguiculata*
	Broad beans	*Vicia faba*
Lima beans	**Butter beans**	*Phaseolus lunatus*
Channa Common gram Garbanzo Yellow gram	**Chick peas**	*Cicer arietinum*
Fansi	**Green beans/French beans**	*Phaseolus vulgaris*
Continental lentils Masur	**Lentils**, green and brown	*Lens esculenta*
Masoor dahl Masur dahl	**Lentils**, red	*Lens esculenta*
Green gram Golden gram Moong beans	**Mung beans**	
	Red kidney beans	*Phaseolus vulgaris*
	Runner beans	*Phaseolus coccineus*
	Soya beans	*Glycine max*
Peas		
Snowpeas	**Mange-tout peas**	*Pisum sativum* var *macrocarpum*

Alternative names	Food names	Taxonomic names
Badla Mattar Vatana	**Peas**	*Pisum sativum*
Other vegetables		
	Asparagus	*Asparagus officinalis* var *altilis*
Baingan Brinjal Eggplant Jew's apple Ringana	**Aubergine**	*Solanum melongena* var ovigerum
	Beetroot	*Beta vulgaris*
Calabrese	**Broccoli**, green	*Brassica oleracea* var *botrytis*
Chote bund gobhi Nhanu kobi	**Brussels sprouts**	*Brassica oleracea* var *gemmifera*
Bund gobhi Kobi	**Cabbage**	*Brassica oleracea*
	Cabbage, January King	*Brassica oleracea* var *capitata*
	Cabbage, white	*Brassica oleracea* var
Gajjar	**Carrots**	*Daucus carota*
Pangoli Phool gobhi	**Cauliflower**	*Brassica oleracea* var *botrytis*
	Celery	*Apium graveolens* var *dulce*
Belgian chicory Witloof	**Chicory**	*Cichorium intybus*
Zucchini	**Courgette**	*Cucurbita pepo*
Kakdi Khira	**Cucumber**	*Cucumis sativus*
Borecole Kale	**Curly kale**	*Brassica oleracea* var *acephala*
	Fennel, Florence	*Foeniculum vulgare* var *dulce*

Alternative names	Food names	Taxonomic names
Lassan Lehsan	**Garlic**	*Allium sativum*
	Gherkins	*Cucumis sativus*
Bitter gourd Balsam apple	**Gourd**, karela	*Momordica charantia*
	Leeks	*Allium ampeloprasum* var *porrum*
	Lettuce	*Lactuca sativa*
	Marrow	*Cucurbita pepo*
	Mushrooms, common	*Agaricus campestris*
	Mustard and cress	*Brassica* and *Lepidium* spp
Bhendi Bhinda Bhindi Gumbo Lady's fingers	**Okra**	*Hibiscus esculentus*
Dungli Kanda Piyaz	**Onions**	*Allium cepa*
	Parsnip	*Pastinaca sativa*
Pimento	**Peppers**, capsicum, chilli, green	*Capsicum annuum*
Bell peppers Motamircha Simla mirch Sweet peppers	**Peppers**, capsicum (green/red)	*Capsicum annuum* var *grossum*
	Plantain	*Musa paradisiaca*
Kumra Lal kaddu Lal phupala	**Pumpkin**	*Cucurbita* sp

Alternative names	Food names	Taxonomic names
	Quorn, myco-protein	*Fusarium graminearum*
	Radish, red	*Raphanus sativus*
Palak Saag	**Spinach**	*Spinacia oleracea*
	Spring greens	*Brassica oleracea* var
	Spring onions	*Allium cepa*
Neeps (England) Rutabaga Yellow turnip	**Swede**	*Brassica napus* var *napobrassica*
Shakaria Yam (USA)	**Sweet potato**	*Ipomoea batatas*
	Sweetcorn	*Zea mays*
	Tomatoes	*Lycopersicon esculentum*
Neeps (Scotland) Shalgam	**Turnip**	*Brassica rapa* var *rapifera*
	Watercress	*Nasturtium officinale*
	Yam	*Dioscorea* sp
Herbs and spices		
	Cinnamon	*Cinnamomum verum* *Cinnamomum aromaticum*
	Mint	*Mentha spicata*
	Mustard	*Sinapis alba* *Brassica hirta*
	Nutmeg	*Myristica fragrans*
	Paprika	*Capsicum annuum*
	Parsley	*Petroselinum crispum*
	Pepper, black	*Piper nigrum*
	Pepper, white	*Piper nigrum*

Alternative names	Food names	Taxonomic names
	Rosemary	*Rosmarinus officinalis*
	Sage	*Salvia officinalis*
	Thyme	*Thymus vulgaris*

Fruit

Alternative names	Food names	Taxonomic names
Tarel	**Apples**	*Malus pumila*
	Apricots	*Prunus armeniaca*
	Avocado	*Persea americana*
Kula	**Bananas**	*Musa* spp
	Blackberries	*Rubus ulmifolius*
	Blackcurrants	*Ribes nigrum*
	Cherries	*Prunus avium*
	Clementines	*Citrus reticulata* var *Clementine*
	Currants	*Vitis vinifera*
	Damsons	*Prunus domestica* subsp *institia*
	Dates	*Phoenix dactylifera*
Gullar	**Figs**	*Ficus carica*
	Gooseberries	*Ribes grossularia*
	Grapefruit	*Citrus paradisi*
	Grapes	*Vitis vinifera*
	Guava	*Psidium guajava*
Chinese gooseberry	**Kiwi fruit**	*Actinidia chinensis*
	Lemons	*Citrus limon*
Chinese cherry Lichee Lichi Litchee Litchi	**Lychees**	*Litchi chinensis*

Alternative names	Food names	Taxonomic names
	Mandarin oranges	*Citrus reticulata*
	Mangoes	*Mangifera indica*
	Melon, Canteloupe-type	*Cucumis melo* var *cantaloupensis*
	Melon, Galia	*Cucumis melo* var *reticulata*
	Melon, Honeydew	*Cucumis melo* var *indorus*
	Melon, watermelon	*Citrullus lanatus*
	Nectarines	*Prunus persica* var *nectarina*
	Olives	*Olea europaea*
	Oranges	*Citrus sinensis*
Purple grenadillo	**Passion fruit**	*Passiflora edulis f edulis*
Papai Papaya	**Paw-paw**	*Carica papaya*
	Peaches	*Prunus persica*
	Pears	*Pyrus communis*
	Pineapple	*Ananas comosus*
	Plums	*Prunus domestica* subsp *domestica*
	Prunes	*Prunus domestica*
	Raisins	*Vitis vinifera*
	Raspberries	*Rubus idaeus*
	Rhubarb	*Rheum rhaponticum*
	Satsumas	*Citrus reticulata*
	Strawberries	*Fragaria* sp
	Sultanas	*Vitis vinifera*
	Tangerines	*Citrus reticulata*

Alternative names	Food names	Taxonomic names
Nuts and seeds		
Badam	**Almonds**	*Prunus amygdalus*
	Brazil nuts	*Bertholletia excelsa*
Kaju	**Cashew nuts**	*Anacardium occidentale*
	Chestnuts	*Castanea vulgaris*
	Coconut	*Cocos nucifera*
	Hazelnuts	*Corylus avellana* *Corylus maxima*
Queensland nuts	**Macadamia nuts**	*Macadamia integrifolia* *Macadamia tetraphylla*
Groundnuts Monkey nuts	**Peanuts**	*Arachis hypogaea*
Hickory nuts	**Pecan nuts**	*Carya illinoensis*
Indian nuts Pignolias Pine kernels	**Pine nuts**	*Pinus pinea* *Pinus edulis*
Pista	**Pistachio nuts**	*Pistacia vera*
Benniseed Gingelly Til	**Sesame seeds**	*Sesamum indicum*
	Sunflower seeds	*Helianthus annuus*
Akhrot Madeira nuts	**Walnuts**	*Juglans regia*

REFERENCES TO THE TABLES

Cashel, K., English, R. and Lewis, J. (1989) *Composition of Foods, Australia. Volume 1.* Department of Community Services and Health, Canberra

Gopalan, C., Rama Sastri, B. V. and Balasubramanian, S. C. (1980) *Nutritive value of Indian foods,* National Institute of Nutrition, Indian Council of Medical Research, Hyderabad

Haytowitz, D. B. and Matthews, R. H. (1984) *Composition of foods: vegetables and vegetable products, raw, processed and prepared.* Agriculture Handbook No. 8-11, US Department of Agriculture, Washington DC

Haytowitz, D. B. and Matthews, R. H. (1986) *Composition of foods: legumes and legume products, raw, processed and prepared.* Agriculture Handbook No. 8-16, US Department of Agriculture, Washington DC

McCarthy, M. A. and Matthews, R. H. (1984) *Composition of foods: nut and seed products, raw, processed and prepared.* Agriculture Handbook No. 8-12, US Department of Agriculture, Washington DC

Marsh, A. C. (1980) *Composition of foods: soups, sauces, and gravies, raw, processed and prepared.* Agriculture Handbook No. 8-6, US Department of Agriculture, Washington DC

Marsh, A. C., Moss, M. K. and Murphy, E. W. (1977) *Composition of foods: spices and herbs, raw, processed and prepared.* Agriculture Handbook No. 8-2, US Department of Agriculture, Washington DC

Pellet, P. L. and Shadarevian, S. (1970) *Food composition tables for use in the Middle East.* American University of Beirut, Beirut

Posati, L. P. and Orr, M. L. (1976) *Composition of foods: dairy and egg products, raw, processed and prepared.* Agriculture Handbook No. 8-1, US Department of Agriculture, Washington DC

Wharton, P. A., Eaton, P. M. and Day, K. C. (1983) Sorrento Asian food tables: food tables, recipes and customs of mothers attending Sorrento Maternity Hospital, Birmingham, England. *Hum. Nutr. : Appl. Nutr.,* **37A**, 378–402

Wiles, S. J., Nettleton, P. A., Black. A. E. and Paul, A. A. (1980) The nutrient composition of some cooked dishes eaten in Britain: A supplementary food composition table. *J. Hum. Nutr.* **34**, 189–223

Wu Leung, W. T., Busson, F. and Jardin, C. (1968) *Food composition table for use in Africa.* Food and Agriculture Organization and US Department of Health, Education and Welfare, Bethesda

Wu Leung, W. T., Butrum, R. R., Chang, F. H., Narayana Rao, M. and Polacchi, W. (1972) *Food composition table for use in East Asia.* Food and Agriculture Organization and US Department of Health, Education and Welfare, Bethesda

FOOD INDEX

- Foods are indexed by their food number and **not** by page number.
- Cross references in this index give access to the individual foods items through this index and to alternative names given in the Alternative and Taxonomic Names list on pages 181–190.

Aduki beans, dried, boiled in unsalted water 693L
Aduki beans, dried, raw 692L
Advocaat 1119L
Adzuki beans see **Aduki beans**
Akhrot see **Walnuts**
Alad see **Black gram**, urad gram
Ale, brown, bottled 1098L
Ale, pale, bottled 1100L
Ale, strong 1103L
All-Bran 65L
Almonds 972L
Almonds, weighed with shells 973L
Aloo see **Old potatoes**
Anchovies, canned in oil, drained 609L
Apples, cooking, raw, peeled 852L
Apples, cooking, stewed with sugar 854L
Apples, cooking, stewed without sugar 855L
Apples, cooking, weighed with skin and core 853L
Apples, eating, average, raw 856L
Apples, eating, average, raw, peeled 858L
Apples, eating, average, raw, peeled, weighed with skin and core 859L
Apples, eating, average, raw, weighed with core 857L
Apple chutney 1156L
Apple juice, unsweetened 1087L
Apricots, canned in juice 864L
Apricots, canned in syrup 863L
Apricots, raw 860L
Apricots, raw, weighed with stones 861L
Apricots, ready-to-eat 862L
Arctic roll 262L
Asparagus, boiled in salted water 738L
Asparagus, raw 737L
Aubergine, fried in corn oil 740L
Aubergine, raw 739L
Avocado, average 865L
Avocado, average, weighed with skin and stone 866L

Baby sweetcorn, canned, drained 823L
Bacon, collar joint, lean and fat, boiled 342L
Bacon, collar joint, lean and fat, raw 341L
Bacon, collar joint, lean only, boiled 343L
Bacon, fat only, cooked, average 339L
Bacon, fat only, raw, average 338L
Bacon, gammon joint, lean and fat, boiled 345L
Bacon, gammon joint, lean and fat, raw 344L
Bacon, gammon joint, lean only, boiled 346L
Bacon, gammon rasher, lean and fat, grilled 347L
Bacon, gammon rasher, lean only, grilled 348L
Bacon, lean only, raw, average 340L
Bacon, rasher, lean and fat, back, fried 353L
Bacon, rasher, lean and fat, back, grilled 357L
Bacon, rasher, lean and fat, back, raw 349L
Bacon, rasher, lean and fat, middle, fried 354L
Bacon, rasher, lean and fat, middle, grilled 358L
Bacon, rasher, lean and fat, middle, raw 350L
Bacon, rasher, lean and fat, streaky, fried 355L
Bacon, rasher, lean and fat, streaky, grilled 359L
Bacon, rasher, lean and fat, streaky, raw 351L
Bacon, rasher, lean only, average, fried 352L
Bacon, rasher, lean only, average, grilled 356L
Badam see **Almonds**
Badla see **Peas**
Baingan see **Aubergine**
Baked beans, canned in tomato sauce 694L
Baked beans, canned in tomato sauce, reduced sugar 695L
Bakers yeast, compressed 1187L
Bakers yeast, dried 1188L
Baking powder 1174L
Balsam apple see **Gourd**, karela
Bananas 867L
Bananas, weighed with skin 868L
Barbecue sauce 1164L
Batata see **Old potatoes**
Bath buns see **Chelsea buns**
Battenburg cake 109L
Beans, aduki see **Aduki beans**
Beans, baked see **Baked beans**
Beans, blackeye see **Blackeye beans**
Beans, broad 702L

Beans, butter 703L
Beans, green see **Green beans/French beans**
Beans, French see **Green beans/French beans**
Beans, mung see **Mung beans**
Beans, red kidney see **Red kidney beans**
Beans, runner see **Runner beans**
Beans, soya see **Soya beans**
Beansprouts, mung, raw 696L
Beansprouts, mung, stir-fried in blended oil 697L
Beef, brisket, lean and fat, boiled 365L
Beef, brisket, lean and fat, raw 364L
Beef, fat only, cooked, average 362L
Beef, fat only, raw, average 361L
Beef, forerib, lean and fat, raw 366L
Beef, forerib, lean and fat, roast 367L
Beef, forerib, lean only, roast 368L
Beef, lean only, raw, average 363L
Beef, mince, raw 369L
Beef, mince, stewed 370L
Beef, rump steak, lean and fat, fried 372L
Beef, rump steak, lean and fat, grilled 373L
Beef, rump steak, lean and fat, raw 371L
Beef, rump steak, lean only, fried 374L
Beef, rump steak, lean only, grilled 375L
Beef, salted, dried, raw 377L
Beef, salted, fat removed, raw 376L
Beef, silverside, lean and fat, salted, boiled 378L
Beef, silverside, lean only, salted, boiled 379L
Beef, sirloin, lean and fat, raw 380L
Beef, sirloin, lean and fat, roast 381L
Beef, sirloin, lean only, roast 382L
Beef, stewing steak, lean and fat, raw 383L
Beef, stewing steak, lean and fat, stewed 384L
Beef, topside, lean and fat, raw 385L
Beef, topside, lean and fat, roast 386L
Beef, topside, lean only, roast 387L
Beef chow mein 539L
Beef curry, retail 540L
Beef curry, with rice 541L
Beef dripping 317L
Beef kheema 542L
Beef koftas 543L
Beef sausages, fried 525L
Beef sausages, grilled 526L
Beef sausages, raw 524L
Beef steak pudding 544L
Beef stew 545L
Beefburgers, frozen, fried 504L
Beefburgers, frozen, raw 503L
Beer, bitter, canned 1094L
Beer, bitter, draught 1095L
Beer, bitter, keg 1096L
Beer, mild, draught 1097L
Beetroot, boiled in salted water 742L
Beetroot, pickled, drained 743L
Beetroot, raw 741L
Belgian chicory see **Chicory**
Bell peppers see **Peppers**, capsicum, green
Belly rashers pork, lean and fat, grilled 418L
Belly rashers pork, lean and fat, raw 417L
Benniseed see **Sesame seeds**
Bhendi see **Okra**
Bhinda see **Okra**
Bhindi see **Okra**
Biriani, mutton 559L
Biscuits, chocolate, full coated 93L
Biscuits, digestive, chocolate 96L
Biscuits, digestive, plain 97L
Biscuits, ginger 99L
Biscuits, homemade, creaming method 100L
Biscuits, sandwich 103L
Biscuits, semi-sweet 104L
Biscuits, short-sweet 105L
Biscuits, wafer, filled 107L
Bitter beer, canned 1094L
Bitter beer, draught 1095L
Bitter beer, keg 1096L
Bitter gourd see **Gourd**, karela
Black gram, urad gram, dried, boiled in unsalted water 699L
Black gram, urad gram, dried, raw 698L
Black pepper 847L
Black pudding, fried 505L
Black treacle 1013L
Blackberries, raw 869L
Blackberries, stewed with sugar 870L
Blackberries, stewed without sugar 871L
Blackcurrant pie, pastry top and bottom 150L
Blackcurrants, canned in juice 874L
Blackcurrants, canned in syrup 875L
Blackcurrants, raw 872L
Blackcurrants, stewed with sugar 873L
Blackeye beans, dried, boiled in unsalted water 701L
Blackeye beans, dried, raw 700L
Blackeye peas see **Blackeye beans**
Blended vegetable oil, average 333L
Boiled eggs, chicken 293L
Boiled sweets 1025L
Bolognese sauce 546L
Bombay Mix 1034L
Borecole see **Curly kale**
Bounty bar 1014L
Bournvita powder 1043L

Bournvita powder, made up with semi-skimmed milk 1045L
Bournvita powder, made up with whole milk 1044L
Bovril 1175L
Bran Flakes 66L
Bran, wheat 1L
Brandy 1122L
Brandy, cherry 1120L
Brawn 506L
Brazil nuts 974L
Brazil nuts, weighed with shells 975L
Bread, brown, average 33L
Bread, brown, toasted 34L
Bread, currant 37L
Bread, currant, toasted 38L
Bread, granary 39L
Bread, Hovis, average 40L
Bread, Hovis, toasted 41L
Bread, malt 42L
Bread, naan 43L
Bread, pitta, white 45L
Bread, rye 46L
Bread, Vitbe, average 47L
Bread, white, average 48L
Bread, white, French stick 53L
Bread, white, fried in blended oil 50L
Bread, white, fried in lard 51L
Bread, white, sliced 49L
Bread, white, toasted 52L
Bread, white, 'with added fibre' 54L
Bread, white, 'with added fibre', toasted 55L
Bread, wholemeal, average 56L
Bread, wholemeal, toasted 57L
Bread pudding 151L
Bread sauce, made with semi-skimmed milk 1145L
Bread sauce, made with whole milk 1144L
Breaded chicken, fried in vegetable oil 444L
Breast lamb, lean and fat, raw 391L
Breast lamb, lean and fat, roast 392L
Breast lamb, lean only, roast 393L
Brie cheese 226L
Brinjal see **Aubergine**
Brisket beef, lean and fat, boiled 365L
Brisket beef, lean and fat, raw 364L
Broad beans, frozen, boiled in unsalted water 702L
Broccoli, green, boiled in unsalted water 745L
Broccoli, green, raw 744L
Brown ale, bottled 1098L
Brown bread, average 33L
Brown bread, toasted 34L
Brown chapati flour 2L
Brown flour 12L
Brown lentils see **Lentils**, green and brown
Brown rice, boiled 19L
Brown rice, raw 18L
Brown rolls, crusty 58L
Brown rolls, soft 59L
Brown sauce, bottled 1165L
Brown trout, steamed 629L
Brown trout, steamed, weighed with bones 630L
Brussels sprouts, boiled in unsalted water 747L
Brussels sprouts, frozen, boiled in unsalted water 748L
Brussels sprouts, raw 746L
Build-up powder 1046L
Build-up powder, made up with semi-skimmed milk 1048L
Build-up powder, made up with skimmed milk 1049L
Build-up powder, made up with whole milk 1047L
Bund gobhi see **Cabbage**
Buns, Chelsea 130L
Buns, currant 133L
Buns, Hamburger 61L
Buns, hot cross 141L
Butter 306L
Butter beans, canned, drained 703L
Butter ghee 335L
Butterhead lettuce, raw 778L

Cabbage, boiled in unsalted water, average 750L
Cabbage, January King, boiled in salted water 752L
Cabbage, January King, raw 751L
Cabbage, raw, average 749L
Cabbage, white, raw 753L
Cake mix, made up 110L
Cake, Battenburg 109L
Cake, Eccles 138L
Cake, fruit, plain, retail 113L
Cake, fruit, rich 114L
Cake, fruit, rich, iced 115L
Cake, fruit, wholemeal 116L
Cake, Madeira 118L
Cake, sponge 119L
Cake, sponge, fatless 120L
Cake, sponge, jam filled 121L
Cake, sponge, with butter icing 122L
Cakes, crispie 111L
Cakes, fancy iced, individual 112L
Calabrese see **Broccoli**, green
Calf liver, fried 484L
Calf liver, raw 483L
Camembert cheese 227L
Candied popcorn 1030L
Canned anchovies, in oil, drained 609L

Canned apricots, in juice 864L
Canned apricots, in syrup 863L
Canned baby sweetcorn, drained 823L
Canned baked beans in tomato sauce 694L
Canned baked beans in tomato sauce, reduced sugar 695L
Canned blackcurrants, in juice 874L
Canned blackcurrants, in syrup 875L
Canned butter beans, drained 703L
Canned carrots, drained 758L
Canned cherries, in syrup 878L
Canned chick peas, drained 706L
Canned cook-in-sauces 1166L
Canned crab 636L
Canned cream of chicken soup, condensed 1125L
Canned cream of chicken soup, condensed, ready to serve 1126L
Canned cream of chicken soup, ready to serve 1124L
Canned cream of mushroom soup, ready to serve 1127L
Canned cream of tomato soup, condensed 1129L
Canned cream of tomato soup, condensed ready to serve 1130L
Canned cream of tomato soup, ready to serve 1128L
Canned curry sauce 1167L
Canned custard 278L
Canned fruit cocktail, in juice 891L
Canned fruit cocktail, in syrup 892L
Canned gooseberries, dessert, in syrup 898L
Canned grapefruit, in juice 901L
Canned grapefruit, in syrup 902L
Canned guava, in syrup 907L
Canned ham 360L
Canned ham and pork, chopped 513L
Canned low calorie soup 1131L
Canned luncheon meat 515L
Canned lychees, in syrup 913L
Canned mandarin oranges, in juice 914L
Canned mandarin oranges, in syrup 915L
Canned mangoes, in syrup 918L
Canned mushy peas 728L
Canned new potatoes, drained 663L
Canned oxtail soup, ready to serve 1132L
Canned paw-paw, in juice 937L
Canned peaches, in juice 940L
Canned peaches, in syrup 941L
Canned pears, in juice 945L
Canned pears, in syrup 946L
Canned peas, drained 733L
Canned pilchards, in tomato sauce 621L
Canned pineapple, in juice 948L
Canned pineapple, in syrup 949L
Canned plums, in syrup 954L
Canned pork and ham, chopped 513L
Canned prunes, in juice 955L
Canned prunes, in syrup 956L
Canned processed peas, drained 736L
Canned raspberries, in syrup 960L
Canned red kidney beans, drained 718L
Canned rhubarb, in syrup 964L
Canned rice pudding 287L
Canned salmon 625L
Canned sardines, in oil, drained 628L
Canned sardines, in tomato sauce 627L
Canned shrimps, drained 643L
Canned stewed steak, with gravy 536L
Canned strawberries, in syrup 968L
Canned sweetcorn kernels, drained 824L
Canned tomatoes, whole contents 832L
Canned tongue 537L
Canned tuna, in brine, drained 632L
Canned tuna, in oil, drained 631L
Canned vegetable soup, ready to serve 1133L
Canteloupe 919L
Canteloupe, weighed with skin 920L
Capsicum peppers, chilli, green, raw 801L
Capsicum peppers, green, boiled in salted water 803L
Capsicum peppers, green, raw 802L
Capsicum peppers, red, boiled in salted water 805L
Capsicum peppers, red, raw 804L
Carrots, canned, drained 758L
Carrots, old, boiled in unsalted water 755L
Carrots, old, raw 754L
Carrots, young, boiled in unsalted water 757L
Carrots, young, raw 756L
Cashew nuts, roasted and salted 976L
Cauliflower cheese 166L
Cauliflower, boiled in unsalted water 760L
Cauliflower, raw 759L
Celery, boiled in salted water 762L
Celery, raw 761L
Channa see **Chick peas**, whole
Channel Island milk, semi-skimmed, UHT 197L
Channel Island milk, whole, pasteurised 194L
Channel Island milk, whole, pasteurised, summer 195L
Channel Island milk, whole, pasteurised, winter 196L
Chapati flour, brown 2L
Chapati flour, white 3L
Chapatis, made with fat 35L
Chapatis, made without fat 36L
Cheddar cheese, average 228L
Cheddar cheese, vegetarian 229L
Cheddar-type cheese, reduced fat 230L
Cheese, Brie 226L

Cheese, Camembert 227L
Cheese, Cheddar, average 228L
Cheese, Cheddar, vegetarian 229L
Cheese, Cheddar-type, reduced fat 230L
Cheese, cottage, plain 232L
Cheese, cottage, plain, reduced fat 234L
Cheese, cottage, plain, with additions 233L
Cheese, cream 235L
Cheese, Danish blue 236L
Cheese, Edam 237L
Cheese, Feta 238L
Cheese, Gouda 243L
Cheese, hard, average 244L
Cheese, Lymeswold 245L
Cheese, Parmesan 247L
Cheese, processed, plain 248L
Cheese, soft, full fat 242L
Cheese, soft, medium fat 246L
Cheese, Stilton, blue 249L
Cheese, white, average 250L
Cheese and egg quiche 303L
Cheese and egg quiche, wholemeal 304L
Cheese omelette 302L
Cheese sauce packet mix, made up with semi-skimmed milk 1149L
Cheese sauce packet mix, made up with whole milk 1148L
Cheese sauce, made with semi-skimmed milk 1147L
Cheese sauce, made with whole milk 1146L
Cheese spread, plain 231L
Cheesecake, frozen 274L
Chelsea buns 130L
Cherries, canned in syrup 878L
Cherries, glacé 879L
Cherries, raw 876L
Cherries, raw, weighed with stones 877L
Cherry brandy 1120L
Cherry pie filling 880L
Chestnuts 977L
Chick peas, canned, drained 706L
Chick peas, whole, dried, boiled in unsalted water 705L
Chick peas, whole, dried, raw 704L
Chicken, boiled, dark meat 437L
Chicken, boiled, light meat 436L
Chicken, boiled, meat only 435L
Chicken, breaded, fried in vegetable oil 444L
Chicken, dark meat, raw 434L
Chicken, leg quarter, roast, meat only, weighed with bone 443L
Chicken, light meat, raw 433L
Chicken, meat and skin, raw 432L
Chicken, meat only, raw 431L
Chicken, roast, dark meat 441L
Chicken, roast, light meat 440L
Chicken, roast, meat and skin 439L
Chicken, roast, meat only 438L
Chicken, wing quarter, roast, meat only, weighed with bone 442L
Chicken curry, retail 549L
Chicken curry, with bone 547L
Chicken curry, with rice 550L
Chicken curry, without bone 548L
Chicken liver, fried 486L
Chicken liver, raw 485L
Chicken noodle soup, dried 1134L
Chicken noodle soup, dried, ready to serve 1135L
Chicken soup, cream of, canned, ready to serve 1124L
Chicken soup, cream of, condensed, canned 1125L
Chicken soup, cream of, condensed, canned, ready to serve 1126L
Chicory, raw 763L
Chilli con carne 551L
Chilli peppers, green, raw 801L
Chilli powder 838L
Chinese cherry see **Lychees**
Chinese gooseberry see **Kiwi fruit**
Chips, fine cut, frozen, fried in blended oil 684L
Chips, fine cut, frozen, fried in corn oil 685L
Chips, fine cut, frozen, fried in dripping 686L
Chips, French fries, retail 680L
Chips, homemade, fried in blended oil 674L
Chips, homemade, fried in corn oil 675L
Chips, homemade, fried in dripping 676L
Chips, oven, frozen, baked 687L
Chips, retail, fried in blended oil 677L
Chips, retail, fried in dripping 678L
Chips, retail, fried in vegetable oil 679L
Chips, straight cut, frozen, fried in blended oil 681L
Chips, straight cut, frozen, fried in corn oil 682L
Chips, straight cut, frozen, fried in dripping 683L
Choc ice 263L
Chocolate, milk 1015L
Chocolate, plain 1016L
Chocolate, white 1017L
Chocolate biscuits, full coated 93L
Chocolate digestive biscuits 96L
Chocolate mousse 285L
Chocolate nut spread 999L
Chocolate nut sundae 264L
Chocolate Swiss rolls, individual 123L
Chocolate, drinking, made up with semi-skimmed milk 1066L
Chocolate, drinking, made up with whole milk 1065L

Chocolate, drinking, powder 1064L
Chocolates, fancy and filled 1018L
Chopped ham and pork, canned 513L
Chops, lamb, loin, lean and fat, grilled 395L
Chops, lamb, loin, lean and fat, grilled, weighed with bone 396L
Chops, lamb, loin, lean and fat, raw 394L
Chops, lamb, loin, lean only, grilled 397L
Chops, lamb, loin, lean only, grilled, weighed with fat and bone 398L
Chops, pork, loin, lean and fat, grilled 420L
Chops, pork, loin, lean and fat, grilled, weighed with bone 421L
Chops, pork, loin, lean and fat, raw 419L
Chops, pork, loin, lean only, grilled 422L
Chops, pork, loin, lean only, grilled, weighed with fat and bone 423L
Chori see **Blackeye beans**
Chote bund gobhi see **Brussels sprouts**
Chow mein, beef 539L
Christmas pudding, homemade 152L
Christmas pudding, retail 153L
Chutney, apple 1156L
Chutney, mango, oily 1158L
Chutney, tomato 1163L
Cider, dry 1104L
Cider, sweet 1105L
Cider, vintage 1106L
Cinnamon, ground 839L
Clementines 881L
Clementines, weighed with peel and pips 882L
Coalfish see **Saithe**
Coca-cola 1080L
Cockles, boiled 644L
Cocktail onions, drained 798L
Coco Pops 67L
Cocoa powder 1050L
Cocoa powder, made up with semi-skimmed milk 1052L
Cocoa powder, made up with whole milk 1051L
Coconut oil 320L
Coconut, creamed block 978L
Coconut, desiccated 979L
Cod, dried, salted, boiled 572L
Cod, fillets, baked 564L
Cod, fillets, baked, weighed with bones and skin 565L
Cod, fillets, poached 566L
Cod, fillets, poached, weighed with bones and skin 567L
Cod, fillets raw 563L
Cod, in batter, fried in blended oil 570L
Cod, in batter, fried in dripping 571L
Cod, steaks, frozen, grilled 569L
Cod, steaks,frozen, raw 568L
Cod liver oil 321L
Cod roe, hard, fried 657L
Coffee and chicory essence 1055L
Coffee, infusion 1053L
Coffee, powder, instant 1054L
Coffeemate 1056L
Coley see **Saithe**
Collar joint bacon, lean and fat, boiled 342L
Collar joint bacon, lean and fat, raw 341L
Collar joint bacon, lean only, boiled 343L
Colostrum human milk 205L
Common gram see **Chick peas**, whole
Common Sense Oat Bran Flakes 68L
Complan powder, savoury 1057L
Complan powder, savoury, made up with water 1058L
Complan powder, sweet 1059L
Complan powder, sweet, made up with semi-skimmed milk 1062L
Complan powder, sweet, made up with skimmed milk 1063L
Complan powder, sweet, made up with water 1060L
Complan powder, sweet, made up with whole milk 1061L
Compound cooking fat 316L
Condensed cream of chicken soup, canned 1125L
Condensed cream of chicken soup, canned, ready to serve 1126L
Condensed cream of tomato soup, canned 1129L
Condensed cream of tomato soup, canned, ready to serve 1130L
Condensed milk, skimmed, sweetened 198L
Condensed milk, whole, sweetened 199L
Continental lentils see **Lentils**, green and brown
Cook-in-sauces, canned 1166L
Cooking apples, raw, peeled 852L
Cooking apples, stewed with sugar 854L
Cooking apples, stewed without sugar 855L
Cooking apples, weighed with skin and core 853L
Cooking fat, compound 316L
Cordial, lime juice, undiluted 1083L
Corn Flakes 69L
Corn Flakes, Crunchy Nut 70L
Corn oil 322L
Corn snacks 1035L
Corn, sweet see **Sweetcorn**
Corn-on-the-cob, whole, boiled in unsalted water 825L
Corned beef, canned 507L
Cornetto 265L
Cornflour 4L
Cornish pastie 508L
Cottage cheese, plain 232L

Cottage cheese, plain, reduced fat 234L
Cottage cheese, plain, with additions 233L
Cottonseed oil 323L
Courgette, boiled in unsalted water 765L
Courgette, fried in corn oil 766L
Courgette, raw 764L
Cowpeas see **Blackeye beans**
Crab, boiled 634L
Crab, boiled, weighed with shell 635L
Crab, canned 636L
Crackers, cream 94L
Crackers, wholemeal 108L
Cream, fresh, clotted 216L
Cream, fresh, double 215L
Cream, fresh, half 211L
Cream, fresh, single 212L
Cream, fresh, soured 213L
Cream, fresh, whipping 214L
Cream, sterilised, canned 217L
Cream, UHT, canned spray 218L
Cream cheese 235L
Cream crackers 94L
Cream horns 131L
Cream of chicken soup, canned, ready to serve 1124L
Cream of chicken soup, condensed, canned 1125L
Cream of chicken soup, condensed, canned, ready to serve 1126L
Cream of mushroom soup, canned, ready to serve 1127L
Cream of tomato soup, canned, ready to serve 1128L
Cream of tomato soup, condensed, canned 1129L
Cream of tomato soup, condensed, canned, ready to serve 1130L
Creme caramel 275L
Creme eggs 1019L
Cress, mustard and see **Mustard and cress**
Cress, water see **Watercress**
Crispbread, rye 95L
Crispie cakes 111L
Crisps, potato 1037L
Crisps, potato, low fat 1038L
Croissants 60L
Croquettes, potato, fried in blended oil 690L
Crumble, fruit 154L
Crumble, fruit, wholemeal 155L
Crumpets, toasted 132L
Crunchy Nut Corn Flakes 70L
Cucumber, raw 767L
Curacao 1121L
Curly kale, boiled in salted water 769L
Curly kale, raw 768L
Currant bread 37L
Currant bread, toasted 38L
Currant buns 133L
Currants 883L
Curried meat 552L
Curry, beef, retail 540L
Curry, beef, with rice 541L
Curry, chicken, retail 549L
Curry, chicken, with bone 547L
Curry, chicken, with rice 550L
Curry, chicken, without bone 548L
Curry, mutton 560L
Curry powder 840L
Curry sauce, canned 1167L
Custard, canned 278L
Custard, made up with skimmed milk 277L
Custard, made up with whole milk 276L
Custard powder 5L
Custard tarts, individual 134L
Cutlet veal, fried in vegetable oil 428L
Cutlets lamb, lean and fat, grilled 400L
Cutlets lamb, lean and fat, grilled, weighed with bone 401L
Cutlets lamb, lean and fat, raw 399L
Cutlets lamb, lean only, grilled 402L
Cutlets lamb, lean only, grilled, weighed with fat and bone 403L

Dairy ice cream, flavoured 268L
Dairy ice cream, vanilla 267L
Dairy spread 307L
Damsons, raw, weighed with stones 884L
Damsons, stewed with sugar 885L
Danish blue cheese 236L
Danish pastries 135L
Dates, dried, weighed with stones 887L
Dates, raw, weighed with stones 886L
Demerara sugar 1010L
Dessert Top 219L
Digestive biscuits, chocolate 96L
Digestive biscuits, plain 97L
Dogfish, in batter, fried in blended oil 573L
Dogfish, in batter, fried in blended oil, weighed with waste 574L
Dogfish, in batter, fried in dripping 575L
Dogfish, in batter, fried in dripping, weighed with waste 576L
Doughnuts, jam 136L
Doughnuts, ring 137L
Draught bitter beer 1095L
Draught mild beer 1097L
Dream Topping, made up with semi-skimmed milk 221L

Dream Topping, made up with whole milk 220L
Dried chicken noodle soup 1134L
Dried chicken noodle soup, ready to serve 1135L
Dried cod, salted, boiled 572L
Dried instant soup powder 1136L
Dried instant soup powder, made up with water 1137L
Dried minestrone soup 1138L
Dried minestrone soup, ready to serve 1139L
Dried mixed fruit 888L
Dried oxtail soup 1140L
Dried oxtail soup, ready to serve 1141L
Dried skimmed milk 200L
Dried skimmed milk, with vegetable fat 201L
Dried tomato soup 1142L
Dried tomato soup, ready to serve 1143L
Drinking chocolate powder 1064L
Drinking chocolate powder, made up with semi-skimmed milk 1066L
Drinking chocolate powder, made up with whole milk 1065L
Drinking yogurt 251L
Dripping, beef 317L
Duck, meat only, raw 445L
Duck, meat, fat and skin, raw 446L
Duck, roast, meat only 447L
Duck, roast, meat, fat and skin 448L
Duck eggs, whole, raw 297L
Dumplings 167L
Dungli see **Onions**

Easy cook white rice, boiled 23L
Easy cook white rice, raw 22L
Eating apples, average, raw 856L
Eating apples, average, raw, peeled 858L
Eating apples, average, raw, peeled, weighed with skin and core 859L
Eating apples, average, raw, weighed with core 857L
Eccles cake 138L
Eclairs, frozen 139L
Edam cheese 237L
Eggs, chicken, boiled 293L
Eggs, chicken, fried in vegetable oil 294L
Eggs, chicken, poached 295L
Eggs, chicken, scrambled, with milk 296L
Eggs, chicken, white, raw 291L
Eggs, chicken, whole, raw 290L
Eggs, chicken, yolk, raw 292L
Eggs, duck, whole, raw 297L
Egg and cheese quiche 303L
Egg and cheese quiche, wholemeal 304L
Egg fried rice 298L
Egg noodles, boiled 28L
Egg noodles, raw 27L
Eggplant see **Aubergine**
Elmlea, double 224L
Elmlea, single 222L
Elmlea, whipping 223L
Evaporated milk, whole 202L

Faggots 509L
Fancy iced cakes, individual 112L
Fansi see **Green beans/French beans**
Fat, cooking, compound 316L
Fat spread 307L
Fennel, Florence, boiled in salted water 771L
Fennel, Florence, raw 770L
Feta cheese 238L
Figs, dried 889L
Figs, ready-to-eat, semi-dried 890L
Filled wafer biscuits 107L
Fish cakes, fried 650L
Fish fingers, fried in blended oil 651L
Fish fingers, fried in lard 652L
Fish fingers, grilled 653L
Fish paste 654L
Fish pie 655L
Flaky pastry, cooked 125L
Flaky pastry, raw 124L
Flapjacks 98L
Flavoured low fat yogurt 256L
Flavoured milk 203L
Flavoured soya milk 210L
Florence fennel, boiled in salted water 771L
Florence fennel, raw 770L
Flour, chapati, brown 2L
Flour, chapati, white 3L
Flour, rye, whole 7L
Flour, soya, full fat 9L
Flour, soya, low fat 10L
Flour, wheat, brown 12L
Flour, wheat, white, breadmaking 13L
Flour, wheat, white, plain 14L
Flour, wheat, white, self-raising 15L
Flour, wheat, wholemeal 16L
Forerib beef, lean and fat, raw 366L
Forerib beef, lean and fat, roast 367L
Forerib beef, lean only, roast 368L
Frankfurters 510L
French beans see **Green beans/French beans**
French dressing 1157L
French fries, retail 680L
French stick, white 53L
Fresh cream, clotted 216L
Fresh cream, double 215L

Fresh cream, half 211L
Fresh cream, single 212L
Fresh cream, soured 213L
Fresh cream, whipping 214L
Fried bread, white, fried in blended oil 50L
Fried bread, white, fried in lard 51L
Fried eggs 294L
Fried rice, white , fried in lard/dripping 24L
Fromage frais, fruit 239L
Fromage frais, plain 240L
Fromage frais, very low fat 241L
Frosties 71L
Fruit 'n Fibre 72L
Fruit cake, plain, retail 113L
Fruit cake, rich 114L
Fruit cake, rich, iced 115L
Fruit cake, wholemeal 116L
Fruit cocktail, canned in juice 891L
Fruit cocktail, canned in syrup 892L
Fruit crumble 154L
Fruit crumble, wholemeal 155L
Fruit fromage frais 239L
Fruit gums 1026L
Fruit mousse 286L
Fruit pie filling 893L
Fruit pie, individual 158L
Fruit pie, one crust 156L
Fruit pie, pastry top and bottom 157L
Fruit pie, wholemeal, one crust 159L
Fruit pie, wholemeal, pastry top and bottom 160L
Fruit salad, homemade 894L
Fruit scones 145L
Fruit yogurt, low fat 257L
Fruit yogurt, whole milk 261L
Full fat soft cheese 242L

Gajjar see **Carrots**
Galia melon 921L
Galia melon, weighed with skin 922L
Gammon joint, lean and fat, boiled 345L
Gammon joint, lean and fat, raw 344L
Gammon joint, lean only, boiled 346L
Gammon rasher, lean and fat, grilled 347L
Gammon rasher, lean only, grilled 348L
Garam masala 841L
Garbanzo see **Chick peas**
Garden peas, canned, drained 733L
Garlic, raw 772L
Gateau 117L
Gelatin 1176L
Ghee, butter 335L
Ghee, palm 336L
Ghee, vegetable 337L
Gherkins, pickled, drained 773L
Gin 1122L
Gingelly see **Sesame seeds**
Gingernut biscuits 99L
Glacé cherries 879L
Glucose liquid, BP 1000L
Goats milk, pasteurised 204L
Gobhi, bund see **Cabbage**
Gobhi, chote bund see **Brussels sprouts**
Gobhi, phool see **Cauliflower**
Golden gram see **Mung beans**
Golden syrup 1012L
Goose, roast, meat only 449L
Gooseberries, raw 895L
Gooseberries, stewed with sugar 896L
Gooseberries, stewed without sugar 897L
Gooseberries, dessert, canned in syrup 898L
Gouda cheese 243L
Gourd, bitter see **Gourd**, karela
Gourd, karela, raw 774L
Gram, black see **Black gram,** urad gram
Gram, common see **Chick peas**
Gram, golden see **Mung beans**
Gram, green see **Mung beans**
Gram, yellow see **Chick peas**
Granary bread 39L
Grape juice, unsweetened 1088L
Grapefruit, canned in juice 901L
Grapefruit, canned in syrup 902L
Grapefruit, raw 899L
Grapefruit, raw, weighed with peel and pips 900L
Grapefruit juice, unsweetened 1089L
Grapes, average 903L
Grapes, weighed with pips 904L
Gravy instant granules 1177L
Gravy instant granules, made up with water 1178L
Greek pastries 140L
Greek yogurt, cows 252L
Greek yogurt, sheep 253L
Green and brown lentils, whole, dried, boiled in salted water 711L
Green and brown lentils, whole, dried, raw 710L
Green beans/French beans, frozen, boiled in unsalted water 708L
Green beans/French beans, raw 707L
Green broccoli, boiled in unsalted water 745L
Green broccoli, raw 744L
Green chilli peppers, raw 801L
Green gram see **Mung beans**
Green peppers, boiled in salted water 803L
Green peppers, raw 802L

Greens, spring see **Spring greens**
Grillsteaks, grilled 511L
Groundnuts see **Peanuts**
Grouse, roast, meat only 450L
Grouse, roast, weighed with bone 451L
Guava, canned in syrup 907L
Guava, raw 905L
Guava, raw, weighed with skin and pips 906L
Gullar see **Figs**
Gumbo see **Okra**

Haddock, in crumbs, fried in blended oil 580L
Haddock, in crumbs, fried in blended oil, weighed with bones 581L
Haddock, in crumbs, fried in dripping 582L
Haddock, in crumbs, fried in dripping, weighed with bones 583L
Haddock, raw 577L
Haddock, smoked, steamed 584L
Haddock, smoked, steamed, weighed with bones and skin 585L
Haddock, steamed 578L
Haddock, steamed, weighed with bones and skin 579L
Haggis, boiled 512L
Halibut, raw 586L
Halibut, steamed 587L
Halibut, steamed, weighed with bones and skin 588L
Ham and pork, chopped, canned 513L
Ham, canned 360L
Hamburger buns 61L
Hard cheese, average 244L
Hard margarine, animal and vegetable fat 310L
Hard margarine, vegetable fat only 311L
Hare, stewed, meat only 466L
Hare, stewed, weighed with bone 467L
Hazelnuts 980L
Hazelnuts, weighed with shells 981L
Heart, lamb, raw 472L
Heart, ox, raw 473L
Heart, ox, stewed 474L
Heart, pig, raw 475L
Heart, sheep, roast 476L
Herring, fried 611L
Herring, fried, weighed with bones 612L
Herring, grilled 613L
Herring, grilled, weighed with bones 614L
Herring, raw 610L
Herring roe, soft, fried 658L
Hickory nuts see **Pecan nuts**
Homemade biscuits, creaming method 100L
Honey 1001L
Honeycomb 1002L
Honeydew melon 923L
Honeydew melon, weighed with skin 924L
Horlicks LowFat Instant powder 1067L
Horlicks LowFat Instant powder, made up with water 1068L
Horlicks powder 1069L
Horlicks powder, made up with semi-skimmed milk 1071L
Horlicks powder, made up with whole milk 1070L
Horseradish sauce 1168L
Hot cross buns 141L
Hot pot 553L
Hovis, average 40L
Hovis, toasted 41L
Hula hoops 1039L
Human milk, colostrum 205L
Human milk, mature 207L
Human milk, transitional 206L
Hummus 709L

Ice cream, dairy, flavoured 268L
Ice cream, dairy, vanilla 267L
Ice cream, non-dairy, flavoured 270L
Ice cream, non-dairy, mixes 271L
Ice cream, non-dairy, vanilla 269L
Ice cream desserts, frozen 266L
Ice cream wafers 272L
Iceberg lettuce, raw 779L
Indian nuts see **Pine nuts**
Indian tea, infusion 1079L
Instant coffee 1054L
Instant dessert powder 279L
Instant dessert powder, made up with skimmed milk 281L
Instant dessert powder, made up with whole milk 280L
Instant potato powder, made up with water 688L
Instant potato powder, made up with whole milk 689L
Instant soup powder, dried 1136L
Instant soup powder, dried, made up with water 1137L
Irish stew 554L
Irish stew, weighed with bones 555L

Jaffa cakes 101L
Jaggery 1003L
Jam, fruit with edible seeds 1004L
Jam, reduced sugar 1006L
Jam, stone fruit 1005L
Jam doughnuts 136L
Jam tarts 142L
Jam tarts, retail 143L
January King cabbage, boiled in salted water 752L

January King cabbage, raw 751L
Jelly, made with water 282L
Jew's apple see **Aubergine**
Juice, apple, unsweetened 1087L
Juice, grape, unsweetened 1088L
Juice, grapefruit, unsweetened 1089L
Juice, lemon 1090L
Juice, orange, unsweetened 1091L
Juice, pineapple, unsweetened 1092L
Juice, tomato 1093L

Kaju see **Cashew nuts**
Kakdi see **Cucumber**
Kale see **Curly kale**
Kanda see **Onions**
Karela gourd, raw 774L
Kedgeree 656L
Keg bitter beer 1096L
Ketchup, tomato 1172L
Kheema, beef 542L
Kheema, lamb 556L
Khira see **Cucumber**
Kidney, lamb, fried 478L
Kidney, lamb, raw 477L
Kidney, ox, raw 479L
Kidney, ox, stewed 480L
Kidney, pig, raw 481L
Kidney, pig, stewed 482L
Kidney beans see **Red kidney beans**
Kipper, baked 615L
Kipper, baked, weighed with bones 616L
Kit Kat 1020L
Kiwi fruit 908L
Kiwi fruit, weighed with skin 909L
Kobi see **Cabbage**
Kobi, nhanu see **Brussels sprouts**
Koftas, beef 543L
Kula see **Bananas**
Kumra see **Pumpkin**

Lady's fingers see **Okra**
Lager, bottled 1099L
Lal kaddu see **Pumpkin**
Lal phupala see **Pumpkin**
Lamb, breast, lean and fat, raw 391L
Lamb, breast, lean and fat, roast 392L
Lamb, breast, lean only, roast 393L
Lamb, chops, loin, lean and fat, grilled 395L
Lamb, chops, loin, lean and fat, grilled, weighed with bone 396L
Lamb, chops, loin, lean and fat, raw 394L
Lamb, chops, loin, lean only, grilled 397L
Lamb, chops, loin, lean only, grilled, weighed with fat and bone 398L
Lamb, cutlets, lean and fat, grilled 400L
Lamb, cutlets, lean and fat, grilled, weighed with bone 401L
Lamb, cutlets, lean and fat, raw 399L
Lamb, cutlets, lean only, grilled 402L
Lamb, cutlets, lean only, grilled, weighed with fat and bone 403L
Lamb, fat only, cooked, average 389L
Lamb, fat only, raw, average 388L
Lamb, lean only, raw, average 390L
Lamb, leg, lean and fat, raw 404L
Lamb, leg, lean and fat, roast 405L
Lamb, leg, lean only, roast 406L
Lamb, scrag and neck, lean and fat, raw 407L
Lamb, scrag and neck, lean and fat, stewed 408L
Lamb, scrag and neck, lean only, stewed 409L
Lamb, scrag and neck, lean only, stewed, weighed with fat and bone 410L
Lamb, shoulder, lean and fat, raw 411L
Lamb, shoulder, lean and fat, roast 412L
Lamb, shoulder, lean only, roast 413L
Lamb heart, raw 472L
Lamb kheema 556L
Lamb kidney, fried 478L
Lamb kidney, raw 477L
Lamb liver, fried 488L
Lamb liver, raw 487L
Lamb sweetbread, fried 496L
Lamb sweetbread, raw 495L
Lamb tongue, raw 497L
Lard 318L
Lasagne, frozen, cooked 557L
Lassan see **Garlic**
Leeks, boiled in unsalted water 776L
Leeks, raw 775L
Leg lamb, lean and fat, raw 404L
Leg lamb, lean and fat, roast 405L
Leg lamb, lean only, roast 406L
Leg pork, lean and fat, raw 424L
Leg pork, lean and fat, roast 425L
Leg pork, lean only, roast 426L
Leg quarter, roast chicken, meat only, weighed with bone 443L
Lehsan see **Garlic**
Lemon curd, starch base 1007L
Lemon juice 1090L
Lemon meringue pie 161L
Lemon sole, in crumbs, fried 592L
Lemon sole, in crumbs, fried, weighed with bones 593L

Lemon sole, raw 589L
Lemon sole, steamed 590L
Lemon sole, steamed, weighed with bones and skin 591L
Lemon sorbet 273L
Lemonade, bottled 1081L
Lemons, whole, without pips 910L
Lentil soup 1123L
Lentils, continental see **Lentils**, green and brown
Lentils, green and brown, whole, dried, boiled in salted water 711L
Lentils, green and brown, whole, dried, raw 710L
Lentils, red, split, dried, boiled in unsalted water 713L
Lentils, red, split, dried, raw 712L
Lettuce, average, raw 777L
Lettuce, butterhead, raw 778L
Lettuce, Iceberg, raw 779L
Lichee see **Lychees**
Lichi see **Lychees**
Lima beans see **Butter beans**
Lime juice cordial, undiluted 1083L
Liquorice allsorts 1027L
Litchee see **Lychees**
Litchi see **Lychees**
Liver, calf, fried 484L
Liver, calf, raw 483L
Liver, chicken, fried 486L
Liver, chicken, raw 485L
Liver, lamb, fried 488L
Liver, lamb, raw 487L
Liver, ox, raw 489L
Liver, ox, stewed 490L
Liver, pig, raw 491L
Liver, pig, stewed 492L
Liver pate 517L
Liver pate, low fat 518L
Liver sausage 514L
Lobia see **Blackeye beans**
Lobster, boiled 637L
Lobster, boiled, weighed with shell 638L
Loin chops, lamb, lean and fat, grilled 395L
Loin chops, lamb, lean and fat, grilled, weighed with bone 396L
Loin chops, lamb, lean and fat, raw 394L
Loin chops, lamb, lean only, grilled 397L
Loin chops, lamb, lean only, grilled, weighed with fat and bone 398L
Loin chops, pork, lean and fat, grilled 420L
Loin chops, pork, lean and fat, grilled, weighed with bone 421L
Loin chops, pork, lean and fat, raw 419L
Loin chops, pork, lean only, grilled 422L
Loin chops, pork, lean only, grilled, weighed with fat and bone 423L
Low calorie soup, canned 1131L
Low calorie yogurt 254L
Low fat potato crisps 1038L
Low fat sausages, fried 531L
Low fat sausages, grilled 532L
Low fat sausages, raw 530L
Low fat yogurt, flavoured 256L
Low fat yogurt, fruit 257L
Low fat yogurt, plain 255L
Low-fat spread 308L
Lucozade 1082L
Luncheon meat, canned 515L
Lychees, canned in syrup 913L
Lychees, raw 911L
Lychees, raw, weighed with skin and stone 912L
Lymeswold cheese 245L

Macadamia nuts, salted 982L
Macaroni cheese 168L
Macaroni, boiled 26L
Macaroni, raw 25L
Mackerel, fried 618L
Mackerel, fried, weighed with bones 619L
Mackerel, raw 617L
Mackerel, smoked 620L
Madeira cake 118L
Madeira nuts see **Walnuts**
Malt bread 42L
Mandarin oranges, canned in juice 914L
Mandarin oranges, canned in syrup 915L
Mange-tout peas, boiled in salted water 726L
Mange-tout peas, raw 725L
Mange-tout peas, stir-fried in blended oil 727L
Mango chutney, oily 1158L
Mangoes, canned in syrup 918L
Mangoes, raw 916L
Mangoes, raw, weighed with skin and stone 917L
Margarine 309L
Margarine, hard, animal and vegetable fat 310L
Margarine, hard, vegetable fat only 311L
Margarine, polyunsaturated 314L
Margarine, soft, animal and vegetable fat 312L
Margarine, soft, vegetable fat only 313L
Marmalade 1008L
Marmite 1179L
Marrow, boiled in unsalted water 781L
Marrow, raw 780L
Mars bar 1021L
Marzipan, homemade 983L

Marzipan, retail 984L
Masoor dahl see **Lentils**, red
Masur see **Lentils**, green and brown
Masur dahl see **Lentils**, red
Mattar see **Peas**
Mature human milk 207L
Mayonnaise, retail 1159L
Meat, curried 552L
Meat paste 516L
Meat samosas 174L
Medium fat soft cheese 246L
Melon, Canteloupe 919L
Melon, Canteloupe, weighed with skin 920L
Melon, Galia 921L
Melon, Galia, weighed with skin 922L
Melon, Honeydew 923L
Melon, Honeydew, weighed with skin 924L
Meringue 299L
Meringue, with cream 300L
Mild beer, draught 1097L
Milk, Channel Island, semi-skimmed, UHT 197L
Milk, Channel Island, whole, pasteurised 194L
Milk, Channel Island, whole, pasteurised, summer 195L
Milk, Channel Island, whole, pasteurised, winter 196L
Milk, condensed, skimmed, sweetened 198L
Milk, condensed, whole, sweetened 199L
Milk, dried skimmed 200L
Milk, dried skimmed, with vegetable fat 201L
Milk, evaporated, whole 202L
Milk, flavoured 203L
Milk, goats, pasteurised 204L
Milk, human, colostrum 205L
Milk, human, mature 207L
Milk, human, transitional 206L
Milk, semi-skimmed, average 185L
Milk, semi-skimmed, pasteurised 186L
Milk, semi-skimmed, pasteurised,fortified plus Skimmed Milk Powder 187L
Milk, semi-skimmed, UHT 188L
Milk, sheeps, raw 208L
Milk, skimmed, average 181L
Milk, skimmed, pasteurised 182L
Milk, skimmed, pasteurised, fortified plus Skimmed Milk Powder 183L
Milk, skimmed, UHT, fortified 184L
Milk, soya, flavoured 210L
Milk, soya, plain 209L
Milk, whole, average 189L
Milk, whole, pasteurised 190L
Milk, whole, pasteurised, summer 191L
Milk, whole, pasteurised, winter 192L
Milk, whole, sterilised 193L
Milk chocolate 1015L
Milk pudding, made with skimmed milk 284L
Milk pudding, made with whole milk 283L
Milk shake powder 1073L
Milk shake powder, made up with semi-skimmed milk 1075L
Milk shake powder, made up with whole milk 1074L
Milk shake, purchased 1072L
Milky Way 1022L
Mince beef, raw 369L
Mince beef, stewed 370L
Mince pies, individual 144L
Mincemeat 1009L
Minestrone soup, dried 1138L
Minestrone soup, dried, ready to serve 1139L
Minestrone soup, low calorie, canned 1131L
Mint sauce 1169L
Mint, fresh 842L
Mixed fruit, dried 888L
Mixed nuts 985L
Mixed peel 926L
Mixed vegetables, frozen, boiled in salted water 782L
Monkey nuts see **Peanuts**
Moong beans see **Mung beans**
Motamircha see **Peppers**, capsicum, green
Moussaka 558L
Mousse, chocolate 285L
Mousse, fruit 286L
Muesli, Swiss style 73L
Muesli, with no added sugar 74L
Mung beans, whole, dried, boiled in unsalted water 715L
Mung beans, whole, dried, raw 714L
Mung beansprouts, raw 696L
Mung beansprouts, stir-fried in blended oil 697L
Mushroom soup, cream of, canned, ready to serve 1127L
Mushrooms, boiled in salted water 784L
Mushrooms, fried in blended oil 785L
Mushrooms, fried in butter 786L
Mushrooms, fried in corn oil 787L
Mushrooms, raw 783L
Mushy peas, canned, re-heated 728L
Mussels, boiled 645L
Mussels, boiled, weighed with shell 646L
Mustard and cress, raw 788L
Mustard powder 843L
Mustard, smooth 1180L
Mustard, wholegrain 1181L
Mutton biriani 559L
Mutton curry 560L
Myco-protein Quorn 811L

Naan bread 43L
Nectarines 927L
Nectarines, weighed with stones 928L
Neeps (England) see **Swede**
Neeps (Scotland) see **Turnip**
New potatoes, average, raw 660L
New potatoes, boiled in unsalted water 661L
New potatoes, canned, re-heated, drained 663L
New potatoes, in skins, boiled in unsalted water 662L
Nhanu kobi see **Brussels sprouts**
Non-dairy ice cream, flavoured 270L
Non-dairy ice cream, mixes 271L
Non-dairy ice cream, vanilla 269L
Noodles, egg, boiled 28L
Noodles, egg, raw 27L
Nutmeg, ground 844L
Nuts, Brazil 974L
Nuts, Brazil, weighed with shells 975L
Nuts, cashew, roasted and salted 976L
Nuts, mixed 985L

Oat and Wheat Bran 75L
Oat Bran Flakes, Common Sense 68L
Oatcakes, retail 102L
Oatmeal, quick cook, raw 6L
Oil, coconut 320L
Oil, cod liver 321L
Oil, corn 322L
Oil, cottonseed 323L
Oil, olive 324L
Oil, palm 325L
Oil, peanut 326L
Oil, rapeseed, high erucic acid 327L
Oil, rapeseed, low erucic acid 328L
Oil, safflower 329L
Oil, sesame 330L
Oil, soya 331L
Oil, sunflowerseed 332L
Oil, vegetable, blended, average 333L
Oil, wheatgerm 334L
Okra, boiled in unsalted water 790L
Okra, raw 789L
Okra, stir-fried in corn oil 791L
Old potatoes, average, raw 664L
Old potatoes, baked, flesh and skin 665L
Old potatoes, baked, flesh only 666L
Old potatoes, baked, flesh only, weighed with skin 667L
Old potatoes, boiled in unsalted water 668L
Old potatoes, mashed with butter 669L
Old potatoes, mashed with margarine 670L
Old potatoes, roast in blended oil 671L
Old potatoes, roast in corn oil 672L
Old potatoes, roast in lard 673L
Olive oil 324L
Olives, in brine 929L
Olives, in brine, weighed with stones 930L
Omelette, cheese 302L
Omelette, plain 301L
Onion sauce, made with semi-skimmed milk 1151L
Onion sauce, made with whole milk 1150L
Onions, boiled in unsalted water 793L
Onions, fried in blended oil 794L
Onions, fried in corn oil 795L
Onions, fried in lard 796L
Onions, pickled, cocktail/silverskin, drained 798L
Onions, pickled, drained 797L
Onions, raw 792L
Onions, spring see **Spring onions**
Orange drink, undiluted 1084L
Orange juice, unsweetened 1091L
Oranges 931L
Oranges, weighed with peel and pips 932L
Ovaltine powder 1076L
Ovaltine powder, made up with semi-skimmed milk 1078L
Ovaltine powder, made up with whole milk 1077L
Oven chips, frozen, baked 687L
Ox heart, raw 473L
Ox heart, stewed 474L
Ox kidney, raw 479L
Ox kidney, stewed 480L
Ox liver, raw 489L
Ox liver, stewed 490L
Ox tongue, boiled 499L
Ox tongue, pickled, raw 498L
Oxo cubes 1182L
Oxtail soup, canned, ready to serve 1132L
Oxtail soup, dried 1140L
Oxtail soup, dried, ready to serve 1141L
Oxtail, stewed 493L
Oxtail, stewed, weighed with fat and bones 494L

Palak see **Spinach**
Pale ale, bottled 1100L
Palm ghee 336L
Palm oil 325L
Pancake roll 561L
Pancakes, savoury, made with whole milk 169L
Pancakes, Scotch 148L
Pancakes, sweet, made with whole milk 162L
Pangoli see **Cauliflower**
Papadums, fried in vegetable oil 44L
Papai see **Paw-paw**

Papaya see **Paw-paw**
Paprika 845L
Parmesan cheese 247L
Parsley, fresh 846L
Parsnip, boiled in unsalted water 800L
Parsnip, raw 799L
Partridge, roast, meat only 452L
Partridge, roast, weighed with bone 453L
Passion fruit 933L
Passion fruit, weighed with skin 934L
Pasta sauce, tomato based 1170L
Paste, fish 654L
Paste, meat 516L
Pasteurised goats milk 204L
Pasteurised semi-skimmed milk 186L
Pasteurised semi-skimmed milk, fortified plus Skimmed Milk Powder 187L
Pasteurised skimmed milk 182L
Pasteurised skimmed milk, fortified plus Skimmed Milk Powder 183L
Pasteurised whole milk 190L
Pasteurised whole milk, summer 191L
Pasteurised whole milk, winter 192L
Pastie, Cornish 508L
Pastilles 1028L
Pastries, Danish 135L
Pastries, Greek 140L
Pastry, flaky, cooked 125L
Pastry, flaky, raw 124L
Pastry, shortcrust, cooked 127L
Pastry, shortcrust, raw 126L
Pastry, wholemeal, cooked 129L
Pastry, wholemeal, raw 128L
Pate, liver 517L
Pate, liver, low fat 518L
Paw-paw, canned in juice 937L
Paw-paw, raw 935L
Paw-paw, raw, weighed with skin and pips 936L
Peaches, canned in juice 940L
Peaches, canned in syrup 941L
Peaches, raw 938L
Peaches, raw, weighed with stone 939L
Peanut butter, smooth 986L
Peanut oil 326L
Peanuts and raisins 1036L
Peanuts, dry roasted 989L
Peanuts, plain 987L
Peanuts, plain, weighed with shells 988L
Peanuts, roasted and salted 990L
Pears, average, raw 942L
Pears, average, raw, peeled 944L
Pears, average, raw, weighed with core 943L
Pears, canned in juice 945L
Pears, canned in syrup 946L
Peas, blackeye see **Blackeye beans**
Peas, boiled in unsalted water 730L
Peas, canned, drained 733L
Peas, chick, canned, drained 706L
Peas, chick, whole, dried, boiled in unsalted water 705L
Peas, chick, whole, dried, raw 704L
Peas, frozen, boiled in salted water 731L
Peas, frozen, boiled in unsalted water 732L
Peas, mange-tout see **Mange-tout peas**
Peas, mushy see **Mushy peas**
Peas, petit pois see **Petit pois**
Peas, processed see **Processed peas**
Peas, raw 729L
Pecan nuts 991L
Pepper, black 847L
Pepper, white 848L
Peppermints 1029L
Peppers, capsicum, chilli, green, raw 801L
Peppers, capsicum, green, boiled in salted water 803L
Peppers, capsicum, green, raw 802L
Peppers, capsicum, red, boiled in salted water 805L
Peppers, capsicum, red, raw 804L
Petit pois, frozen, boiled in salted water 734L
Petit pois, frozen, boiled in unsalted water 735L
Pheasant, roast, meat only 454L
Pheasant, roast, weighed with bone 455L
Phool gobhi see **Cauliflower**
Pickle, sweet 1160L
Pickled beetroot, drained 743L
Pickled gherkins, drained 773L
Pickled onions, cocktail/silverskin, drained 798L
Pickled onions, drained 797L
Pie, blackcurrant, pastry top and bottom 150L
Pie, fish 655L
Pie, fruit, individual 158L
Pie, fruit, one crust 156L
Pie, fruit, pastry top and bottom 157L
Pie, fruit, wholemeal, one crust 159L
Pie, fruit, wholemeal, pastry top and bottom 160L
Pie, lemon meringue 161L
Pie, pork, individual 520L
Pie, steak and kidney, individual 534L
Pie, steak and kidney, pastry top only 535L
Pie, with pie filling 163L
Pie filling, cherry 880L
Pie filling, fruit 893L
Pies, mince, individual 144L
Pig heart, raw 475L

Pig kidney, raw 481L
Pig kidney, stewed 482L
Pig liver, raw 491L
Pig liver, stewed 492L
Pigeon, roast, meat only 456L
Pigeon, roast, weighed with bone 457L
Pignolias see **Pine nuts**
Pilchards, canned in tomato sauce 621L
Pimento see **Peppers**, capsicum, chilli, green
Pine kernels see **Pine nuts**
Pine nuts 992L
Pineapple juice, unsweetened 1092L
Pineapple, canned in juice 948L
Pineapple, canned in syrup 949L
Pineapple, raw 947L
Pista see **Pistachio nuts**
Pistachio nuts, weighed with shells 993L
Pitta bread, white 45L
Piyaz see **Onions**
Pizza 170L
Pizza, frozen 171L
Plaice, in batter, fried in blended oil 597L
Plaice, in batter, fried in dripping 598L
Plaice, in crumbs, fried, fillets 599L
Plaice, raw 594L
Plaice, steamed 595L
Plaice, steamed, weighed with bones and skin 596L
Plain scones 146L
Plantain, boiled in unsalted water 807L
Plantain, raw 806L
Plantain, ripe, fried in vegetable oil 808L
Plums, average, raw 950L
Plums, average, raw, weighed with stones 951L
Plums, average, stewed with sugar, weighed with stones 952L
Plums, average, stewed without sugar, weighed with stones 953L
Plums, canned in syrup 954L
Poached eggs, chicken 295L
Polony 519L
Polyunsaturated margarine 314L
Popcorn, candied 1030L
Popcorn, plain 1031L
Porage see **Porridge**
Pork, belly rashers, lean and fat, grilled 418L
Pork, belly rashers, lean and fat, raw 417L
Pork, chops, loin, lean and fat, grilled 420L
Pork, chops, loin, lean and fat, grilled, weighed with bone 421L
Pork, chops, loin, lean and fat, raw 419L
Pork, chops, loin, lean only, grilled 422L
Pork, chops, loin, lean only, grilled, weighed with fat and bone 423L
Pork, fat only, cooked, average 415L
Pork, fat only, raw, average 414L
Pork, lean only, raw, average 416L
Pork, leg, lean and fat, raw 424L
Pork, leg, lean and fat, roast 425L
Pork, leg, lean only, roast 426L
Pork, trotters and tails, salted, boiled 427L
Pork and ham, chopped, canned 513L
Pork pie, individual 520L
Pork sausages, fried 528L
Pork sausages, grilled 529L
Pork sausages, raw 527L
Porridge, made with water 76L
Porridge, made with whole milk 77L
Port 1113L
Potato crisps 1037L
Potato crisps, low fat 1038L
Potato croquettes, fried in blended oil 690L
Potato hoops 1039L
Potato powder, instant, made up with water 688L
Potato powder, instant, made up with whole milk 689L
Potato waffles, frozen, cooked 691L
Potato, sweet see **Sweet potato**
Potatoes, new, average, raw 660L
Potatoes, new, boiled in unsalted water 661L
Potatoes, new, canned, drained 663L
Potatoes, new, in skins, boiled in unsalted water 662L
Potatoes, old, average, raw 664L
Potatoes, old, baked, flesh and skin 665L
Potatoes, old, baked, flesh only 666L
Potatoes, old, baked, flesh only, weighed with skin 667L
Potatoes, old, boiled in unsalted water 668L
Potatoes, old, mashed with butter 669L
Potatoes, old, mashed with margarine 670L
Potatoes, old, roast in blended oil 671L
Potatoes, old, roast in corn oil 672L
Potatoes, old, roast in lard 673L
Prawns, boiled 639L
Prawns, boiled, weighed with shell 640L
Processed cheese, plain 248L
Processed peas, canned, drained 736L
Prunes, canned in juice 955L
Prunes, canned in syrup 956L
Prunes, ready-to-eat 957L
Pudding, bread 151L
Pudding, Christmas 152L
Pudding, Christmas, retail 153L
Pudding, milk, made with skimmed milk 284L

Pudding, milk, made with whole milk 283L
Pudding, rice, canned 287L
Pudding, sponge 164L
Puffed Wheat 78L
Pumpkin, boiled in salted water 810L
Pumpkin, raw 809L
Purple grenadillo see **Passion fruit**

Queensland nuts see **Macadamia nuts**, salted
Quiche, cheese and egg 303L
Quiche, cheese and egg, wholemeal 304L
Quick cook oatmeal, raw 6L
Quorn, myco-protein 811L

Rabbit, raw, meat only 468L
Rabbit, stewed, meat only 469L
Rabbit, stewed, weighed with bone 470L
Radish, red, raw 812L
Raisin Splitz 79L
Raisins 958L
Raisins and peanuts 1036L
Rapeseed oil, high erucic acid 327L
Rapeseed oil, low erucic acid 328L
Raspberries, canned in syrup 960L
Raspberries, raw 959L
Ravioli, canned in tomato sauce 172L
Ready Brek 80L
Red kidney beans, canned, drained 718L
Red kidney beans, dried, boiled in unsalted water 717L
Red kidney beans, dried, raw 716L
Red lentils, split, dried, boiled in unsalted water 713L
Red lentils, split, dried, raw 712L
Red peppers, boiled in salted water 805L
Red peppers, raw 804L
Red wine 1107L
Reduced calorie salad cream 1162L
Reduced sugar jam 1006L
Rhubarb, canned in syrup 964L
Rhubarb, raw 961L
Rhubarb, stewed with sugar 962L
Rhubarb, stewed without sugar 963L
Ribena, undiluted 1085L
Rice, brown, boiled 19L
Rice, brown, raw 18L
Rice, egg fried 298L
Rice, savoury, cooked 21L
Rice, savoury, raw 20L
Rice, white, easy cook, boiled 23L
Rice, white, easy cook, raw 22L
Rice, white, fried 24L
Rice Krispies 81L
Rice pudding, canned 287L
Rich fruit cake 114L
Rich fruit cake, iced 115L
Rich iced fruit cake 115L
Ricicles 82L
Ring doughnuts 137L
Ringana see **Aubergine**
Risotto, plain 173L
Roast chicken, dark meat 441L
Roast chicken, light meat 440L
Roast chicken, meat and skin 439L
Roast chicken, meat only 438L
Roast turkey, dark meat 465L
Roast turkey, light meat 464L
Roast turkey, meat and skin 463L
Roast turkey, meat only 462L
Rock eel see **Dogfish**
Rock salmon see **Dogfish**
Roe, cod, hard, fried 657L
Roe, herring, soft, fried 658L
Rolls, brown, crusty 58L
Rolls, brown, soft 59L
Rolls, white, crusty 62L
Rolls, white, soft 63L
Rolls, wholemeal 64L
Rosé wine, medium 1108L
Rosehip syrup, undiluted 1086L
Rosemary, dried 849L
Rum 1122L
Rump steak beef, lean and fat, fried 372L
Rump steak beef, lean and fat, grilled 373L
Rump steak beef, lean and fat, raw 371L
Rump steak beef, lean only, fried 374L
Rump steak beef, lean only, grilled 375L
Runner beans, boiled in unsalted water 720L
Runner beans, raw 719L
Rutabaga see **Swede**
Rye bread 46L
Rye crispbread 95L
Rye flour, whole 7L

Saag see **Spinach**
Safflower oil 329L
Sage and onion stuffing 177L
Sage, dried, ground 850L
Sago, raw 8L
Saithe, raw 600L
Saithe, steamed 601L
Saithe, steamed, weighed with bones and skin 602L
Salad cream 1161L
Salad cream, reduced calorie 1162L
Salami 521L

Salmon, canned 625L
Salmon, raw 622L
Salmon, smoked 626L
Salmon, steamed 623L
Salmon, steamed, weighed with bones and skin 624L
Salt, block 1183L
Salt, table 1184L
Salted beef, dried, raw 377L
Salted beef, fat removed, raw 376L
Samosas, meat 174L
Samosas, vegetable 175L
Sandwich biscuits 103L
Sardines, canned in oil, drained 628L
Sardines, canned in tomato sauce 627L
Satsumas 965L
Satsumas, weighed with peel 966L
Sauce, barbecue 1164L
Sauce, Bolognese 546L
Sauce, bread, made with semi-skimmed milk 1145L
Sauce, bread, made with whole milk 1144L
Sauce, brown, bottled 1165L
Sauce, cheese, made with semi-skimmed milk 1147L
Sauce, cheese, made with whole milk 1146L
Sauce, cook-in-sauces, canned 1166L
Sauce, curry, canned 1167L
Sauce, horseradish 1168L
Sauce, mint 1169L
Sauce, onion, made with semi-skimmed milk 1151L
Sauce, onion, made with whole milk 1150L
Sauce, pasta, tomato based 1170L
Sauce, soy, dark, thick 1171L
Sauce, tomato 1173L
Sauce, white, savoury, made with semi-skimmed milk 1153L
Sauce, white, savoury, made with whole milk 1152L
Sauce, white, sweet, made with semi-skimmed milk 1155L
Sauce, white, sweet, made with whole milk 1154L
Sauce packet mix, cheese, made up with semi-skimmed milk 1149L
Sauce packet mix, cheese, made up with whole milk 1148L
Sausages, beef, fried 525L
Sausages, beef, grilled 526L
Sausages, beef, raw 524L
Sausages, low fat, fried 531L
Sausages, low fat, grilled 532L
Sausages, low fat, raw 530L
Sausages, pork, fried 528L
Sausages, pork, grilled 529L
Sausages, pork, raw 527L
Sausage roll, flaky pastry 522L
Sausage roll, short pastry 523L
Saveloy 533L
Savoury complan powder 1057L
Savoury complan powder, made up with water 1058L
Savoury pancakes, made with whole milk 169L
Savoury rice, cooked 21L
Savoury rice, raw 20L
Savoury white sauce, made with semi-skimmed milk 1153L
Savoury white sauce, made with whole milk 1152L
Scampi, in breadcrumbs, frozen, fried 641L
Scones, fruit 145L
Scones, plain 146L
Scones, wholemeal 147L
Scotch eggs, retail 305L
Scotch pancakes 148L
Scrag and neck lamb, lean and fat, raw 407L
Scrag and neck lamb, lean and fat, stewed 408L
Scrag and neck lamb, lean only, stewed 409L
Scrag and neck lamb, lean only, stewed, weighed with fat and bone 410L
Scrambled eggs, with milk 296L
Semi-skimmed Channel Island milk, UHT 197L
Semi-skimmed milk, average 185L
Semi-skimmed milk, pasteurised 186L
Semi-skimmed milk, pasteurised, fortified plus Skimmed Milk Powder 187L
Semi-skimmed milk, UHT 188L
Semi-sweet biscuits 104L
Sesame oil 330L
Sesame seeds 994L
Shakaria see **Sweet potato**
Shalgam see **Turnip**
Sheep heart, roast 476L
Sheep tongue, stewed 500L
Sheeps milk, raw 208L
Shepherd's pie 562L
Sherry, dry 1114L
Sherry, medium 1115L
Sherry, sweet 1116L
Short-sweet biscuits 105L
Shortbread 106L
Shortcrust pastry, cooked 127L
Shortcrust pastry, raw 126L
Shoulder lamb, lean and fat, raw 411L
Shoulder lamb, lean and fat, roast 412L
Shoulder lamb, lean only, roast 413L
Shredded Wheat 83L
Shreddies 84L
Shrimps, canned, drained 643L
Shrimps, frozen, shell removed 642L
Silverside beef, lean and fat, salted, boiled 378L

Silverside beef, lean only, salted, boiled 379L
Silverskin onions, drained 798L
Simla mirch see **Peppers**, capsicum, green
Sirloin beef, lean and fat, raw 380L
Sirloin beef, lean and fat, roast 381L
Sirloin beef, lean only, roast 382L
Skate, in batter, fried 603L
Skate, in batter, fried, weighed with waste 604L
Skimmed condensed milk, sweetened 198L
Skimmed milk, average 181L
Skimmed milk, pasteurised 182L
Skimmed milk, pasteurised, fortified plus Skimmed Milk Powder 183L
Skimmed milk, UHT, fortified 184L
Smacks 85L
Smartie-type sweets 1023L
Smoked haddock, steamed 584L
Smoked haddock, steamed, weighed with bones and skin 585L
Smoked mackerel 620L
Smoked salmon 626L
Snowpeas see **Mange-tout peas**
Soft margarine, animal and vegetable fat 312L
Soft margarine, vegetable fat only 313L
Sole, lemon, in crumbs, fried 592L
Sole, lemon, in crumbs, fried, weighed with bones 593L
Sole, lemon, raw 589L
Sole, lemon, steamed 590L
Sole, lemon, steamed, weighed with bones and skin 591L
Sorbet, lemon 273L
Soup, instant, dried 1136L
Soup, instant, dried, ready to serve 1137L
Soup, chicken noodle, dried 1134L
Soup, chicken noodle, dried, ready to serve 1135L
Soup, lentil 1123L
Soup, low calorie, canned 1131L
Soup, minestrone, dried, ready to serve 1139L
Soup, minestrone, dried 1138L
Soup, oxtail, canned, ready to serve 1132L
Soup, oxtail, dried 1140L
Soup, oxtail, dried, ready to serve 1141L
Soup, tomato, dried 1142L
Soup, tomato, dried, ready to serve 1143L
Soup, vegetable, canned, ready to serve 1133L
Soy sauce 1171L
Soya bean tofu, steamed 723L
Soya bean tofu, steamed, fried 724L
Soya beans, dried, boiled in unsalted water 722L
Soya beans, dried, raw 721L
Soya flour, full fat 9L
Soya flour, low fat 10L
Soya milk, flavoured 210L
Soya milk, plain 209L
Soya oil 331L
Soya yogurt 258L
Spaghetti, canned in tomato sauce 176L
Spaghetti, white, boiled 30L
Spaghetti, white, raw 29L
Spaghetti, wholemeal, boiled 32L
Spaghetti, wholemeal, raw 31L
Sparkling white wine 1111L
Special K 86L
Spinach, boiled in unsalted water 814L
Spinach, frozen, boiled in unsalted water 815L
Spinach, raw 813L
Spirits, 40% volume 1122L
Sponge cake 119L
Sponge cake, fatless 120L
Sponge cake, jam filled 121L
Sponge cake, with butter icing 122L
Sponge pudding 164L
Spread, chocolate nut 999L
Spread, dairy/fat 307L
Spread, low-fat 308L
Spread, very low fat 315L
Spring greens, boiled in unsalted water 817L
Spring greens, raw 816L
Spring onions, bulbs and tops, raw 818L
Sprouts, Brussels see **Brussels sprouts**
Squid, frozen, raw 647L
Start 87L
Steak, rump, lean and fat, fried 372L
Steak, rump, lean and fat, grilled 373L
Steak, rump, lean and fat, raw 371L
Steak, rump, lean only, fried 374L
Steak, rump, lean only, grilled 375L
Steak, stewed, canned, with gravy 536L
Steak, stewing, lean and fat, raw 383L
Steak, stewing, lean and fat, stewed 384L
Steak and kidney pie, individual 534L
Steak and kidney pie, pastry top only 535L
Sterilised cream, canned 217L
Sterilised whole milk 193L
Stew, beef 545L
Stew, Irish 554L
Stew, Irish, weighed with bones 555L
Stewed apples, cooking, stewed with sugar 854L
Stewed apples, cooking, stewed without sugar 855L
Stewed blackberries, stewed with sugar 870L
Stewed blackberries, stewed without sugar 871L
Stewed blackcurrants, stewed with sugar 873L
Stewed damsons, stewed with sugar 885L

Stewed gooseberries, cooking, stewed with sugar 896L
Stewed gooseberries, cooking, stewed without sugar 897L
Stewed plums, average, stewed with sugar, weighed with stones 952L
Stewed plums, average, stewed without sugar, 953L
Stewed rhubarb, stewed with sugar 962L
Stewed rhubarb, stewed without sugar 963L
Stewed steak, canned, with gravy 536L
Stewing steak beef, lean and fat, raw 383L
Stewing steak beef, lean and fat, stewed 384L
Stilton cheese, blue 249L
Stout, bottled 1101L
Stout, extra 1102L
Strawberries, canned in syrup 968L
Strawberries, raw 967L
Stuffing mix 178L
Stuffing mix, made up with water 179L
Stuffing, sage and onion 177L
Suet, shredded 319L
Sugar Puffs 88L
Sugar, demerara 1010L
Sugar, white 1011L
Sultana Bran 89L
Sultanas 969L
Sundae, chocolate nut 264L
Sunflower seeds 995L
Sunflowerseed oil 332L
Swede, boiled in unsalted water 820L
Swede, raw 819L
Sweet peppers see **Peppers**, capsicum, green
Sweet pickle 1160L
Sweet potato, boiled in salted water 822L
Sweet potato, raw 821L
Sweetbread, lamb, fried 496L
Sweetbread, lamb, raw 495L
Sweetcorn, baby, canned, drained 823L
Sweetcorn, kernels, canned, drained 824L
Sweetcorn, on-the-cob, whole, boiled in unsalted water 825L
Sweets, boiled 1025L
Swiss rolls, chocolate, individual 123L
Syrup, golden 1012L
Syrup, rosehip, undiluted 1086L

Table salt 1184L
Tahini paste 996L
Tangerines 970L
Tangerines, weighed with peel and pips 971L
Tapioca, raw 11L
Taramasalata 659L
Tarel see **Apples**
Tart, treacle 165L
Tarts, custard, individual 134L
Tarts, jam, homemade 142L
Tarts, jam, retail 143L
Tea, Indian, infusion 1079L
Teacakes, toasted 149L
Thyme, dried, ground 851L
Til see **Sesame seeds**
Tip Top 225L
Toasted bread, brown 34L
Toasted bread, white 52L
Toasted bread, white, with added fibre 55L
Toasted bread, wholemeal 57L
Toasted currant bread 37L
Toasted Hovis 41L
Toasted teacakes 149L
Toffees, mixed 1032L
Tofu, soya bean, steamed 723L
Tofu, soya bean, steamed, fried 724L
Tomato based pasta sauce 1170L
Tomato chutney 1163L
Tomato juice 1093L
Tomato ketchup 1172L
Tomato purée 826L
Tomato sauce 1173L
Tomato soup, dried 1142L
Tomato soup, dried, ready to serve 1143L
Tomato soup, low calorie, canned 1131L
Tomato soup, cream of, canned, ready to serve 1128L
Tomato soup, cream of, condensed, canned 1129L
Tomato soup, cream of, condensed, canned, ready to serve 1130L
Tomatoes, canned, whole contents 832L
Tomatoes, fried in blended oil 828L
Tomatoes, fried in corn oil 829L
Tomatoes, fried in lard 830L
Tomatoes, grilled 831L
Tomatoes, raw 827L
Tongue, canned 537L
Tongue, lamb, raw 497L
Tongue, ox, boiled 499L
Tongue, ox, pickled, raw 498L
Tongue, sheep, stewed 500L
Topside beef, lean and fat, raw 385L
Topside beef, lean and fat, roast 386L
Topside beef, lean only, roast 387L
Tortilla chips 1040L
Trail Mix 1041L
Transitional human milk 206L
Treacle tart 165L
Treacle, black 1013L

Treacle, golden syrup 1012L
Trifle 288L
Trifle, with fresh cream 289L
Tripe, dressed 501L
Tripe, dressed, stewed 502L
Trotters and tails pork, salted, boiled 427L
Trout, brown, steamed 629L
Trout, brown, steamed, weighed with bones 630L
Tuna, canned in brine, drained 632L
Tuna, canned in oil, drained 631L
Turkey, dark meat, raw 461L
Turkey, light meat, raw 460L
Turkey, meat and skin, raw 459L
Turkey, meat only, raw 458L
Turkey, roast, dark meat 465L
Turkey, roast, light meat 464L
Turkey, roast, meat and skin 463L
Turkey, roast, meat only 462L
Turkish delight, without nuts 1033L
Turnip, boiled in unsalted water 834L
Turnip, raw 833L
Turnip, yellow see **Swede**
Twiglets 1042L
Twix 1024L
Tzatziki 259L

UHT Channel Island milk, semi-skimmed 197L
UHT cream, canned spray 218L
UHT semi-skimmed milk 188L
UHT skimmed milk, fortified 184L
Urad see **Black gram**, urad gram
Urad gram black gram, dried, boiled in unsalted water 699L
Urad gram black gram, dried, raw 698L

Vatana see **Peas**
Veal, cutlet, fried in vegetable oil 428L
Veal, fillet, raw 429L
Veal, fillet, roast 430L
Vegetable ghee 337L
Vegetable oil, blended, average 333L
Vegetable samosas 175L
Vegetable soup, canned, ready to serve 1133L
Vegetable soup, low calorie, canned 1131L
Venison, roast 471L
Vermouth, dry 1117L
Vermouth, sweet 1118L
Very low fat fromage frais 241L
Very low fat spread 315L
Vinegar 1185L
Vintage cider 1106L
Vitbe, average 47L

Wafer biscuits, filled 107L
Wafers, ice cream 272L
Waffles, potato, frozen, cooked 691L
Walnuts 997L
Walnuts, weighed with shells 998L
Water 1186L
Watercress 835L
Watermelon 925L
Weetabix 90L
Weetaflake 91L
Weetos 92L
Wheat and Oat Bran 75L
Wheat bran 1L
Wheat flour, brown 12L
Wheat flour, white, breadmaking 13L
Wheat flour, white, plain 14L
Wheat flour, white, self-raising 15L
Wheat flour, wholemeal 16L
Wheatgerm 17L
Wheatgerm oil 334L
Whelks, boiled, weighed with shell 648L
Whisky 1122L
White bread, average 48L
White bread, French stick 53L
White bread, fried in blended oil 50L
White bread, fried in lard 51L
White bread, sliced 49L
White bread, toasted 52L
White bread, 'with added fibre' 54L
White bread, 'with added fibre', toasted 55L
White cabbage, raw 753L
White chapati flour 3L
White cheese, average 250L
White chocolate 1017L
White flour, breadmaking 13L
White flour, plain 14L
White flour, self-raising 15L
White pepper 848L
White pitta bread 45L
White pudding 538L
White rice, easy cook, boiled 23L
White rice, easy cook, raw 22L
White rice, fried in lard/dripping 24L
White rolls, crusty 62L
White rolls, soft 63L
White sauce, savoury, made with semi-skimmed milk 1153L
White sauce, savoury, made with whole milk 1152L
White sauce, sweet, made with semi-skimmed milk 1155L
White sauce, sweet, made with whole milk 1154L

White sugar 1011L
White wine, dry 1109L
White wine, medium 1110L
White wine, sparkling 1111L
White wine, sweet 1112L
Whitebait, fried 633L
Whiting, in crumbs, fried 607L
Whiting, in crumbs, fried, weighed with bones 608L
Whiting, steamed 605L
Whiting, steamed, weighed with bones 606L
Whole Channel Island milk, pasteurised 194L
Whole Channel Island milk, pasteurised, summer 195L
Whole Channel Island milk, pasteurised, winter 196L
Whole condensed milk, sweetened 199L
Whole evaporated milk 202L
Whole milk yogurt, fruit 261L
Whole milk yogurt, plain 260L
Whole milk, average 189L
Whole milk, pasteurised 190L
Whole milk, pasteurised, summer 191L
Whole milk, pasteurised, winter 192L
Whole milk, sterilised 193L
Wholegrain mustard 1181L
Wholemeal bread, average 56L
Wholemeal bread, toasted 57L
Wholemeal crackers 108L
Wholemeal flour 16L
Wholemeal fruit cake 116L
Wholemeal fruit pie, one crust 159L
Wholemeal fruit pie, pastry top and bottom 160L
Wholemeal pastry, cooked 129L
Wholemeal pastry, raw 128L
Wholemeal rolls 64L
Wholemeal scones 147L
Wholemeal spaghetti, boiled 32L
Wholemeal spaghetti, raw 31L
Wholemeal wheat flour 16L
Wine, red 1107L
Wine, rosé, medium 1108L
Wine, white, dry 1109L
Wine, white, medium 1110L
Wine, white, sparkling 1111L
Wine, white, sweet 1112L
Wing quarter, roast chicken, meat only, weighed with bone 442L
Winkles, boiled, weighed with shell 649L
Witloof see **Chicory**

Yam (USA) see **Sweet potato**
Yam, boiled in unsalted water 837L
Yam, raw 836L
Yeast, bakers, compressed 1187L
Yeast, bakers, dried 1188L
Yellow gram see **Chick peas**
Yellow turnip see **Swede**
Yogurt, drinking 251L
Yogurt, Greek, cows 252L
Yogurt, Greek, sheep 253L
Yogurt, low calorie 254L
Yogurt, low fat, flavoured 256L
Yogurt, low fat, fruit 257L
Yogurt, low fat, plain 255L
Yogurt, soya 258L
Yogurt, whole milk, fruit 261L
Yogurt, whole milk, plain 260L
Yorkshire pudding 180L

Zucchini see **Courgette**